Rehearsal for Living:
Psychodrama

Rehearsal for Living:

Psychodrama

ILLUSTRATED THERAPEUTIC TECHNIQUES

Adaline Starr

NELSON HALL/CHICAGO

RC
489
P7
S7

Copyright © 1977 by Adaline Starr

Manufactured in the United States of America.

Library of Congress Cataloging in Publication Data

Starr, Adaline.
  Rehearsal for living.

  Bibliography: p.
  Includes index.
  1. Psychodrama. I. Title. [DNLM: 1. Psy-
chodrama.   WM430 S796r]
RC489.P7S7   616.8'915   76–49045
ISBN 0–88229–224–2 (cloth)
ISBN 0–88229–468–9 (paper)

To my daughter, Helene, and her children,
who keep me in the mainstream of life;
and to Rudolf Dreikurs,
who encouraged me to write this book.

Contents

Preface

This book is primarily a manual on the use of psychodrama, a guidebook for readers who want to apply this action technique in a clinical or school setting. But it is not intended just for the professional practitioner; others, too, may find it an interesting and helpful way to learn more about human dynamics and relationships. Psychodrama bridges the gap between the practitioner and the patient. In the psychodramatic session, the members of the audience become actors and leaders; just as the audience of a typical session learns a great deal, so may the reader benefit from this book.

The influences behind my becoming a psychodramatist are many; first of all, Dr. Rudolf Dreikurs, a well-known Adlerian psychiatrist, saw value in the uses of psychodrama and suggested that I go to Beacon, New York, to study with Dr. Jacob L. Moreno in preparation for working in the Chicago community child guidance centers, as well as with patients in Dreikurs' private practice. Moreno, a pioneer of group psychotherapy and innovator of therapeutic psychodrama and sociometry, expected his students to move quickly into directing, playing an auxiliary ego, and testing their social involvement with the student group. But Moreno always advised that this action be reinforced by reading about what others were doing and thinking and by writing about one's own experiences. I have drawn on Moreno's theory and practice and quoted freely from his writings.

Dr. Jules Masserman, psychoanalyst and clear and penetrating thinker, also considers psychodrama, when properly used, to be a valuable therapy for hospitalized patients. He invited me to become a member of Northwestern University Medical School's residency training program, a part of which was stationed at Downey Veterans Hospital, Downey, Illinois. I enjoyed this extraordinary opportunity to work and study with the most respected people in the field and to learn how psychodrama is valuable as a therapy in all disciplines. By sharing my experiences with the reader I hope to demonstrate psychodrama's wide range of application.

Until recent times, only the poet and philosopher had the ability to show the individual as he lived, acted, and died to be an indivisible whole, whose existence had the closest connection with his total environment. Following that tradition, I hope to introduce an orientation to therapy that depends on the joy of learning about oneself and others.

My special thanks to Thelma Howell, who carefully typed the manuscript of my book, and to Dorothy Anderson, my editor, whose practical advice and warm encouragement I deeply appreciate.

Introduction

Many techniques of group therapy are currently being used successfully. Typical are: (1) discussion groups, in which selected patients meet regularly with a therapist and explore the relevance of their life experiences to their present predicament and to each other; (2) family therapy, in which people related to each other meet to work out their problems (sometimes family groups are divided into couples and sibling groups) as their interactions are observed and interpreted by one or more therapists; (3) psychodrama, which can be used in discussion and family therapy groups, but which primarily emphasizes communication by acting and sociometric testing of group interaction; (4) dancing, music, and art; and (5) the homogeneous groupings of Alcoholics Anonymous and Synanon.[1] These techniques have inspired growing interest in action group therapies.

With this enthusiasm for and application of psychodramatic practices, many current psychiatric therapies adapt, modify, and augment role playing, sociometric techniques, and dream therapy. Because there are few well-trained director-therapists, this book emphasizes therapeutic options and goals of the psychodramatic session. It does not attempt to introduce a new theory of action techniques; rather, it presents, without psychiatric or effusive jargon, the methods and procedures that are operationally effective. The vehicle for identifying relationship problems with and outside the group is the drama, which, existentially, makes the patient an actor, a spontaneous person capable of solving problems.

Therapists have a great need for techniques to implement change. Man resists change and needs incentives to accomplish it. The tools to effect change are few. One technique for helping patients see how they behave, the Indian wrestle, is drawn from sports, and illustrates the competitiveness of mankind. Bertolt Brecht, the German playwright, studied the sports arena and used it to describe symbolically the fight of man against man.[2] The value of these confronting experiences is that they clarify problems an individual is required to solve.

Psychodrama, as I have directed it during the past thirty years, has never been a single treatment; no treatment ever is. Sessions have been staged in hospitals, in private offices, as training at the Alfred Adler Institute, and as recorded sessions in the home of the patient. In a hospital, psychodrama is part of an overall treatment plan and usually takes place regularly on a weekly basis. These hospital sessions seem to have a profound impact on patients and staff as they are confronted with the behavior of a particular patient and recognize all too well the games that are being played. Psychodrama may be used to introduce a new patient to the unit and to help a patient focus on significant events in his or her life. At other times, it may be used to help the patients understand the staff or to help the staff understand the patients.

The cases presented in this book have been selected to make explicit the application of psychodrama. One example describes its use in individual therapy. Some cases explain how it is employed in exploring the problems of a family group. Others demonstrate techniques that may be used effectively to elicit interaction in a group of people who are unrelated except for the fact that they meet together to help or to be helped.

The patients involved in these groups vary greatly, as do the size and composition of the groups. A state hospital group is usually large and has a liberal share of chronically regressed patients. A private hospital has a smaller group of patients and a proportionately larger staff, and most of the patients also have private therapists. The length of stay there is usually much shorter than in a state hospital. A day psychiatric hospital offers part-time or outpatient treatment programs.

Chapter 2 answers the question, What is the relationship of traditional drama to therapeutic techniques used in psychodrama? The drama remains, today, an effective vehicle of communication. In the opening scene of Luigi Pirandello's play *Six Characters in Search of an Author*, a theatrical company is rehearsing one of Pirandello's comedies. The rehearsal is interrupted by the arrival of six characters: a father, a mother, their step-daughter and their son, a boy, and a child. They have come to the manager in search of an author, for they want to be put into a play with a connected plot.

FATHER	(*To the manager.*) We carry within us the story of a great drama. Find us an author, and we will bring you a fortune.
MANAGER	But this sounds crazy.
FATHER	Of course, it is. So is all drama crazy. It makes life fantastic and fantasy lifelike. Can anything be more crazy than that?
MANAGER	Nonsense. But what's the relationship amongst you?

The manager is persuaded to take a stab at it. The six characters are to play out their drama by way of rehearsal, and the actors are then to re-enact the scenes. The rehearsal turns out to be better than the play, for the six characters *feel* their parts, whereas the actors merely imagine them.[3]

This ironic tragedy deals with an experience common to most of us: we feel the drama of our own lives and want to have it "connected" into a meaningful plot. The psychodrama experience can do this. It exerts an influence on the emotional, cognitive, and behavioral aspects of the participants and connects their past to the present and future.

1

What Is Psychodrama?

Psychodrama is a form of psychotherapy that uses acting to help a patient solve his problems. With the help of a director and other trained therapists, the patient acts out situations and relationships that are disturbing to him. Sometimes the actual people involved in the patient's problems are present. When they are not, others in the group play their roles.

The patient is encouraged to walk around the stage, talk, and act out a series of episodes that are almost spontaneously produced—a direct expression of various life situations related to his difficulties. He may play out a dream. Several group members may take the roles of hallucinatory characters imagined by a schizophrenic patient.

The many techniques of the method elicit responses that reveal personality traits and particular modes of action. Role taking, role playing, and role creating are referred to as *acting out*.[1] The simplicity of the production disguises its complexity, but somehow explains its attractiveness to students of human behavior.

Essentially, this therapeutic method has three aspects: psychodrama, sociometry, and group psychotherapy.[2] It is important in the beginning to make clear that each facilitates and is an instrument of the others and is, in turn, related to still other therapeutic techniques. Each aspect is introduced to clarify the various dimensions of psychodrama rather than to separate and distinguish one aspect from another. The

1

reader will quickly recognize the connection to drama; behavior is vividly experienced by the actor and by the viewer of dramatic situations.

Sociometry, a method of investigation, helps take the guesswork out of relationships as attitudes of attraction and rejection are graphically portrayed. Frequently, this aspect of psychodrama is treated as a separate science, but it is, in fact, one of the essential ingredients of a psychodrama session. The third aspect, group psychotherapy, is related to psychiatry and defines the philosophy of treatment; one member of the group is a therapeutic agent to the other in a "therapeutic society."

Psychodrama

Psychodrama has a close relationship to the drama and to individual therapy. In 1909, Jacob L. Moreno became interested in treating Viennese school children by having them act out little plays written for them about various problems of behavior. Soon the children were spontaneously presenting their own plays, which more directly represented their individual experiences. Moreno applied this impromptu playing to adults at his Theatre of Spontaneity (1922).

Playwrights, directors, and actors in Austria and Germany, directly after World War I, experimented with new dramatic forms designed to reach and teach the public, to alert them to the social predicament of a defeated nation, and to inspire them to act, to find a new order. There was a proliferation of small experimental theaters. Moreno's Theatre of Spontaneity was part of this development. He used the stage to study impromptu behavior, the warming up of the actor without any emphasis on his private life situation. The method produced was the living newspaper technique.[3] Moreno joined news items and impromptu role playing to elicit individual and group reaction to a specific incident.

A cast of actors were dispatched to the scene of a news event. The information that they gathered was brought back to the theater, and, just as news reporters take a story to the news desk, they described the situation, the characters involved, and the high points of the event to a cast of impromptu players, who then acted the roles and the situation before an audience. Since the roles were drawn from the cultural organization of the community, patterns of behavior and attitudes toward issues became apparent. The audience could see, for example, a student uprising. The roles and the relationship among roles were staged, and angry students, the dean, parents of the students, the police, and the university community battled it out.

Such impromptu acting is role playing; in its use for individual growth, it was spontaneity training. Eventually Moreno gave the name *sociodrama* to the technique. There were two lines of development, one in the direction of diagnosis and therapy of the individual, and the other in the direction of roles presented as the collective image of a social stereotype.

During World War II, soon after the race riots in Harlem, a new concept for meeting social problems developed. No longer was a group of actors sent out into the community. The people in the audience, reacting to the violence on the streets, *became* the community. As people gathered in Moreno's psychodrama theater in New York, the director encouraged them to demonstrate the situation of the conflict. Through role taking in the group, they influenced one another toward violence or away from it as they reexperienced the conflict. Wrote Moreno, "The stage is not a stage but a part of the actual world."[4] This format was used in later years to discover and treat the potential Hitlers and Oswalds in the audience as Moreno staged sociodramas of the Eichmann trial and the assassination of John F. Kennedy.

Sociodrama has also been developed as a form of social learning in classrooms, industry, churches, and community organizations. It focuses on solving group problems, with the emphasis on retraining rather than on release of emotional tension. Sociodrama makes it possible to describe, analyze, partially reexperience, and objectify human reaction to social communications as the dynamics of the group structure are explained and treated.

The word *Catharsis*, meaning a cleansing and purifying, is frequently used in connection with the clinical aspects of psychodrama. Historically the word is associated with Aristotelian ideas about tragic drama. Tragedy, Aristotle believed, deeply affects the spectator by arousing both pity and fear and eventually produces a catharsis of emotions in the spectator as he watches the unfolding of human conflict. The attention of the audience is captured through the plot, and solutions to problems influence the audience vicariously.[5]

As used today, catharsis has a variety of meanings, but a release of tension is its primary goal and benefit. Action catharsis brings relief as an individual relives events that he has not been able to understand. The means for finding solutions, however, are not vicarious but direct, as the individual defines and understands his own behavior and the motives underlying it. There is an integrative catharsis in psychodrama therapy as the individual is encouraged to identify with the positions and problems of others. In this manner, persons who previously were unable to break out of emotional isolation see themselves as part of a relationship with the other actors of the plot. Action learning takes place as the exaggerated strength of the other becomes modified when the various situations surrounding the difficulty are acted out. A patient's difficulty may be compared to a golf swing in which there is no follow-through; the body moves and hits the ball, but the ball doesn't reach the desired goal. It is the director's task to help the patient address himself to the ball and follow through to reach the goal.

Activity is vital to psychodrama, as it is to all group psychotherapies. The therapist works to advance the relationship of the audience, the patient, and the assistants (auxiliary egos). This is quite different from such situations as psychological testing, where rapport is necessary and where the aim is to structure the situation so that the interviewer does not influence it. The activity of the therapist in the psychodrama has practical advantages. Since personality is expressed in terms of interaction and in relation to a specific situation, it becomes clear that psychodramatic activity advances the therapeutic process.[6] It encourages confrontation, so that the patient perceives the presence and purpose of his behavior.[7] By the therapist's activity the patient is guided through the exploration of meaningful areas of the present, past, and future in order to repair his relationships with the people with whom he or she is involved—sometimes face-to-face with the people associated with the problem. The spontaneity of the director results in freer expression of the patient.

Action involves the interaction of psychological states and motor behavior. The connection between emotional states and behavior is individually expressed. To a certain degree, every emotion finds some bodily expression, in either a frankly visible way or an imperceptible way, perhaps the twitching of a muscle, the clenching of a fist, the trembling of the voice, or the rigid compression of the lips. Emotions and their physical expressions tell us how the mind is acting and reacting to a situation that it interprets as either favorable or unfavorable.[8]

Acting is the personal behavior of the individual expressed by action with words, feelings, and thoughts. The close connection between motor and psychological states is quickly seen in the language—the verbal idioms—that an individual uses to describe a phenomenon. An individual might say, "I was struck dumb," "I can't stomach it," or "I'm dragging my feet." This may be carried further as the motor elements expressing the emotional states become neurotic symptoms. Thus, patients in psychodrama are able to see and to understand the relation of emotion to behavior.

Acting out in psychodrama differs from *acting out* in psycho-analysis, where the term refers to oppositional behavior. While this may be seen in the psychodramatic role playing of hostile attitudes, it should be stressed that role playing is a cooperative act that may lead to an integration of behavior. It can contribute to the recognition of current emotional problems and the unconscious past.[9]

The term *action method* has come to mean that form of therapy that stimulates the patient to move from narration to motor representation. The effectiveness of these techniques is clearly demonstrated during a psychodrama production. As the patient begins to act, it is possible for him to hold back and conceal his attitudes (and perhaps some of his dysfunctional behavior), but as the production gets under way, the "make-believe process" disappears as the patient becomes involved and begins to think, feel, and act the way he does in actual life situations. The cues and clues that he communicates to the group include all his expressive movements, words, and motor responses. The auxiliary ego picks up on the messages that the patient sends out to further involve the patient in revealing his own personality. He begins to identify himself as a particular personality type in a specific situation. Many techniques are employed in the production to motivate the patient to disclose other aspects of his personality. These techniques are so useful that a separate section has been devoted to them, both as they are derived from the drama and as they apply in a therapy session.

Sociometry

During the 1930s, one of the chief concerns of social scientists was the scientific investigation of the group. Sociometry, the investigation of interpersonal relationships, was established in 1934 with the publication of *Who Shall Survive?* by Moreno. This book resulted from applying a sociometric approach to the social structure of a community —in this case, the New York Training School for Girls at Hudson, under the auspices of William Alanson White. Sociometric technique was developed first as a therapeutic maneuver with role-playing situations in a psychodrama or sociodrama; but soon it became a scientific tool of measurement used extensively by sociologists and educators as a method of research.

Sociometry guides the therapist to an identification of the patient's problem. When a patient enters a group, he brings with him not only his immediate feelings toward its members but also his attitudes toward those outside the group who have affected his life—mother, father, siblings, spouse. These role relationships are the building blocks of a life history. Since an emotional problem is considered to be a disturbance in role relationships, relief comes as the therapist directs the patient in revealing the roles involved in the problem.

Sociometry rests on two concepts, the social atom and tele. Units of social interaction develop between an infant and mother and grow to involve all the people intimately or casually connected to an individual to form his psychosocial network; in other words, his *social atom*. The size of a person's social atom varies considerably, as some people are emotionally expansive and others may be more drawn to objects or symbols. Group and individual development is the result of this expansion.[10]

Tele is the impulse or current of feeling that flows between person and person, from person to object, and from person to symbol. The sensitivity a person has to persons, objects, and symbols is culturally influenced as well as biologically derived. In a well-functioning person, the sensitivities are evenly developed in a positive arrangement to each other. But when there is a disturbance in the role development, the sensitivities may likewise be disturbed; for example, a schizophrenic patient on a ward may prefer a chair to the person who sits next to him, or a person may be attracted to a sex organ regardless of the person to whom it belongs. Or an overly intense emotional expression may spring from a person who cares deeply for people. Telic sensitivity is trainable and can be improved through role playing, spontaneity tests, improvisation, and the many other structured situations designed to "free" the individual.

Since it is obvious that we never deal with the individual alone, a procedure for exploring the pattern of social relatedness between individuals, and a way of acting on it, can be helpful. A sociometric test asks each member of a group to express preferences towards the other members. It clarifies for the individual and the therapist the area of disturbed relationships and offers clues to repairing it.

Group therapists have long discussed whether to place patients with similar psychopathology together or to form groups whose patients have differing pathologies. In contrast, sociometric tests can show that every group, beneath its superimposed selection, has an unofficial structure, which is what the therapist has to consider. Diagnostic considerations about grouping, then, are not of paramount importance, since "good results occur with even the most diverse grouping of patients where the psychopathology is patently different."[11] Sociometry and its principles can guide the therapist through the maze of relationships within the group and help him map a course of therapeutic action. Later chapters will demonstrate the use of this technique with the family, adolescent groups, marital pairs, and alcohol and drug addiction groups.

Group Psychotherapy

Group psychotherapy, the third aspect of psychodrama, is a development of psychiatry. The idea of the importance of the group in the treatment of mental distress has its roots in antiquity; in recent times, however, there has been systematic study by many persons of the potential value of group therapy. It is not the discovery of a single man. Simultaneously in Europe and America physicians were responding to the increased demands for relief from behavior disorders and writing of their experiences, variously calling their techniques "class method," "collective analysis," and "group psychoanalysis." Moreno called it "group psychotherapy," and in 1932 that name was accepted.

Group psychotherapy, Moreno pointed out, ushered in the third revolution in psychiatry. The first occurred during the French Revolution when Pinel unchained the inmates at Bicêtre and released them to the community—symbolically a forerunner of an open-door policy. The second was achieved by the ideas of Freud and his followers as they advanced individual analysis and psychoanalysis and applied the medical model to psychiatry: the dyadic encounter—one patient with one doctor, privacy with diagnosis preceding therapy. In a transition from individual to group therapy, the approach included individual psychotherapy and psychodrama. The group became the therapeutic agent with less emphasis on individual therapy. Sharing replaced privacy. The multiplied interactions within the group replaced the one-to-one relationship of patient and doctor. The nonmedical therapist replaced the psychiatrist as the agent of therapy. Psychiatry lost its exclusive right to the methods it developed.[12]

The group creates change, and the relationships within the group also change. The authoritarian aspect of the therapist's role is modified and diminished through group interaction. But in psychodrama, the therapeutic influence of group members is transferred to the action on the stage. This procedure utilizes a director's skill and the participation of group members in a common effort resulting in interpersonal rapport.

As the patient reexamines his old patterns of behavior and tries out new ones, he is both an observer and a participant in the group treatment. He can, through trial and error stemming from this inter-action, ready himself for the more difficult environment of the com-munity outside.

The group may meet in a variety of places. They may gather at the point of trouble (at home, on the playground, in a dayroom of a hospital), in an office, or in a specially designed area such as a stage in a hospital or in the community. As an evaluation of diagnosis, a patient may be observed in group interactions in order to learn more about the extent and nature of the personality problem, in order to place his behavior in one or another descriptive category of mental illness.

The application of the principles of the three aspects of psycho-drama is of particular therapeutic value. The drama reflects everyday life and affords an opportunity for attitude change by giving the indi-vidual in the group the time necessary to examine and understand his personal experiences. Sociometry explores and works with the recipro-cal feelings in the group as each person tends to look to others for validation of his feelings and attitudes. A feeling of group belonging-ness develops as each person becomes a therapeutic agent to the other, giving group members opportunities to help each other.

2

The Relation of Psychodrama to Traditional Drama

As an outward sign of thought,
action is more immediate than words.
—Ypo Him

Drama has long been of interest to the social scientist as a mode of treatment since its concepts are derived from intuitive group techniques that influenced behavior in the past. At first, the emphasis was on the individual and his intrapersonal dynamics. But more recently, the focus has been on the individual as he coordinates his inner self with his social group. Currently, dramatizing emotionally significant events is recognized as important to the quality of a person's development.

Historical Perspective

From earliest times, people have gathered together in dance, rhythm, and song to express their feelings over an event of local concern: the tapping of the feet and the swaying of the body became a dance form, a rhythm that further expressed itself as music and then developed into poetry and became drama. Man's desire to invest himself temporarily with a fictitious character or characteristic is the basis of drama.[1] Man needs to tell of his experiences and try to understand them. He does this in action, for that is the principal vehicle of communication—"the conversion of a mood into a relationship."[2]

The early function of drama, which included music and dance, was to provide a means for the individual to become engaged in a group experience—to lament capture by the enemy, to praise a successful hunt, to have an orgy. Each was an act of identification with the group. Ancient peoples did not sit and view the ritualistic chantings or the expressions of erotic or aggressive feelings as in the Dionysian mysteries or the sadistic rites of Kali. They participated in them. The inhibiting forces of our times have isolated and cut people off from regarding themselves as sources of creativity. Self-expression and integrative catharsis have become submerged as social stereotypes replace spontaneity in a society where science and technology, through automobiles, high-rise buildings, radio, television, and other developments, have further encouraged passive withdrawal. Alienation has become a gigantic problem. When so many natural forms of communication have failed, the creative arts may be used to bring to mankind a sense of humanness.

The ancients recognized this. The Greek theater at Epidaurus, which still stands and is in use, was a temple dedicated to Asclepius, god of healing and therapist demigod. People came to this and other sanatoriums to be relieved of mental and physical distress, and the course of treatment included music, drama, discussions with a philosopher, and other forms of stimulation and relaxation. In the cultural history of mankind there is an art form, a vehicle, that is solely devoted to the "acting out of the problems of society, the human society in miniature."[3] That form is the drama.

When Moreno's idea of a "theater of spontaneity" was transformed into an experimental theater of sociological concern, it led to formal development of the technical uses of psychodrama. There are other instances in which the drama was used as a curative instrument in the treatment of the mentally ill. The Marquis de Sade wrote plays for the patients to enact while he was interned at Charenton. J. C. Reil advocated the enactment of plays in which angels and devils arise from graves with the "utmost verisimilitude" to treat and help the patient in a form of noninjurious torture.[4] Pierre Janet role played with his patients some of their traumatic experiences; he entered the patient's drama as a second actor.[5]

Goethe's interest in mental disorders made others keenly aware of the relevance of literature and psychology. Both Freud and Adler acknowledged his influence on them. It is in a musical play (written for the birthday of Duchess Louise) called *Lila* that Goethe offered a psychological cure for the treatment of a psychotic depression by having the family members act out the victim's delusions.[6] This may be regarded as a forerunner of hallucinatory psychodrama.[7]

Elements Related to Traditional Theater

Dramatic forms that were at first spontaneous and characteristic of a simple social group became traditional and preserved. A formula for writing and producing plays evolved, and technical skill developed in each period and in each country to solve the problems confronting the playwrights: the audience, stage design, costumes, and the available talent. It is helpful to consider some of the solutions to these problems for a better understanding of a therapeutic production.

Audience

Plays are written not to be read but to be seen and heard, to be experienced and accepted by the audience. The playwright depends on audience approval. In fact, the audience has always been the most important influence on the kind of theatricals produced. From the time of the early Greeks to the present, there have been vast differences in taste and interest, due perhaps not to individual human nature, but to the preoccupations of people at the time. For this reason, we find changes in the theater, in techniques, and in how the playwright makes contact with the audience.

In the time of Shakespeare, audiences clustered around the stage, sometimes sitting on the stage itself. Before the French Revolution, Rousseau involved the audience in riotous participation as part of what he called a "democratic process." At other times, the audience was physically separated from the actors by a curtain, or the audience felt separated from the stage because a playwright ignored the viewers' spontaneity level and wrote in abstract symbolism. The French and German Expressionists and Goethe in his philosophical dramas did this. The experimental playwright's ambition was to make the audience aware of issues and move it to political action. Often the audience wasn't sure what it came for—entertainment or education.

In psychodrama, the audience plays a vital role, but a different one from that in conventional theater. In fact, there may be no audience at all. But if there is one, it becomes a part of the social organization of the actor-patient. The audience provides: (1) the protagonist; (2) the dramatis personae, that is, the auxiliary egos; and (3) reactors. There is no separation between the actors and the audience, no curtain, nothing to maintain distance between the stage and the audience. The audience has come for help, for revelation, to share in a production of its own making. What excites the audience is therapeutic involvement of being a double to the actor-patient on the stage.

Staging

Plays are limited by the mechanical developments of their period —curtains, scenery, lighting, and stage size. Think of the effect electricity had on the theater! The theater of Dionysius at Athens was an immense outdoor area, large enough for processions and games as well as plays. The dramatist met this problem by putting words into the actors' and chorus's mouths. Since the Greek drama evolved from the lyrics of the chorus, the audience expected the chorus to be helpful in depicting the past, present, and future. We find the same device in the Shakespearean theater, since, as far as we know, there was no scenery or curtain at that time. It was the obligation of the playwright to have the words of the actors establish time, location, and space. When an actor walked on stage, he had to tell the audience who and where he was; a scene ended by an actor's simply walking off.

In the respect that there is no scenery and no curtain, production aspects of psychodrama are similar. The actor-patient is placed on a stage—any area will do—and the director helps him place himself in time, space, and location, not only for the benefit of the audience, but also, and more importantly, for warming up the actor-patient to the outward aspects of the situation to be enacted. This is called an *action* or *physical warm-up*.

Psychodrama does not require a theatrical setting. Although Moreno designed a circular, three-level stage, any space may be designated as the stage. The acting area is neutral ground that the actors can magically transform into a living room, a campfire, an executive's suite, or even heaven or hell.

Writing and Directing

The dramatist is sensitive to the actors' talent. Many dramatists wrote their plays for a particular actor: *Cyrano de Bergerac* was written by Edmond Rostand for the French actor Benoît Constant Coquelin; Molière wrote for his acting company and his own special acting skills. The plot of the story is less important than the character that is drawn and the players who surround him (it has been pointed out that there are, in all of human experience, about thirty-six basic plots). The real drama is the treatment of the story line. There must be sympathy between the writer and the actor so that the actor can extract and recreate the meaning intended by the playwright.

This is equally true for the director of psychodrama. There must be good rapport between the protagonist-patient and the director if the patient is to become productive. The director selects the protagonist from the audience and guides him in portraying his world and how he adapts to it, by the words he uses, the movements he makes, and the emotions he shows. The director becomes the playwright-producer.

Techniques Derived from Traditional Theater

Time passes quickly in both the legitimate theater and on the therapeutic stage; it is necessary to condense the events of living to a semblance of real life, to perceive as soon as possible the relationship of the chief characters to one another. A play usually runs two or three hours and a psychodrama somewhat less; therefore, each selects the vital areas of conflict and presents them in such a way that all can see and understand the happenings. The dramatist not only condenses the episodes taken from the life of the protagonist, but also clarifies them. Each drama heightens the facts of life; in psychodrama, this is called a surplus of reality. Clarification and enlargement are achieved through techniques such as the double, role reversal, and the mirror.

The soliloquy, the aside, and the confidant are some of the conventional theatrical techniques that have served for centuries as ways to further the plot as well as to unveil the souls of the characters. These techniques are revived and modified for use in the therapeutic theater (as the auxiliary ego, the double ego, the soliloquy aside, and the monologue) to show unspoken thoughts as well as the spoken, to free the actor-patient, and to help him and the audience better understand the riddle of human nature.

The Soliloquy and Aside

One effective technique used by dramatists for delineating character is the soliloquy, which Brander Matthews, in 1910, described as "the speech in which a character talks aloud, not to any person on the stage with him, but directly to the audience." Matthews continued, "The most striking changes have taken place in the drama of our time with the sudden disappearance of the soliloquy. No longer does a character come down to the footlights for a confidential communication to the audience, telling them his thoughts, declaring his intentions, and defending his acts. So sharp is the reaction against the practice, that the French writer of a eulogistic study of the later German naturalistic dramatists, after praising the technique of Hauptmann, asserts positively that the soliloquy and the aside are hereafter banished from the stage."[8] Henrik Ibsen was against any technique that interrupted the realism of the play. Allowing a character to step out of the living room and talk to the audience Ibsen called an "unnatural technique." Many theatrical devices that are unnatural, however, can be effective.

Two major uses of the soliloquy are found in the dramatic literature: (1) to give information to the audience as the plot unfolds and (2) to expose to the audience the thoughts of the character when he is alone. Shakespeare and Molière didn't hesitate to use the soliloquy, for when they became playwrights, it was an acceptable technique found in the comedies and tragedies of the Greeks and Romans. Even though a soliloquy was originally a man talking aloud when he was alone, later other characters often were present when the soliloquy began. It is only modern theater that considers the soliloquy too simplistic a technique. (However, certain experimental playwrights have begun to revive it.)

In psychodrama, the soliloquy is used whenever it is important for the audience to hear what the patient is thinking. It doesn't matter if he speaks to the audience in a lowered voice or turns his head to the side (*an aside*); the patient and the spectators hear his association to the situation at the moment. The value of this is apparent to anyone who is interested in associative ideation.

The Confidant

In the French classic tragedy of Jean Baptiste Racine, *Phèdre*, the chorus has been reduced to a single attendant for each of the leading characters. These shadowy figures are called *confidants*; they are other dimensions of the chief characters who talk and unveil themselves. This technique replaced the soliloquy as the seventeenth-century French playwrights Corneille and Racine experimented with different forms. The confidant has no purpose of his own except to be talked to, to hear the plans, and to resonate the feelings of the subject. A confidant enters into a psychological dialogue; he shares the same fate as the character he accompanies. "And in the tragedy which is rehearsed in [English playwright Richard] Sheridan's *Critic* where the heroine goes mad in white satin, the confidant unhesitatingly goes mad in white muslin."[9] Audiences, however, found this theatrical device for exploring character even more disagreeable than the soliloquy.

The Double and Multiple Doubles

The double is a psychological device that has been described in both ancient and modern literature. One example known to many is in Stevenson's play *Dr. Jekyll and Mr. Hyde*. The two characters represent man as having a dual nature, one part good, the other bad, which is presented as man's eternal conflict. In *Lila* we have the hallucinated double of mental illness. Pierre Janet differentiates between the double of madness and of prayer. Both are internal dramas. The double or demon of madness takes over and is in charge of the subject. It exists outside the patient. In prayer, the double is a voluntary act and may be turned off at will, since the individual is "master of the inward drama."[10] These internalizations originated the idea of a double or spirit existing invisibly behind the visible actions of the individual.

The confidant is parallel to the double of psychodrama, for an actual person is placed beside the patient and becomes one with him. The double is an auxiliary ego who becomes not an absentee family member or friend but the external form of the internal imaginings of the actor-protagonist. They share the enactment and speak to each other in the first person. The double may encourage the musings of the patient in order to understand him better, but the patient remains in charge of the drama. The double draws on the patient for signals to confirm that they act as one. He begins by assuming the same physical stance and receives from this a clue to the feeling state of the patient. The double may have read the patient's history, and been informed of instances of significant behavior. He may use this information to arouse the patient to respond to the interaction. The dialogue begins. The invisible part of the individual becomes visible.

Some forms of drama endeavor to represent the full truth as the dramatist perceives it, to present not only the tangible aspects of man but also the philosophies of existence. At such times a drama of symbols evolves. During the Middle Ages, drama became a moralistic teaching tool, attempting to translate the concepts of Christian thought into common experience by realistic personification and concrete examples. The morality plays were the final form of this effort.

In modern times, the drama of the German Expressionists, influenced by August Strindberg, addressed itself to the individual and portrayed the subjective psychological experience. The whole man is the individual as well as all the forces that created him. Frequently each part is represented symbolically, as in the morality play. In a play of George Kaiser, *From Morn Till Midnight*, there is a scene that shows this technique: The chief character changes from a bank clerk to a thief to a sexual debaucher and reaches the last stage of his progress in a Salvation Army hall. "From the assembled men and women a number of penitents come forward to confess their sins; and each sin forms a part of the clerk's own guilt, which is distributed among them."[11] We see here how a concrete form depicts the complex inner life of the character. This is also found in Goethe's *The Triumph of Sentimentality*, for he too was concerned with the inner experiences of man, the use of multiple doubles, the splitting of the fantasy into parts. This diffuses the realization of a feared object or event and, according to Freud, is a mechanism of paranoia.[12] Similarly, in Shakespeare we find that "Macbeth's thoughts are *witches*, these subhuman figures are the dramatic objectification of his subjective state."[13]

The psychodramatic use of multiple doubles is one technique used to handle the problem of identity: A person feels all alone, yet needs other humans. The feeling of belonging is restored when one receives a confirmation of identity.

A patient, at a critical moment in his drama, is joined by several parts of himself (auxiliary egos), as many as the anxiety indicates, to represent his childhood, adulthood, mother, future hopes, and so forth. They talk, one at a time, to communicate to the patient the inner significance of his life experience.

The Mirror

A person sits in the audience of the theater, a spectator of the drama that reproduces the nature of human society and the foibles of the individual. The play becomes a mirror held up to the spectator, so that he recognizes in it some of his own problems and "reaches his own solutions in this vicarious way."[14]

In the mirror technique, a patient—one who needs to be aroused to life and to an awareness of his behavior patterns—sits in the audience as an auxiliary ego reflects his behavior. This is accomplished by the auxiliary ego's carefully miming the gestures and expressions of the patient, using a series of situations experienced by the patient and the group. These scenes are often effective in bringing the patient to a realization of his inadequate behavior. The play within a play is the dramatist's use of this principle. Hamlet, wanting to force a confession from the king, had the murder of his father played out in the court theater.

Role Reversal

Of the many techniques to be found in the literature, two are of prime importance: (1) *role reversal*, which is probably the most popular of the action methods, and which is used in education, industrial

training, and clinical situations, and (2) *pantomime,* which is nonverbal.

A major theatrical plot, and a favorite of playwrights, is role reversal, or the exchange of identities—the mix-up. The exchange may take place during infancy as part of a sinister scheme, or as a matter of choice, of wanting to experience the life of the other, as in *The Prince and the Pauper* by Mark Twain. The loss of identity is anxiety producing, and the dramatist makes good use of it.

Kaiser's play *Die Korall* (*The Coral,* 1917) contains an example of reversing roles, of a person's stepping into someone else's shoes to change the feelings of one of the characters. In this play, "the millionaire owner of a factory changes roles with his secretary during business hours."[15] The secretary protects his employer from all contact with the poor and wretched that the millionaire wants to forget, for they remind him of his poverty-stricken youth. In a way, the millionaire believes in the illusion of his creation, since the secretary's past was serene and peaceful. The play ends when the millionaire kills his secretary in order to assume the role permanently. But eventually the secretary is found guilty of the murder of the millionaire. The illusion cannot become reality.

We find in Shakespeare's *Henry IV* an example of role playing in which two intimates, the young and exuberant Prince Hal and the old and bawdy Falstaff, rehearse Prince Hal's approaching interview with his irate father, King Henry, to save Falstaff's neck and reconcile father and son. Falstaff plays at being the king and Prince Hal is the son; the two change places, and Prince Hal plays his father and Falstaff, the son. Shakespeare's goal was comedy, not therapy, but the dramatic device of reversing roles increases role perception, not of the actors but of the audience. This is called a *future projection technique* when the rehearsal is for meeting a real-life situation.

Role reversal is the foundation of role-playing theory and the signal of the functioning personality. While a complete role reversal is not possible, one can try to feel a way into another's situation and search for understanding through the experience of "being" the other person.

Pantomime

Pantomime is a kind of drama in which a story is told entirely by action and gestures, without words. The elaborate and detailed body movements and facial responses make the plot understandable to the audience, for emotions are often best expressed in gesture and movement. It is believed that pantomime originated at Roman festivals.

Andronicus, a Roman player who had lost his voice from too much shouting over the noise of the crowd, assigned his words to a boy in the chorus. Music and the chorus accompanied him as he changed masks and gestured the different parts.[16]

Although speech is the most direct way to give information to an audience, much can be done without it. Pantomime is a way to eliminate verbiage and make a point quickly. Body movements, facial expressions, and exaggerated gestures convey the actions and emotions of the actors. Such gestures have meaning because the action is rounded out by the association made by the spectator. Think of fatigue. If you lose some muscle tone and drag your feet, you are recognized as tired. Drop your shoulders and lower your head, and fatigue becomes defeat or despair. Essential information regarding one's immediate mental state is implicitly expressed in one's body stance. In pantomime, all the necessary information is conveyed with body language.

Body Language

Body posture and attitude make up the sign language of the body. An individual tells about himself in expressive movements; for example, he may move aggressively toward another or lean in dependency. This behavior is total. The mind and body act on each other. Kenneth Burke writes: "The body is an actor; as an actor, it participates in the movements of the mind, producing correspondingly; in styles of thought and expression we embody these correlations and the recognition of this is, as you prefer, either 'scientific' or 'poetic.' "[17]

Conclusion

In drama, communication skills of speech, gesture, and movement natural to man are considered as primary data. Drama imitates life; it may be a spontaneous expression of an event, a great drama from the Greek period, or an impromptu enactment on the street, at a fair, or at a festival, as was common in the Middle Ages. All that happens to man is as he sees or perceives it. The techniques of the drama evolved to show ever more clearly a certain personality—his interpersonal values, anxieties, major goals, and private logic.

Therapeutic drama utilizes all the theatrical conventions, even playwriting. It differs from other drama in that it is usually spontaneously enacted and the plots are cooperatively developed. But differences are more superficial than basic.

The action techniques of psychodrama, verbal and nonverbal, are derived from dance, music, and drama. Using psychodrama and its action techniques, therapists and allied mental health workers reach, teach, and change patients and themselves. These techniques may be used (often without the direct participation of the psychiatrist but with auxiliary helpers and aides) to improve patient care and achieve a more satisfactory resocialization of patients in many settings.

3

Roles, Role Playing, and Role Training

All the world's a stage;
And all the men and women merely players;
They have their exits and their entrances;
And one man in his time plays many parts.
—WM. SHAKESPEARE, *As You Like It*, II, 7

Playwrights provide us with dramatic characters that are referred to as *roles*. The character reveals himself by what he does. Shakespeare created roles recognizable as living human beings even though some of them were supernatural, such as the witches in *Macbeth*, the ghost in *Hamlet*, and the fairies in *Midsummer Night's Dream*. Anyone who sees *Hamlet* forgets that the Dane's existence is a fiction; the role becomes reality.

Webster's New Twentieth Century Dictionary gives this definition of *role*: "A part, or character performed by an actor in a drama, hence, the part or function taken or assumed by anyone." The social anthropologist and the sociologist use the word to mean the function an individual assumes in society, not a specific behavior. "Used in connection with communication, the term 'role' refers to nothing but the code which is used to interpret the flow of messages."[1]

Psychodrama is based on a concept of roles, role playing, and role training. While the terms *role* and *role playing* are closely identified with Moreno, Theodore Sarbin reminds us that George Herbert Mead, in *Mind, Self, and Society*, made role taking the foundation of his system of social psychology.[2] Mead stresses the importance of the social act and its development through language and role taking; whereas Moreno emphasizes tele, an interactional emotional process. Both men study what goes on between people in order to understand the person.

21

Henri Ellenberger remarks on the similarity between Mead and Pierre Janet, though they were separated by language and distance.[3] Mead's theory of the development of the self is as follows: The infant is born into a social system with its values and attitudes formed and organized in advance of the baby's arrival. The newborn infant has a tendency to act, and through the development of gestures and symbols, the infant learns to internalize these values and attitudes. This process of internalization is behaviorally expressed in role taking. Roleless at first, the infant, after acquiring his basic reaction patterns, learns first one role, then another. The role taken by the child is a symbol that calls out a group or learned response in the other person. At the same time this response elicits the group (learned) response in the child. Communication takes place through this sharing of significant symbols. Through language and role development, the child learns to distinguish the "me" and the "generalized other" from the "I," and in this way learns to "take the role of the other."[4]

Moreno differs from Mead in that he considers role playing to exist in the absence of significant symbols, that language is not of primary importance. "The infant's tendency to act is termed spontaneity, a cerebral function with an internal locus."[5] "The S [spontaneity] factor can animate a gesture even if there is no 'self' yet and no social 'other' involved. . . . It is possible, as we see with infants and psychotics, for the individual to operate with several alter egos."[6] Moreno concludes: "Role is the final crystallization of all the situations in a *special* area of operations through which the individual has passed (for instance the eater, the father, the airplane pilot)."[7] The role, then, is a unit of behavior that is the spontaneous result of the self with the group.

Roles

Man is an actor, a role player who progressively adds the roles necessary to his survival and creates other roles out of his responsiveness to the environment. First, a set of private roles emerges that is shaped and modified by the collective roles in the environment. As the actor grows and meets new challenges, the number and kinds of roles he takes continuously change. Some roles are adequate, productive, and useful. Some are not. And other roles never develop. The pattern and development of a person's repertoire of roles, then, describe, in part, his personality.

There are four categories or basic types of roles:

1. *Psychosomatic or physiologic roles.* The newborn enters the world helpless and incomplete and passes through an orderly succession of stages as it obtains mastery over its body. It must breathe, eat, eliminate, sleep, and move in order to survive. These physical functions, which meet the bodily needs of the infant, are to some extent self-initiated, but require the continuous attention of the mother, an auxiliary ego. It is in this first interaction with the mother that the infant develops a set of psychosomatic roles—the eater, the sleeper, the eliminator, the mover.[8] This places role playing at the nonverbal period. Each infant and mother interacts in this early "scene" in a style unique to them, and binds the social roles to the physical; in this interaction, the infant's first social role emerges.

The infant has the services of his universe at his beck and call. His cry is a demand for comfort. Without pointing or explaining, it summons help. If the infant is to survive, it must receive help. The mother-child relationship is built from the beginning on mutual roles: the mother in the role of giver and the infant in the role of receiver. Development and change in role-taking behavior continue throughout life, but in this early infancy period, we can observe the beginning of a continuing process. The infant begins to distinguish the nipple from the self and finally recognizes the mother as the source of nutritive care. Once the infant is able to merge reality and fantasy roles successfully, he is ready to organize his role performance towards persons, objects, and goals outside himself.[9]

2. *Fantasy or psychodramatic roles.* These are the roles that the individual imagines are outside himself—God, the devil, witches, animals, and objects such as trees or tables. As roles begin to crystallize, there is less dependency on the mother and an increase in the independent role playing of the infant. Reality occurs in the form of controls from within and without. This marks the end of the first infantile period, that time when the infant experiences self only in terms of his needs, which must be met by others. One never gives this up entirely. Fantasy life is at first perfectly normal, but as the child matures, he is expected to be able to shift to reality. As he is successful in this, new roles are added in orderly progression.

As the individual shifts from fantasy to reality, he continues to imagine and, in imagining, is able to share feelings with others, as well as to have an image of himself. He lives in both worlds. It is perhaps for this reason that the techniques of psychodrama—the double, the soliloquy, and the mirror—are effective in exploring attitudes in adult behavior. According to Adler, a person's fantasies "can be used as entrance gates to gain insight into the workshop of the mind."[10] These roles are psychological, the conceptual form of behavior.

3. *Social roles.* Essentially, social roles are the relationships with the real people in an individual's life. The infant-mother relationship is the first social role. Even though the umbilical cord is cut, the child is connected to his mother, and this is the foundation of the individual's ability to interact with others. This first experience of another person is the basis of a person's ability to trust or fear others. An individual needs people, and social roles develop out of this need, whether it is to seek cooperation with others or to dominate them out of fear.

Many adult roles are aborted in the early development of the child. If the mother is too concerned with keeping the child close to her, it may be hard for the child to interest himself in others later on. Early deprivation of normal love in the infant will prevent the development of normal social relationships. When there is a protective and meaningful contact with adults, the child quickly grows and acquires interpersonal skills, as well as self-confidence in motor and exploratory skills.

4. *Cultural roles.* Every culture produces social roles that distinguish it from other groups, races, or nations. The role of the policeman in American culture is different from that of a policeman in an authoritarian state; the policeman has power in America because the citizens have given it to him, and they can also take it away from him. A doctor is expected to be a healer and a teacher, to follow established customs of behavior. He would be considered bizarre, if, like a witch doctor, he uttered incantations and danced. The cowboy is no longer seen as glamorous or the Indian as a savage. Cultural roles that develop in a society are too numerous to itemize, but a person is influenced by these collective elements in his life situation.

The performance of a telephone operator or of a punch-press operator contains little variation. These roles are clear and well defined. It is not so easy to put a collective stereotype on the roles of mother, father, wife, husband, male, and female, but each person creates a generalized image of these roles. That image becomes a part of the person. Personal experiences and private goals of the person exist together and produce a role, either in conflict or merging comfortably, but always in interaction, with his group and culture.

Roles may be assessed and a person's attitudes discovered when these factors are considered: (1) the warm-up, (2) spontaneity, (3) creativity, and (4) role taking.[11]

The Warm-Up

The warm-up is the psychological experience of focusing one's attention on a task, an attitude, or an activity. As a person is faced with a situation and prepares for action, he gives clues by expressive body movements (his posture, his facial expression, his breathing) as to the amount of spontaneity available to reach a solution by acting. From these outward indications, one may assess whether or not there is adequate warm-up to the situation.

One characteristic of the warm-up is the amount of time it takes for a role to emerge, for a person to become a role player. Here is an example:

Two girls are walking along the street at night, and as they turn to enter their apartment, a man grabs both of them from behind. As his arm encircles her, one girl turns quickly, screams "Help! Help!" and fights to free herself. The other is frozen to the spot; she doesn't cry out or try to disengage herself from the stranger. A fast response is in order. One girl warms up quickly and frightens the attacker away; the other warms up slowly to the danger.

The factor of speed is relevant to the requirements of an emergency situation. We find among the plays of Shakespeare, who had such a great gift for role creation, a variety of pace: *Macbeth* is a fast-moving drama; *Hamlet* is slow and thoughtful; and *King Lear* starts as a storm and grows into a hurricane. A person interacts in his own way with the environment, the problem facing him, and the people within the situation. This visible expressive movement is his role behavior.

The time it takes for a role to emerge is poetically but accurately expressed in Hamlet's brooding in the role of a bereaved son who must overcome his culturally learned respect for God's law against suicide but not murder, for it was expected that a prince would avenge his father's murder. He has to whip himself into a posture and belief that the victim should get what is coming to him. Hamlet's delay before the final act of murder is caused by a need for time to justify it to himself, or perhaps by his desire to commit the perfect crime, a reflection of his perfectionist attitude. He reflects as he is warming up to the justification of vengeance and murder, and carefully brings himself to view the roles of mother and stepfather, the roles with which he is in conflict, as insidious, dangerous, and worthless. Listen as he broods:

> O! that this too too solid flesh would melt,
> Thaw, and resolve itself into a dew;

Or that the Everlasting had not fix'd
His canon 'gainst self-slaughter! O God! O God!
How weary, stale, flat, and unprofitable,
Seem to me all the uses of this world!
Fie on't! O fie! 'Tis an unweeded garden,
That grows to seed: things rank and gross in nature
Possess it merely. That it should come to this!
But two months dead: nay, not so much, not two:
So excellent a King; that was, to this,
Hyperion to a satyr: so loving to my mother,
That he might not beteem the winds of heaven
Visit her face too roughly. Heaven and earth!
Must I remember? Why, she would hang on him,
As if increase of appetite had grown
By what it fed on; and yet, within a month,
Let me not think on't: Frailty, thy name is woman!

The brooding is long, but the final execution of the act is swift.

A fast reaction is not always the best reaction, since many roles require a slow, careful, and pedantic approach. Consider the roles of scholarly historian, philosopher, physicist, and mathematician, for example. View the rate of warm-up as unique to an individual.

A pause is an indication that a person is selecting a response. With the schizophrenic, the pause is one of the chief characteristics of communication; when the pause is too long, the listener speculates about the message that is being sent and the act that is not being faced.

Involvement is a basic and desired goal of the warm-up. Anyone who has worked on a psychiatric ward has observed both the extremes of involvement and the absence of it. There are patients who sit in a lifeless row along the walls of the dayroom; they seldom move when called to meals or bat an eyelash if a fight is taking place a few feet away. In this example, the lack of responsiveness is taken as uninvolvement. "We notice with interest that, while the group removes its criminal members for what they *do*, it usually removes its schizophrenic members for what they *do not do*."[12] A superficial involvement is apparently achieved when a psychiatric aide goes to them and helps them get to meals, to bed, or out of range of the fighting. The movement of the patients is slow, mechanical, and resistant.

Still other patients are easily involved in anything and everything, running from person to person, looking for a breast to lean against or someone to talk to. At the least invitation, the storm within becomes a hurricane of words and actions. It is in this instance, where controls are gone, that a short and quick warm-up is not followed by effective action.

Another type of involvement that is intense and active can be seen in the following example. A training group in psychodrama met regularly to experience its techniques and to familiarize themselves with the method. A spontaneity test was set up as follows:

A young woman imagined herself to be on tne deck of a pleasure cruiser. As she sat sunning and enjoying herself, a ship's mate delivered a cablegram revealing that her mother had just died. The young woman broke into convulsive sobbing. Her reaction was noticeably and vividly real—*the situation had meaning to her.* She was an exchange student from Greece and had left her children in the care of her mother in Athens; the possibility of such a tragic event touched her present (unexpressed) concern and she was able, in a moment, to drop the eager student role and become the homesick mother who missed her family. The members of the group responded to her sadness with warmth and reassurances. The fast warm-up led to the emergence of her real feelings. Here we see how a hypothetical situation became a vehicle of catharsis and allowed the student to adequately portray the daughter role.

Role involvement is naturally limited when a person has to warm up to two separate life situations at the same time. A recent story reported in the news provides an example of a mixed warm-up:

A mother of five children was much admired by her neighbors for the intensity of her involvement with her children and her neighbor's children as well. Christmas week was the time for caroling, so she left the house with her children and went from house to house gathering other children to join the caroling group. As she reached the middle of the block, someone looked up and saw smoke and flames bursting into the air. It was her house, and it burned completely to the ground. That evening, as she and her family were in a neighbor's house, the neighbor looked on with amazement as the woman calmly sat reading Christmas stories to the children. When the reporters called to check the story of the fire, this woman commented, "I must have forgotten to blow out one of the candles around the Christmas tree. I hope other mothers don't make the same mistake."

In this story, the change of focus from one area of action to another indicates that one had primacy over the other. Two life situations had to be met and one area suffered because of the difficulty in warming up to two situations simultaneously. The role of the mother and the activities of caroling and Christmas took precedence over the role of the housekeeper, but the forfeiture was costly. Did the woman warm up intensely and directly only to roles away from the house? Did she reject the role of housekeeper and wife? And were those roles in need of development? Without seeing the mother, one can only hazard a guess.

Spontaneity and Creativity

Spontaneity is the readiness and ability to meet new situations adequately and old ones with a new vitality. Spontaneity is self-initiated behavior at the moment of action and allows a person to move freely, without compulsion, into a task or situation. The moment a person faces any situation, his choice of behavior shows whether his spontaneity has a creative, adequate form or not.

It is helpful in understanding role behavior to have some idea of the kind and degree of spontaneity a role requires and the role player produces. Each role requires a certain amount of spontaneity: a leader is expected to be sincere, to influence others, to mobilize action; a writer is expected to communicate by putting thoughts on paper. Some roles require more spontaneity than others. All people are faced with the act of awakening; it is a requirement of social living (invalids excepted) to get out of bed. When an alcoholic awakens with a big head and a sick stomach and musters just enough energy to ask his wife to call the boss and make some excuse for his not going to work, his spontaneity is weak and the solution is disruptive. The boss is disappointed, the wife is angry at her husband, and the alcoholic feels guilty. If a person awakens with chills and fever and goes to work anyway, his spontaneity may be considered adequate, but the solution lacks originality, since he is meeting a new situation (sickness) with a stereotypic pattern.

Another form of spontaneity is exemplified in the case of a woman who awakens early, perhaps at 4:00 A.M., because of pressure to complete all that needs to be done. She rushes around the house, turns on all the lights, starts to vacuum, takes a shower, awakens the entire household, and then rushes out of the house to knock on a neighbor's door to borrow something. Her spontaneity is overheated and leads to confusion. Psychotic behavior takes this form.

An example of pathological spontaneity is demonstrated by a member of a group of hospitalized adults who began their psychodrama session with introductions. One woman said, "I'm Esther and I'm nine years old." One of the disbelieving patients asked her how she figured that out. "Well," said Esther, "I was born twenty-nine years ago and I'm losing two years at a time. That makes me nine." This was a novel response, but the regressive behavior was pathological, and the arithmetic was bad. The patient at that moment established her relationship to the group thus: "I am a crazy woman who wants to be treated as a child. Don't ignore me, but don't expect too much of me, either." The spontaneity was too great and diffuse. One should not expect this patient to learn much at this point.

An uncreative response describes a wide variety of behavior, from compliance ("yes, thank you") to excessive rigidity of ritualistic mannerisms. In a person who gives such uncreative responses, interpersonal relationships are poorly developed. The role of the "other" is too threatening to allow him to satisfactorily enact a role, or he has feelings of being inadequate to perform a task that seems bigger than his talents. Here is an example: A patient, a salesman, complained that whenever he had to meet with the sales manager of his firm in a planning session, he experienced extreme discomfort. The sales manager was successful, abrupt, and evasive, and never looked at the salesman as he talked. This was so disconcerting that the salesman was unable to disagree with any marketing plan proposed by the sales manager, even when he was against it. He felt like a "yes" man. When this attitude becomes overwhelming, the individual experiences a loss of spontaneity and feels depressed. Another person in this situation might respond with "yes, but," a neurotic response. The patient thereby makes an attempt at self-realization, but it is frustrated, and this results in immobilization.

The highest form of spontaneity produces creative productivity. It leads to something, perhaps a more efficient resolution of a life situation.

Role Taking

Creativity is the goal of spontaneity, that moment when a person causes something to happen—an idea, a new form, a new role, or a new attitude. As soon as the new element exists, it becomes a role conserve, a part of the role repertoire. This new behavior is satisfying since the actor has created a new experience.

The best example of a fully established role that permits no change —is the part that an actor plays in the legitimate theater. This is the final form of the role conserve, or repetitious role playing. Unlike the theater, life never presents a situation in which the role enactment is exactly the same each time the situation occurs. Life tests the spontaneity of an individual, and the roles he creates show how effectively he improvises in an encounter with others. Life not only tests spontaneity, but may train it in a constricted and mistaken way towards oneself and others. Role playing in a therapeutic situation is a reliable way to test and train spontaneity—to learn by recognizing the meaning of behavior.

Summary and Inferences

A role is a pattern of behavior that a person develops from his life experiences in order to cope with the situations he faces. He develops and perceives his roles in terms of the anticipatory roles of other persons. The number and kinds of roles a person takes vary, as do the intensity and completeness with which the roles are executed.

Role taking is the ability to place oneself imaginatively or actually in a situation and to share it with others in their frame of reference. Role playing is the process of assuming the role or character of another person, an animal, an inanimate object, or oneself at another time and of acting accordingly. Psychodrama is a method that utilizes role playing in conjunction with other techniques.

Behavior may be studied by using the formulation of the role as a unit of observable behavior. Man is seen as a role player; he observes, imitates, improvises, and transforms roles and is identified and evaluated by his role behavior. A role is a form of communication that is easily recognized by others but that has a personal as well as a group meaning.

4

Further Analysis
of Role Concepts

A psychodrama session begins with role playing. A minimum of two persons participate—a patient and a therapist-director; but it is more usual to have three—a patient, a director, and an auxiliary ego. An audience (the group) may be present as in the following example. This example shows that a role as a unit of behavior is interactional, and the acting of it is both diagnostic and, perhaps, therapeutic as the patient suddenly sees himself. As the patient begins to play a role, the two elements (private and collective) of the role merge so that the enactment is experienced as a whole.

The Technique of One Role

When the director of the psychodrama meets a patient, he explains that each individual lives out many different roles, as a mother or father, a son or daughter, a basketball player, a student, and so on. Then the director asks, "Will someone in the group show us one of his roles?" Whether the group is large or small, it is easy for a patient to respond, since a role permits an individual to select any part of his living circumstance he wishes to show the group. The patient, of course, is the focus of attention.

PATIENT I will show you my role as picketer.

DIRECTOR Show us this situation of picketing. Who will you need? Is this something you do? Is it a real role or an imagined one?

PATIENT It's a real one when I'm not in the hospital. I'll need some other people picketing and some hecklers. I need a heckler. (*Starts marching, pretending to hold up a sign.*)

HECKLER 1 Why don't you get a haircut? You look like a furry thing. Why are you picketing this store? I don't like to cross a line, but I love to shop here.

This is good, for it uses the audience too.

PICKETER The practices of this chain of stores are unfair.

HECKLER 2 There's nothing wrong with this store; maybe other stores show prejudice.

PICKETER You may be right, but we found it ineffective to picket just the offending store. We have to picket the whole chain.

HECKLER 3 It would be a good idea if you just went in and bought some soap. You could really use it.

DIRECTOR Is this the way picketing goes?

Director checks the validity of the scene.

PICKETER	Yes, I'm really bushed at the end of my time, and then I hand my picket sign to another guy.	
DIRECTOR	Where do you go after you're through?	*Director is exploring another role.*
PICKETER	I go home to my wife and is she burned up!	*Here's a clue to conflict.*
DIRECTOR	Then you also have the role of husband. Let's see that. Choose someone to be your wife.	
PICKETER	I'll choose Heckler 2. She sounds a little like that, always throwing in arguments against my picketing.	*This gives a clue to the auxiliary ego in playing the wife: to be argumentative, but to use reason rather than slurs.*
WIFE	I don't feel that you're justified in coming home so tired—you'll not get any sympathy from me.	*The wife is not specific enough.*
PICKETER	*(To the group.)* She's from Hungary.	
DIRECTOR	Let's switch roles. You know your wife, so show us what she's like. How does she talk to you when you come home sweaty and tired after you've picketed?	*Director helps the husband portray wife's attitude by reversing roles.*
PICKETER *(as wife)*	You're too idealistic. We took it for granted in Hungary that if we picketed, we would get shot, not clubbed. What you're doing is ridiculous. You don't know how well you have it.	

DIRECTOR	Switch roles. Be yourself again.	*Auxiliary ego has sufficient information.*
PICKETER	You would not want me to go against my convictions, would you? There are many changes that have to be made, many indignities.	
WIFE	(*Heatedly.*) Oh, my goodness. You act as if you're the only one who has ideals. There are other things you can do besides standing in the line with pickets in order to show your idealism.	
AUXILIARY EGO (*as wife*)	You are fighting with me. You may call it an intellectual argument, but this is a fight without an end. I could shake you—I'm so angry.	*The wife and the auxiliary ego move closer and closer to the fight.*
PICKETER	You are just like all women. You become emotional when reason is indicated.	
WIFE	There you go again, so high and mighty. The only feeling you have is for the poor miserable undertrodden. What about me?	*The picketer has no more to say, so stops role playing, which ends the scene. This type of termination of the scene usually indicates that the actor has reached his limit for performance for the moment.*

Comment on the Role-Playing Technique

Whichever role the patient selects can be portrayed as a sample of an interpersonal relationship. The husband's relationships are shown in the diagram. Generalizations are made based on the actual behavior the patient demonstrated, a valid expression of the external forms of interaction, but perhaps not of the total personality. *Figure 4.1* shows the roles the patient enacted in this scene.

Figure 4.1

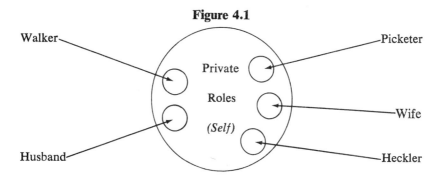

Figure 4.2 shows the way in which the patient enacted the roles: solid lines represent unconflicted feelings between his private self and the roles of picketer and walker; broken lines represent the conflicted character of the feelings of husband and heckler.

Figure 4.2

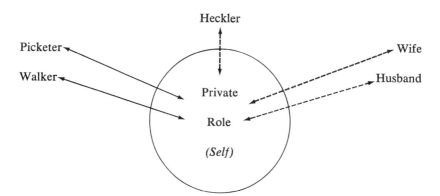

The patient selected a role in which he hoped to gain respect and admiration from the group: "Look at what a good man I am and the pain and humiliation I endure from the hecklers." In his private role as a husband, his wife became a heckler. He used the same condescending explanation with her that he gave to the street hecklers. His positive feelings were toward the sign and toward what it symbolized. In the role playing, he was confronted with his assumed superiority and he withdrew. The role of the picketer may have satisfied his need to use idealism as a way of looking down on others. The role, however, interfered with his relationship to his wife and probably interfered with his relationships with other people.

In general, then, a collective role can lead into the patient's private world and give the first diagnostic clues of a problem.

The Auxiliary Ego

The auxiliary ego is a trained person (a staff member or a patient) who portrays the actual or imagined people needed by the protagonist to act out events of the past, present, or future that are to be dealt with in the present. It is always the current behavior that is the focus of attention. The auxiliary ego represents the patient's ego and responds intuitively (guesses). His responses are based on his prior experience or, more immediately, on the way he warms up to the patient. He may represent a person, a dream figure, a hallucinatory or delusional character, or another symbol. He assists the director by eliciting information from the patient. The player of the auxiliary ego may give guidance within the role, as he is a co-therapist and his skill in responding leads both to diagnosis and therapy.

The auxiliary ego must be sensitive to the patient's description of the person he is to portray if he is to be able to translate it into a role. The following is an example of the flexible behavior of the auxiliary ego as he begins with a stereotype and then becomes the symbol of the patient's absentee person.

Tom, a twenty-two-year-old, opened the meeting in a loud, blustery voice: "I need to know whether I should take an apartment with my boyfriend and his girlfriend and her baby. We are going to share and share alike, but my mother thinks it's crazy, and they will take advantage of me."

An auxiliary ego was given the role of boyfriend and the scene began.

AUXILIARY EGO *(as Tom's friend)*	Listen, Tom, if we are to live together, I expect that you'll give us some privacy.	*Begins with a* *straightforward* *discussion of issues.*

TOM	*(To director before director has had time to check the distortion of the auxiliary ego's role playing.)* No, no. That's not the way he said it.	
DIRECTOR	Switch roles. Tom, you be the friend.	
TOM *(as friend)*	No problem, Tom. We'll have a great time. Find a girl for you so we'll be even. Smoke a little pot, drink, have parties. After all, you're my best friend.	
AUXILIARY EGO *(as Tom's friend)*	Tom, don't worry. Anita will do all the cooking, cleaning, and shopping. She won't pay rent—just work out her and the baby's share.	*Corrects the role of Tom's friend.*
TOM	I don't want to cause trouble between you and Anita, but what if we get drunk and I end up in bed with her? I don't want you to knock me around.	
AUXILIARY EGO *(as Tom's friend)*	No problem. If it happens, it happens.	*Portrays the role as defined by Tom.*
TOM	I don't want to end up being a babysitter for you and Anita.	
AUXILIARY EGO	Never. I promise. Do you have your money together? I need a pad and so does Anita.	*Clarifies the interpersonal situation.*

Tom	Sounds good, but I won't sign a lease.	
Auxiliary Ego	No problem. I'll sign. Come on. Take a chance. It'll be trading one crib for another, only this one is *real*, man. You'll have everything you want—food, drinks, sex.	*The auxiliary seductively offers complete pampering.*

The auxiliary ego, within the role, reflected the goal of the patient, which seemed to be to get everything he wanted—his needs took precedence over all other considerations. With this as his goal, he wasn't asking for advice about whether or not he should move in with his friends, but rather how to get his mother to agree that the arrangement was workable. He needed professional permission to influence his mother to finance it.

In the role playing, the auxiliary ego adopted some of his own conclusions of Tom's behavior drawn from prior experiences with Tom. He also included in the presentation his knowledge of Tom's relationship to his mother. If he had spoken to the best friend and had some actual reactions to the plan, he would be expected as a co-therapist to bring this out in the open. It is a devastating experience—to the audience, the patient, and the director—to withhold information that could easily remove the distortions that develop because of misinformation.

We can see that the auxiliary ego's reaction to the patient's behavior stimulated the patient to show more than he intended: The unrealistic terms of the arrangement for living together portrayed Tom's confusion. As the auxiliary ego role played Tom's best friend, he probably helped create a realistic picture of what happened. This could lead to exploring other relationships between Tom and his mother, Tom and Anita, and so on.

The auxiliary ego in this illustration was a member of the staff; his acting helped not only the patient but himself, as it added to his role repertoire. Understanding comes from playing another's role. This function may be called a helping ego, an assistant, a co-therapist, as well as an auxiliary ego, and it may be performed either by another patient or by someone professionally trained. Whoever performs this function benefits from the role playing. A patient may be asked to role play with another patient as part of his own development.

An auxiliary ego can refuse to play a role, but he should be made aware that the refusal may interrupt the patient's willingness to go on with the situation and cause a loss of spontaneity. An explanation should be made to the patient if another refuses to come to his assistance. A valid excuse would be that the role to be enacted is the same as an unresolved one of the auxiliary ego and therefore seems too overwhelming to the auxiliary. For example, in one session a woman recently divorced from an alcoholic husband accepted this role in relation to an alcoholic male patient. At a crucial moment in the situation, she overreacted and slapped his face, which shocked him into hitting her back. She had been unable to separate her own unresolved attitude toward her ex-husband from her role vis-à-vis the patient.

Willingness to use body contact as an outward expression of the role is a desirable characteristic of the auxiliary ego. He should be able to touch, hold, embrace, rock, and wrestle. To enter into contact with genuine warmth is therapeutic, as the patient needs to interact with a reasonable representative of the real person. When a patient has suffered a loss, whether early in life or recently, it is usually therapeutic for the auxiliary ego to portray the lost fantasy figure with tender regard and sincere concern for the patient. Touching should be carefully considered in the case of certain patients, however. For some, it is a threatening gesture and may be something less than therapeutic for both the patient and the auxiliary ego. Body movements communicate an attitude, and the auxiliary ego should be aware if the patient pulls away, averts his glance, or shifts his body weight. He may feel uncomfortable with the intimacy of touch.

There are, of course, occasions when the auxiliary ego simply stands or sits and lets the patient project the image of an absent person. This may occur when the patient is unable to interact or the auxiliary ego is too inexperienced to do otherwise, as when a student is having a first experience as an auxiliary ego. No harm is done, as the patient's effort in helping the student often has a beneficial effect. There is no therapeutic gain when the touching is done only to satisfy the erotic needs of one party.

The auxiliary ego, then, is skilled in the psychological meaning of behavior and is able to accept cues from the director and translate them into a meaningful role for the patient and the audience.

The Audience

The patient with a problem is first a member of the audience. As he moves to the stage, the audience begins to act as his social reality and helps him as it reacts to the presentation with criticism or approval. This communication may be expressed by comments, laughter, or deadly silence. In the interaction between the audience and the patient, the audience participates both as a giver and a receiver of help as members of the audience see themselves in the roles being portrayed. A member of the audience may join the action on the stage as a double when the warm-up reaches some part of his own experience. There is no one way in which the members of the audience react to the performed problem. For some, it is a matter of deep concern; for others, a time for quiet musing; for still others, a matter of indifference.[1]

At the end of each episode the director invites the audience to a discussion. There may be a spontaneous expression of identification if the life situation touched someone in the audience. Or the director may guide the discussion with questions. The following is an example of a spontaneous reaction from members of the audience:

AUDIENCE 1   Tom, it'll never work. He's
              just after rent money.

TOM   His mother kicked him out of
              her house. Maybe you're
              right.

AUDIENCE 2   Go ahead, Tom; take a
              chance. What have you got
              to lose?

AUDIENCE 1   It'll last less than a week.   *The audience is drawn*
              He'll knock the shit out of   *into the situation and*
              you.   *tries to help Tom*
                                                  resolve the problem.

TOM   Not me. Not out of me.
              Anita maybe, but not me.

DIRECTOR   (*To auxiliary ego.*) How did
              Tom make you feel?

AUXILIARY EGO Like his mother was listening
              somewhere, and he was
              showing her he knew how to
              drive a hard bargain.

DIRECTOR | Neither one of us was trying to make a workable arrangement.

Tom, do you agree? Is that what was going on?

A directed viewing helps the members of the audience place themselves in the interaction by encouraging identification with the players at some level of the problem. For example, the director might ask if someone in the group understood—as a mother or as a son or daughter —the mother's resistance to her son's moving in with a friend. As the audience is carefully questioned about its reactions to what has gone on, the role identity is being tapped, and each member of the audience has a chance to discover for himself whether anything that happened on the stage reminds him of his own experience with other people. This may lead to a rearrangement of the cast as the patients in the audience play out the problem of a young man's desire to become part of a world larger and livelier than a mother's apartment.

Basic Techniques

All the techniques of psychodrama increase the involvement of the individual and the group and thereby create a clearer understanding of self and others. These techniques, when used flexibly, can reach patients who might be accessible in no other way. "In fact, they tap what Jurgen Ruesch has called nonanalogic communication or what Moreno calls infantile spontaneity, the role playing that is established with deep and permanent significance through acts and gestures between the infant and its environment" long before the child has learned the significance of words and symbols.[2] However, psychodrama can also generate stresses disruptive to patterns of self-control and to adaptations to reality. For example, the director must avoid having the patient act out homicidal or suicidal acts except in a carefully controlled environment, such as an institution, and even then the director must have sufficient training and experience to know the suitability of one set of techniques over another.[3] These disadvantages may often be counteracted by a suitable combination of group and individual sessions.

The Double Ego

In the double ego technique, an auxiliary ego stands beside the patient and acts like him—at times, *for* him—in an attempt to simulate the mental state of the patient.[4] The double may speak in the first person singular to express the patient's thoughts. This technique is especially valuable for the isolate, as he needs to feel that someone understands him. It is also effective with the patient who has difficulty communicating. The double ego sits beside him, or walks along with him, and speaks as if they were one. He might say, "I'm lonesome. I wish people were nicer to me." When the patient is withholding anger, as depressed patients often do, the double can become explosive and rage in the patient's place or show the love the patient is unable to express.

Two doubles may be used if the patient is struggling with ambivalence. The doubles can verbalize both sides of the conflict, and the battle between them can help the patient to act, to be assertive, to make a decision. Here is an example: A hospitalized seventeen-year-old girl, a drug user, had failed during her first pass into the community by walking directly from the hospital to join a group of old friends in the park to smoke some joints, mixed with a little hash. She returned to the hospital sick, hysterical, and screaming, wanting a pill to quiet her down. Her parents arrived at this inopportune time, and she dramatically ordered them out of her life. The problem she brought to the psychodrama group was whether or not she should call her parents and make peace with them.

The situation described above was reenacted and two doubles were produced. The first double pushed for reconciliation, and the second pointed out the cost of making peace with the folks—being obedient and giving up drugs. As the fight went on, the patient joined in with, "That's the way I feel!" The director had a phone ring; it was the mother (auxiliary ego). The patient answered it, and the mother, in a sweet voice, said, "Do you feel better, baby?" The patient stopped, looked at the group, and said, "That's just the way it is; I don't have to decide whether to call her or not. She'll call me. If just once she would tell me how stupid I am. I'm stupid. Stupid." It may be that this patient began to understand her ambivalent feelings. She waited for others to act first, for she knew she didn't have to. The ambivalence (indecision) kept the engine running while the vehicle stood still.

The Mirror

The second important technique is the mirror. In this technique, as the name implies, the auxiliary ego reflects the actions of the patient for the patient to observe and react to. This works well with patients who have been unable to interact with other people appropriately—the depressed individual, the misbehaving child, or the fantasy-ridden person. The individual needs to have his behavior portrayed by another so that he can stand at a distance from it. This is similar to the feedback provided by videotaping a group therapy session.

In one psychodrama session on a ward with an actively hallucinating patient, one of the patients in the group said, "Let's work with Jim; he's driving us batty." The group was warmed up and involved with this problem. It was obvious that Jim was actively hallucinating and was not ready to work on anything but his fantasies. The director asked, "Who will be Jim?" At the same time, she moved alongside Jim, checking all the while with him by means of his body movements if it were all right to do this. Since Jim did not say no, or get up to leave, he presumably agreed.

The auxiliary ego (in this case one of the patients) used two chairs to form a bed, then began shaking imaginary sheets and muttering, "The devil is here someplace—I must find him." He went from bed to bed, waking up all the patients. Since all the men had been involved in this, they were invited to show how they responded to his pushing them out of bed in his search for the devil. The director kept in close contact with Jim, the hallucinatory patient who was being mirrored, until she detected that Jim was responding to the action. The director asked, "Is this what you do?" "I guess so," Jim replied.

Jim was asked to come to the stage, and his mirror (auxiliary ego) left. The mirror, in this case, was used to capture the attention and interest of a psychotic patient. The group was able to clarify the meaning of this behavior by asking Jim, "When did you start looking for the devil?" and to move in the direction of defining the pressures in Jim's life that forced him to deal with his problems symbolically.

Sometimes when the mirror technique is used, it becomes clear, as the patient's behavior is being enacted, that he does not recognize himself and objects to the enactment. When this happens, he is invited to come up and correct it. This may frighten him, or he may feel ridiculed. The director must deal with the patient's response until some understanding is reached.

Role Reversal

The third technique is role reversal, sometimes called switching roles. Two people exchange roles with one another at a crucial moment of the scene or the situation. The better each person knows the other, the easier it is to reverse roles. Roles that can be reversed rather easily are husband and wife, mother and child, and student and teacher.[5] Young people usually perceive a "generation gap," which really means that they feel that their elders are unable to reverse roles with them. Likewise, black militants feel that no white man can reverse roles with a black. The psychological and social distance is too great. This may or may not be true; it depends on the individuals involved.

Role reversal is helpful in correcting the disturbed attitudes between intimates. Often it leads to an improved relationship as the other person's position and reactions are understood.[6] For example, disturbance between husband and wife is vividly portrayed by the following:

A husband and wife are driving along in a car. The windows are up. The two are discussing a trivial matter. She lowers the window on her side of the car. The husband makes a cutting remark and the wife points it out. An argument ensues.

The roles are switched. The wife, in the role of the husband, discovers that the husband's anger and sarcasm are not with the content of the discussion but with the fact that she was inconsiderate when she lowered the window. Her husband is hard of hearing and she knows (or should know) that he can't hear when the window is lowered.

It would have been difficult, as in real life, to have gotten from the husband his perception of an inconsiderate wife except as he role-played her in the car.

Each person has a particular position in relationship to the other, and with the role reversal technique, there is the possibility of understanding the other person's thinking, feeling, and behavior when the identification with the other takes place. As a result of this insight, the attitudes of both may be changed.

Role reversal is also helpful in moving a story plot along. When the patient blocks because the auxiliary ego inaccurately responds to the situation, roles can be reversed so that a correction can be made without stopping the action and losing spontaneity. Blocking on the part of the patient is usually a signal for reversing roles.

Some patients are unable to role-reverse. For example, role reversal is not indicated with psychotic patients. Some patients can enact a person in authority but not one who accepts authority. Many psychotic patients are unwilling to play the role of the other and either respond with terror, taking the role as real, or make no effort to influence or change the course of events. Role reversal is a technique of socialization that requires a certain amount of self-integration in order to benefit from the viewpoint of the other person.[7]

Role reversal can define and clarify an issue. Exchanging roles helps the role player see another's point of view. It also makes it possible for the role player to move into the other role and show how he wants to be treated. In a way, then, reversing roles not only establishes the area of conflict, but also in many instances leads the way out of the conflict.

Soliloquy

Another technique mentioned earlier is the soliloquy. The player shares with the group his normally censored feelings and thoughts and thereby associates his feelings to the ongoing event. He turns his head to one side, and in a different voice tone associates his feelings to the behavior he is experiencing. This is helpful in communicating how certain kinds of behavior arouse feelings which may not be observable. When he returned, he was asked to discuss some of the difficulties he experienced. He acted out the situation of going to a restaurant. Two girls sat down next to him at the counter and talked to each other. Their conversation confused him. Were they referring to him or to someone else? The conversation went like this:

FIRST GIRL   I'm glad we got rid of him.

SECOND GIRL   I'm not sure if we got rid of him or he got rid of us.

PATIENT   (*To the girls.*) You're alone. What happened?

FIRST GIRL   (*To the patient.*) Oh, we picked this guy up at the station, but he was a fink.

PATIENT   What do you mean?

DIRECTOR   Tell the group, John. Talk out loud, not to the girls.

PATIENT	I have never been married.	*John expresses ideas*
	It is a good thing I never did.	*that indicate he*
	Look how mean girls are.	*thought the girls were*
	It's pretty dangerous to get	*referring to him. His*
	involved with people like this.	*words focus on the*
	I wonder what the word	*relationship of the*
	fink means.	*event to his feelings.*

Another patient who had gone out on a pass was asked what had happened to him, and he admitted to speaking to no one, although he had sat next to a girl on the train. The scene was set up, and the patient was asked to talk out loud, to soliloquize his thoughts as he was riding along. In this case, the soliloquy was used to show this young man how to talk to a girl, and the auxiliary ego substituted for the passenger on the train.

The Monologue

Monologue is a form of the soliloquy in which the patient moves into the roles of others. The patient plays the roles of all the people involved in a scene. As he shifts from role to role, he moves around the stage. This self-directed psychodrama may work better for a patient who finds the spontaneity of the auxiliary ego too disturbing, or when a patient insists on playing a situation *exactly* as he remembers it. It is better for him to reach a feeling of completeness and a continuity of progression in a monologue, or monodrama.

Conclusion

Part of the skill in directing a psychodramatic session is in learning to use the basic techniques consistently before attempting the many variations and formats that finally become the repertoire of a psychodramatist. The better he understands how and why things happen, the more effectively he can control what happens. This chapter attempts to show how to translate role theory into practice. Any role is only a part of a system of interdependent roles and must flow easily into other roles, which is the basic foundation of a psychodrama session. The next step is applying role playing to family problems.

5

Psychodrama with the Family Group

The influence of the family in the personality development of the child has been acknowledged in scientific literature, folklore, and elegant prose and poetry. But a rapidly growing collection of historical data shows that parents have not always aspired to teach children mutual respect and cooperation as they do today. The further back in time one goes, the more it is apparent that patterns of childhood training have differed from ours.[1]

The Greek poets were not averse to humanizing their gods and reported this instance of parental anger and abandonment. Vulcan, the celestial artist, was the son of Jupiter and Juno. He was born lame, according to one account, and his mother was so displeased at the sight of him that she flung him out of their sky dwelling. In another account, Jupiter was the one that rejected the child; Jupiter threw Vulcan out for siding with Juno in a family quarrel, and Vulcan's lameness was the result of his subsequent fall to earth.[2] The ideal of people coping with disappointment without showing anger, accepting without emotion whatever fate brings, isn't true to life, as one discovers when one looks at any family and its ordinary and extraordinary problems.

By examining the dynamics of the family group, students of human nature hope to discover the healing as well as the crippling effects of its structure. While each family group is unique, it is a part of the fabric of a society and its culture. The family is a natural social grouping with a psychological organization which influences each member of the family, directly and indirectly. A child born into a family adapts to that family and learns to interact with its members. Experiences are tempered by the environment into which a child is born (the attitudes and the tele phenomenon of family interaction) and his perception of it.

In the ideal family, the husband and the wife are of similar age and mental capacity and are sexually and socially attracted to one another. To this sexual group or union, children are added, forming a second group and activating in the original pair the roles of mother and father. The children are daughters and sons to the parents and, at the same time, are brothers and sisters to each other. This is the beginning for the children of their social relatedness (social atom), which develops to include persons outside the family. These two groups with separate functions live together in what Moreno calls a sexual grouping and a monastic grouping.[3] A sociogram of the family group is shown in *Figure 5.1*.

Figure 5.1

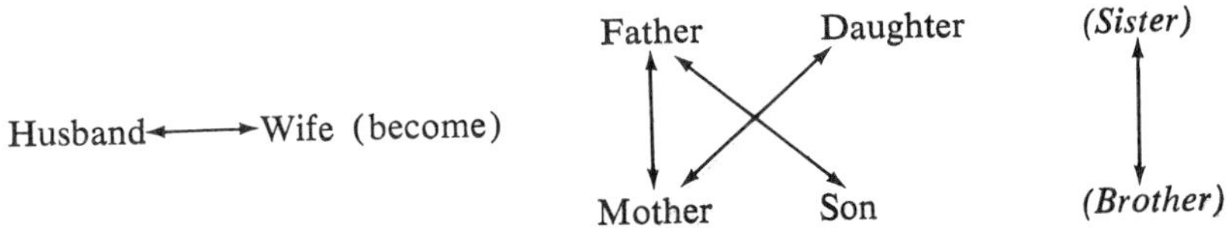

A further development (*Figure 5.2*) of the sociogram pictures the attraction to others outside the family.

Figure 5.2

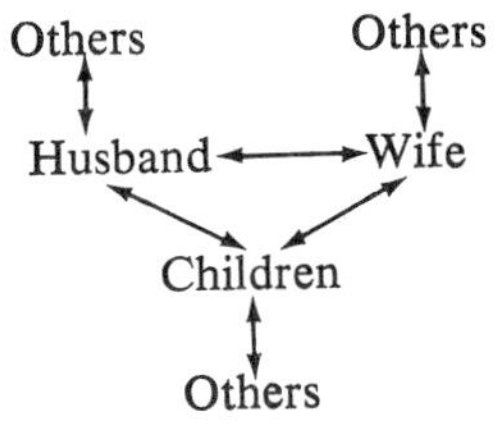

The Approach of Family Therapy

Family therapy is of value at any period of the human drama; the target of therapy may be a child, several children, an adolescent, a young or middle-aged adult, or a senior citizen. When the director meets with the entire family, aspects of a difficult situation may be enacted as the pattern of interaction is seen and discussed, and the family history becomes known. The approach presented here is an integrated application of sociometry and psychodrama. It is used to uncover the unique structure of a group with a continuing life and organizations such as is found in the family. "Therapy of families on an outpatient basis may be viewed as an intermediate milieu therapy. These intermediate forms may possess greater promise than the traditional therapies."[4]

Development of Family Therapy

Family therapy as a tactic or strategy has been used by therapists for the last twenty-five years. It has become a common treatment technique for all levels of family problems. Through family meetings, the problem of the patient can be understood as a problem in the communication and behavior of the whole family; all the family members need to change.

Some therapists work only with the entire family, refusing to see the individual patient alone. This is a complete reversal of technique from the time when a patient was seen only in individual therapy, without the other members of his family being included or consulted. This dramatic change began with the social psychology of Alfred Adler and the interpersonal psychiatry of Harry S. Sullivan. The interest in group therapy was furthered by the followers of Kurt Lewin and his field theory and of Jacob Moreno and his small-group experiments. Family therapy ties individuals to cultural and social factors in treatment as well as in theory.

Over fifty years ago, Adler's formulation that a child's love life is directed toward others[5] (not, as Freud would say, upon his own body) opened the door to the importance of the cultural and economic surroundings of the child. Man is a social being concerned with and striving to correct the difficulties he encounters in his life situation. He wants to belong to the group, to have friends, and to feel that others are responding to him. Adler established community clinics and laid the groundwork for the family approach. He believed that the therapist's role was to complete the job of the mother—to teach the patient cooperation. This was the beginning of a trend which rapidly changed the focus of therapy.

Sullivan found the roots of mental disease in a "transpersonal reality, requiring that we study at the same time the person and his life situation; it is not the one or the other who is sick—it is the form of the interaction."[6] Sullivan's innovations in interpersonal psychiatry were principally with psychotic patients, and while he never invited the families into the treatment, he accepted that "the situation is not any old thing, it is you and someone else integrated in a particular fashion that can be converted in the alembic of speech into a statement that A is striving towards so-and-so from B; B is highly significant in the situation."[7]

The professional experiences of these two men were different, so many of their conclusions seem at variance. Sullivan spent most of his time as a doctor ministering to hospital patients, principally psychotics; it does not seem strange, then, that his goal of treatment—mental health—would be expressed as intimacy. Adler dealt more with neurotics and problem children on an ambulatory basis and moved beyond psychiatric contacts into educational and lay circles.[8] As pointed out earlier, his criterion of mental health was social interest, expressed operationally as cooperation.

Group Therapy and the Family

Group therapy is based on the dynamics of the group; the similarity between the dynamics of a small group and those of a family is obvious. Both groups are powerful value forming instruments. Gardner Murphy and Elizabeth Cattell find "a close parallel here both to the conception of sociatry as developed by Moreno and to the conception of group dynamics as developed by the followers of Kurt Lewin . . . and Sullivan's conception of the rebuilding of the patient's world as a first step in interpersonal therapy."[9] While there are differences in these three movements, each recognizes the significance of intergroup dynamics.

All groups have areas of interaction occurring simultaneously "within the individual, between the members of the group, and within the total situation."[10] Change in one area affects the individuals within the total group situation and the climate of the group as well.

Diagram of a Sociometric Triangle

The complex configuration of a family with one child becomes apparent when a few of the possible sociograms are drawn (see Figure 5.3).

To understand the individual, we first make a general assumption which may be clarified or changed by further observation, study, or role playing. Some probabilistic statements about "only" children are:

Figure 5.3

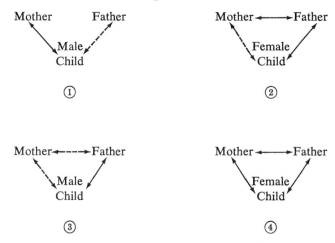

1.   The only child bears the brunt of the feelings, negative and positive, of the parents and usually suffers because of it.

2.   Parents of only children may be timid people who deal cautiously with the child, demonstrating much anxiety.

3.   An only child may receive too much pampering (diagram 4).

4.   The only child is the sibling rival of the father when the child is a boy; or of the mother, if the child is a girl (diagrams 1 and 2), and must strive to be an adult.

5.   The only child likes being the center of the parents' love and has difficulty in later life in finding this Utopia (ex. 4).

6.   When an only child chooses the father, the child is complaining about the mother (diagram 3).

7.   A mother is related not only to her child but also to her husband. When the attraction between mother and father is weak or negative, the child may never develop positive feelings for the father. We see this on sociogram 1, a negative feeling expressed either overtly by a desire to be rid of the father, or by withdrawing from him. This is not the Oedipus drama (or in the case of the girl, the Electra), but a response attitude of a child who has been pampered and is reluctant

to release his maternal servant.[11] This reluctance is expressive of the child's attitude toward satisfaction of all his needs, at times even sexual.

8. In the therapeutic management of the only child, it is a good idea to provide him with activities with other children by sending him to nursery school and camp at as early an age as possible. Venus found a solution to this problem in the advice of Themis, the goddess of law who counseled Jove. Venus complained to Themis that her son Eros (Cupid) continued to be a child. Themis said that this was because Eros was solitary—if he had a brother he would "grow apace." Venus soon thereafter bore Anteros, and Eros immediately was seen to increase rapidly "in size and strength."[12]

Each firstborn child lives for a time as an only child. When the second baby is born, there is a change involving the parents who now have two children and the firstborn who must adapt to this new circumstance. The second child becomes the baby of the family until a third child arrives, and then he becomes a middle child. As the family becomes larger, each child adapts to the change through a pattern of interaction which defines who the child is in relation to the family constellation. For example, when there are four children, a coalition of two and two may form, or the eldest may retain his firstborn status by remaining separate and aloof from the other three.

There is a tendency for each child in a family to select some quality or attribute that is lacking in the others. The first child may find his place as a conforming, studious person and the second may be more interested in excelling in sports, leaving the area of studying strictly alone. The youngest in a family may stay in the baby role or work hard at overcoming that role. Each child experiences the helplessness of infancy that brings love or rejection; he never completely loses that feeling of helplessness and the sense of the response of others to that helplessness.

The Mother Role

The mother has a twofold function: to give the child an experience of love and to guide the child into having this feeling for others. The mother role is a cluster of roles—housekeeper, hostess, chauffeur, sexual partner, complement to her husband's vocation, and often wage earner. It is not surprising, then, that children find it difficult to identify with the mother role.

The Father Role

The father's adequacy furthers the socialization of the children. Ideally, and without becoming a policeman directing traffic, he helps teach the children the "rules of the road" and that outside the family exist trustworthy human beings. This prepares the children to enter into contact with others.

The father role is rooted in a man's occupational life, which is crucial to the man's self-esteem and preempts other demands on his time. However, when all the father's satisfactions are derived from activities outside the family and he excludes them, especially his wife, the family, of course, suffers.

Parental Influence

The relationship between the mother and father usually creates the value system in the home. The husband and wife are a team with the necessary authority to establish respect for themselves and for the others in the family. This is carried out by parents respecting their children's freedom of action to perform their functions without undue interference and receiving in return children who contribute to the family harmony.

Parents influence but do not determine a child's behavior. Children also respond to the sibling system, and when parents understand the meaning of this interaction, many of the failures in family functioning may be corrected.

The family group has a natural feeling of relatedness, of continuity, and of anchorage in relationships that may stimulate responsibility, cooperation, and intellectual growth. The two groups within the family operate through patterns of interaction: parent to child, child to parent, child to child, and husband to wife. The family group trains an individual in the attitudes that will later determine that person's role and behavior in adult society.

Applications of Role Playing in Family Problems

Because the problems of the child (or children) usually result from family transactions, we try to work with all the family members at the same time. Often the mother is, at first, the only parent who attends with the children, and the father begins to attend after he notices some positive improvement. It is important, regardless of disparate ages, that all the siblings attend.

The psychodramatist should know something about the family—names, ages, and chief difficulty—before he meets with them. He tentatively draws the family roles as the child shows through his behavior how he achieves recognition in the family. This places the misbehaving or dysfunctioning child in the role of chief protagonist, with the rest of the family in supporting roles.

Planning the Family Session

The family sits in a circle with the psychodrama director. The relationship of the director to the family is important and must be based on mutual trust and respect. The director conveys to the family that all people have problems and that many problems are not easy to solve. In order to be helpful, the director needs the cooperation of the family. He recognizes that there may be some apprehension being experienced, not only by the children but also by the parents, who are perhaps wondering if counseling is necessary.[13] The family becomes the chief resource in this cooperative problem-solving venture and must be made aware that each family member has something to contribute to improve communication. This is accomplished by each person's (1) being willing to show himself in a frank and open way and (2) reporting back on what is changing in the family and what is not changing. Communication provides both the director and the family with the necessary feedback, the information about family transactions that are improving and those that are still in need of change.

The first contact with the family is often easy, especially if the disturbances in the family are the usual misbehaviors that frequently erupt in all families. If the members of the family are able to respond readily to this meeting as a potentially interesting experience, perhaps they will even enjoy the hour together. Look for evidence of a willingness to trust a new approach.

When parents bring children into the room, it is easy to observe if their attitude toward being in the situation is fearful, embarrassed, tense, or broadly indifferent. The first contact of the director with the family is important. A friendly atmosphere can be established and personal interest expressed through introductions: names and ages can be exchanged, playfully when the children are preadolescent. With the adolescent, a deliberate professional role with friendly concern is preferred to the friendly camaraderie one can express with younger children. If the children do not respond quickly, visiting in the circle should be prolonged. The interviewing of one another may take an active form and continue until a problem is agreed upon as suitable for enactment. An example of this approach (usually used with a large family) is as follows: After the introductions and when there seems to be a lag in responsiveness, the director says, "There are many ways to get to know one another besides giving names and ages. Let's arrange ourselves as liking or disliking something. Who likes to eat? Who is the one in this group who likes to eat the most? [Everyone points to mother.] All the good eaters join mother and the not-so-good eaters sit opposite them."

The family alignment can be estimated from this situation since this interaction uncovers the competitors in the family: an eater may be competing with a noneater. Or it may be that all the children eat well; the parents do not make a fuss over the eaters or noneaters. Dinner time is not battle time.

Then the director suggests: "Now show how you seat yourself at meal time. Let's make it a time when you usually are all eating together." The director helps the family arrange themselves around a real or imaginary table by calling attention to their movements: "Mother sits next to baby, and father sits across from Joe. I see that the two men in the family sit across from each other. Is that the way it is?" With this comment the director notes that the "problem child" chooses to sit next to a certain family member and that the father places himself across from his son. Often parents keep a corrective eye on the misbehaving child.

The director asks the family to think a moment and to rearrange themselves in terms of preferences that they have for sitting near one another at dinner time. With Joe in the lead, the three children leave the table and seat themselves in front of the imaginary TV. This leaves mother and father alone at the table. The mother laughs and remarks, "We can't compete with TV." This has the effect of separating the family into two parts, the chosen and the unchosen. The director may introduce any other area of liking or disliking, for example, reading, sleeping, or washing dishes, and invite the family to suggest other family tasks. To have the family share in the production of ideas is important. This portion of the interview explores the family pattern of accepting and rejecting tasks.

When the exploration of tasks reaches a problem area, the director may ask, "Does anyone wish to play the role of one of the persons facing you?" The speed and timing of moving to this step, of course, is related to the warm-up of the family to working together.

Another way to lead into a problem is to have the members of the family, as they sit together, make a single statement of complaint about something that happens in the family that bothers, angers, or frustrates them. Young children may have trouble in identifying a problem, but after a few sessions, the young child is usually able to express himself more clearly. The complaints are a manifestation of the compatibility and conflict between the persons in the family and define an individual's perception of the family values.

Role Playing of Family Problems

Family problems are worked out in steps. First, the director should discuss and select the problem to be enacted. Second, he should put the various family transactions into context and cast the family roles as quickly as possible. During the enactment, the transactional pattern is manifest in the conflict and in the way it is resolved. A variety of responses are possible to a conflict situation, and the enactment should include not only the tensions of the conflict but also what each family member does about it.[14] To check the validity of the interaction, the various aspects of the situation may be tested at this time through role changing and mirroring. Third, the director should analyze and discuss with the family the pattern of relationship as shown in the role playing, that is, the actual behavior of the family group during the discussion, the unstructured interaction on entering, and the ease of participation or lack of it. The discussion may be started with a tentative hypothesis of the family dynamics, putting a conclusion in the form of a question, such as, "Do you usually feel sorry for the little one when the bigger child hits him?" The child's self-concept, as shown in the playing, is explored. This may lead into other situations that the family feels are stressful. Fourth, the problem that is the most urgent one in the family's estimation should be reenacted to discover a better solution to the difficulty.

The corrective treatment of the relationships existing in the family depends, of course, on what is shown in the reenactment and the various psychological attitudes and interpretations of the director toward reconciliation of dysfunction. However, one psychodramatic approach is to cast the child-with-a-problem in several different family roles—the father, the mother, the other siblings—with the family members assuming the other roles. The fighter-in-the-family becomes the umpire or mediator. A series of roles may be developed: a truant girl may be cast in roles of authority such as nurse to patient and prosecuting attorney to defendant. The director interacts spontaneously with the family to make recommendations that can change the family atmosphere and the individual's attitudes.

Every family has its own particular characteristics that some family therapists call the lifestyle of the family. A sociometrist calls them the characteristics of the group. These characteristics reflect the influence, or the impact, of each family member on the others. Everyone in his own way through his behavior contributes to the particular climate that prevails in the family. If change takes place in one, the effect is felt in all. This is why family therapy works so well. Good results may be reached by changing the experience of one member of the family, even though all members may not be present.

In one example in this chapter, a six-year-old boy whose disruptive behavior was preventing the session from progressing was given the choice of staying with the group or leaving it. He chose to leave. This circumstance had the beneficial effect of shifting the parents' attention to each other, albeit to work on the management of the child. During this interaction, the mother was shown how to sidestep the son's maneuvering the father out of the picture. The family had a need to learn how to negotiate new family rules. These were offered as corrective measures and were included in the discussion which followed the role playing. At this time the parents were told what they were doing that seemed to be ineffective and what they should do to be helpful.

The Child Who Makes Excessive Demands

Mr. and Mrs. Jones arrived at the office with their only child, Don, aged six, and explained that he was a difficult child to manage: he talked incessantly, especially at mealtime, refused to go to bed until his parents did, continually roamed about the apartment, and had a temper tantrum whenever his mother wanted to leave the house or he had to go to school. Often the episodes ended with vomiting. However, once he got to school, he was well behaved.

What precipitated taking the child for help was concern expressed by close relatives at the sight of the mother, father, and son dancing as a threesome at a social event to which no children had been invited. The relatives felt the Joneses needed help in raising their child and offered to pay for therapy, and the Joneses accepted their arrangements.

The psychodramatist is interested in what parents do when, for example, the child or children respond negatively to staying home with a babysitter when the parents spend an evening out with each other. It may be deduced from the above anecdote that these parents gave in to the child's insistences and that this action describes the social reward that the child received from his behavior. They danced to his tune.

Many children find it difficult to understand that the mother-father roles grow out of a husband-wife relationship with roles that exclude them. When the couple has only one child, unless the parents help him to develop some independence, to form relationships outside the family, the tendency to cling to the mother is usually more pronounced and is expressed in a variety of ways. The child has no one close to him in age or capability and must therefore orient himself to the parents. He lacks the stimulation of siblings and takes longer to relate socially to his peers. While this does not necessarily affect his ability to adjust as an adult, it does result in competition between the same-sex members of the family for the favorable attention of the parent of the opposite sex.[15] How the parents react to this is of crucial importance, as the following example shows:

Mother is a semi-invalid who stays at home caring for the child and her failing health. Father has taken to working many evenings and the weekends. These events are important, but, the meaning each family member attaches to them provides a clue to the kinds of changes and alterations that are necessary to influence and help the family. The child has discovered the mother's sensitivity to being left alone and is able to control her by wildly running about and making her believe that he is suffering. The important thing to look for here is how the parents respond to the child.

A pattern of role interaction develops when the role of the child meets and interacts with the role of the parent. Parenthood, in addition to previously developed roles, calls into being parenting roles that Salvador Minuchin points out "require the capacity to nurture, guide, and control." He adds, "Parents cannot carry out their executive function unless they have the power to do so."[16] The spontaneity of a six-year-old is sporadic, and the roles he has are poorly structured. When the parents meet these loosely formed roles, the director should watch the actions of the child as a guide to understanding the messages which are being sent, since the child communicates, at this age, principally non-verbally. The body acts the thought; words are accompanied with mimetic gestures, exploring activity, and explosive sound. This can be observed in the following excerpt from a group role playing the familiar family scene of getting up in the morning.

The director set the scene by arranging chairs in twos to form a bed for each member and asked the players to put themselves on the "beds" in a sleep position.

DIRECTOR	You are all sleeping soundly. It is morning. Who gets up first?	
DON	Me. *(Suiting the action to the word, he jumps up, stretches, and starts moving around.)* I go to the toilet and brush my teeth. *(Brushes.)*	*He is saying, "I'm a good boy who knows the right way to behave."*
MOTHER	That isn't what he does. He runs barefoot into the living room, turns on the TV . . .	
DIRECTOR	*(Interrupts.)* Now, you be Don and show us what Don does. Crawl into bed as Mother, Don. Show what she does. *(Don puts an arm over his head.)*	*The director asks mother and son to reverse roles to stop the criticism by mother; she is using the roles to make rules for her son, who is being portrayed as antagonizing the father and trying to involve the mother.*
MOTHER *(as Don)*	I'm catching cold by running around without my robe on. *(Runs wildly around the room and jumps up and down on the bed.)* Wake up. Watch TV with me. I'm hungry. Mother, you wake up, too. *(Shakes Don.)* I don't want Daddy to fix breakfast. You do it, Mother. *(Pulls and yanks at her son who is playing the sleeping mother.)*	
DON	I don't want to be Mother. I'll be Daddy.	*He rejects the mother role as he realizes the unfavorable review of his behavior and jumps out of bed.*

FATHER (as mother)	*(After he is prompted by the director.)* I'll be Mother. Don, put on your shoes. I don't want you to get sick. You can't go to school if you do. Did you brush your teeth?	
MOTHER (as Don)	Yes, I did. Don't go shopping while I'm in school. I don't want you out of this house while I'm away. Promise me; promise me.	*She feels the tyranny of her son. Don watches the interaction out of the corner of his eye.*
FATHER (as mother)	*(Leans over and smells his wife's breath.)* Let me see if you really brushed your teeth. You didn't. You'll get cavities. Go in and brush them right now.	*Father confirms the mother's overly protective attitude and registers his resentment of it.*
DON	I don't like this play. Let's do something else.	*He resists role playing, thereby stopping the performance.*
DIRECTOR	What are you thinking, Don?	
DON	I don't always do that. I'm a good boy. *(He stuffs his ears with his thumbs and covers his eyes with his fingers.)*	

The director got the nonverbal message and asked for a discussion. "What is Don showing in closing his ears to what's being said and shutting his eyes? Let's copy what Don is doing. How does it feel?"

MOTHER	I feel alone.
FATHER	You can't make me listen to you.
DIRECTOR	Who's the boss in this family? Don, are you?

DON	*(Taking his hands away from his eyes.)* No, Mom is.
DIRECTOR	Mother, what do you think about that? Are you the boss?
MOTHER	I can't get Don to do anything. I don't call that being a boss, do you?
DIRECTOR	A boss is a person who tries to make and enforce rules that others may rebel against.

The child's nonverbal response might have indicated that the power struggle had gone beyond the power fight and into a revenge motive: "I won't look at or listen to you, and I'll get even by doing something even worse." Or it might have signaled complete discouragement: "It hurts to listen and look, so I won't even try to be better!" The mother tried too hard to influence the child, which led to her excessive talking and ordering him about. The boy reacted negatively.[17]

DIRECTOR	You say you can't get Don to do anything. Think, now, of one thing you *can* get him to do. What is it?	*The director is trying to find the mother's area of effective action to have the family experience a pleasant interaction: acting out a fairy tale; playing a game; or doing some painting together.*

Role Reversal to Correct Misbehavior

After a whining appeal to the husband, which he ignored, the mother decided on taking her son to the playground (what he liked doing and the mother disliked). As the scene was getting started, Don became a human talking machine—checking and stopping all action as he rushed back and forth between one parent and the other. He stood in front of his mother and clapped his hand over her mouth, then rushed to the father and did the same thing, talking all the while as they tried to stop him. The picture of their interaction was clear. The personal feelings of each one in the family (mother's being unsure and afraid of life, father's sense of defeat) had turned the situation into endless conflict. Don felt that the situation was progressing contrary to his wishes and protected himself with a battery of words and actions—a temper tantrum. To the shocked father the director requested a role reversal, "Dad, be Don. Clap your hand over his mouth and yak away. Louder, the way Don does it. Get your body into it like Don does. Don, be Dad." The son was experiencing his own behavior for the second time during the session. He still didn't like the exposure, but he was determined to control the group: the parents didn't know how to stop him. The role reversal was an effective intervention.

DIRECTOR	Would you like to learn a different way to listen to each other?	
DON	No, no, no!	
MOTHER AND FATHER	Yes.	
DIRECTOR (to Don)	You may stay and watch us work it out in a play, or you may go to the outer office and play with some toys. Which do you want to do?	*The director is utilizing the therapeutic technique of choice and the child's capacity to decide.*
DON	Go home.	
DIRECTOR	Mom and Dad, are you ready to leave? No? If you want to go home and think you can manage it, you are free to go. We'll be through in a short time. (Don leaves the room but continues to interrupt periodically by banging on the door. He is ignored.)	
MOTHER	See, that's what I go through all day long.	

DIRECTOR   Was there anything different in the way you think I responded to Don from the way you usually do?

DAD   You stuck to your guns. We don't.

DIRECTOR   What have you done to get Don's cooperation?

PARENTS   Everything. You name it and we've done it.

The following explanation and recommendations were given to Don's parents: "It is understandable for parents to worry about their child's catching cold and getting cavities. You want to spare your child all sorts of discomforts, you especially Mrs. Jones, since you have a weak constitution. But parental concern frequently boomerangs. It can frighten the child and make him afraid to move away from the side of the all-protective mother. Isn't this what we saw here? Don became angry when the person he wanted acceptance from was critical of him and wouldn't do exactly as he said. Now, in order to change this we move in steps, one step at a time."

Because parents must give their children a lot of attention, for a child needs this, Don's parents were asked to acknowledge when Don was behaving himself—to play games with him, to talk to him, and love him—but to ignore him when he demanded their attention. The parents were advised to devote a week to building a good relationship with Don by giving him a lot of attention and agreeing with him. "Agreeing" meant that they would agree that it was all right not to brush his teeth if he did not do it, to let him run barefoot without warning him that he would catch cold. These seem like little things, but they were big in the total relationship. By allowing Don to do as he wished, the parents were practicing having confidence in their child and trusting him to take care of himself. The mother was not to argue when Don objected to having his father fix breakfast, and she was not to give in to Don. The two men in the family were to settle their differences themselves.

The rest of the session was devoted to the mother playing her son as the father played the mother, to develop some attitudes that would lower the tension between them and prepare the way for a good relationship. This additional role playing was necessary because a child who is used to winning a power fight with his parents won't give up without more fighting. Many parents fail to recognize the value of withdrawing, not from the child, but from the fight.

Other Problems

No amount of talk shields the child from the rough and tumble of individual experience, of unfair treatment at the hands of peers. During his early years, a child's attention is focused on his relationship to his parents and siblings. As he grows older, at about age ten or eleven, his peer relationships become important; he tries to find his place in this group. Disturbing behavior patterns frequently show up at this time. It is especially difficult for children to meet the unfair treatment evidenced in peer groups when the parents' fundamental attitudes toward life block the natural development of problem-solving and exploratory skills and give the children the impression that the problems are bigger than they are. Children then are unable to take frustrations in stride. As we saw in the case of Don, fear was communicated to the child and resulted in his helpless fury against the parents.

Another type of parental attitude that leads to disillusionment and anger—not only against the parents but also against life—is that of overoptimism, an excess of idealism that denies difficulties: "Everything will work out; don't worry." The therapist's approach is to get family members to acknowledge and then examine the problem, to search for the answer to the question, What can be done about it? This refers to what the child can do, not the parent.[18] Spontaneity training, both at home and in the therapist's office, confronts the family with the issues that are disturbing the child, and role playing provides an opportunity for learning what may be done about the problem.

The Temper Tantrum

Mr. and Mrs. Smith were a fortunate couple. They enjoyed each other. Both were high-ranking professionals, well organized, involved in private and public affairs, knowledgeable and active in the management of their only child Jim, age ten. After a move into a new neighborhood (a move is a test situation), the trouble started. Jim began to have discipline and learning problems in school, and after school he frequently got into fights. One day, he rushed into his room and began throwing chairs, books, and the radio in a burst of violence. He swore and threatened to kill the black boy who had jumped him on his way home from school. Mrs. Smith was terrified and called her husband, who rushed home. The three had a long talk. Mr. and Mrs. Smith were appalled by Jim's expressed racial prejudice and threats, since they had worked hard in support of the rights of all people and were against violence in any form. What had happened to their son? They wanted to help, but they were stumped by Jim's rage and afraid that he would act out his threats. So they sought outside help.

A Flashback

Since Jim was a talented actor, both in school plays and at home, the director asked for a "flashback," a reenactment of the after-school episode that had led to his rage at home. Jim's mother and father, as well as the director, became auxiliaries. The scene ended with the mother and father warning Jim of the danger of broken glass as he destroyed his radio set. Jim swaggered out of the office, still showing the exhilaration he felt when he threw things and swore. This response indicated his desire to show how powerful he was. The destruction bothered his parents, not him.

MOTHER	Wasn't that frightening?	
DIRECTOR	He needs an audience to play that role. You must remove yourself from the house the next time he goes on a rampage.	*The family is often an audience that satisfies the goals of a misbehaving child.*
MOTHER	I can't. He'll hurt himself or destroy the house.	
FATHER	I'll go along with your idea. He's a showoff. It usually isn't in this way, but he's always performing.	
DIRECTOR	We pressure our children into feeling that it is important to be somebody special. And when a child can't achieve it by studying or in another acceptable, worthwhile way, he can feel exceedingly important when he fights and throws his weight around.	

Changing Role Behavior through Role Reversal

Jim was invited back into the room and given a summary of what was said. He was told that he had shown a lot of guts in tackling and fighting his classmates and asked whether he was ready to make friends with them. Jim was delighted by the possibility that there was a way to get home from school without fighting. "Let's begin with the fight at the water fountain," said the director. With the parents as auxiliary egos, Jim played all the roles involved in the fight. First he showed his response to the "bully who pushed him," the black child Jim was so angry at. Then he showed how each boy in the group managed the "bully"—some confronted him, some ignored him, others ran away. The scene ended with Jim doing a soliloquy on how the "bully" felt about the fights he was having. Did he like it, or did he, too, wish it wouldn't happen? Jim became the black boy who went home to his parents and was soundly spanked for fighting (the director and father played the black parents). The antagonist's role was humanized for Jim through his role playing it.

Jim warmed up too quickly to excitement and needed a more useful way to feel important. He needed a task that would interest him and keep him busy, thereby ending the after-school fighting and the rages at home. He accepted the "job" of a TV news reporter, gathering data during the week and describing the after-school events for us in the office the following week.

Changing Roles at Home

To increase Jim's understanding of the effects of one person's behavior on another, it was suggested that Mrs. Smith change roles with her son at home for a short period of time—through the evening meal to bedtime. Carl Whitaker finds that "such role flexibility makes it possible not only for each member to play psychodrama games with the family situation" but also for each member to select the roles he wants.[19] Since the relationship between Mrs. Smith and Jim was positive, the objective was to help Jim discover techniques and attitudes for sizing up his own behavior in terms of acceptance by those he wanted as friends. Mrs. Smith reported back the following week.

It was awkward at first, she said, as they kept correcting their role playing, but as soon as the novelty wore off, Jim was responded to as mother, and Mrs. Smith as Jim. After dinner, as was customary, Jim (mother) stretched out in front of the TV. Mother (Jim) and father began reading. Jim (mother) began interrupting with, "Look at this!"

Mother (Jim), after the third interruption, said, "It's pretty hard to read when I bust in like that. Right, mom?" The subtle difference between role experience and lecturing helped Jim see how *disturbance* was his method of achieving group acceptance. Don's next problem was to channel his activity to accommodate a group of peers.

Spontaneity Training at Home

Action techniques can be used with children at home. It is a mistake to regard role playing as a memory exercise or an excuse to rely on what has worked before. The goal is not to teach a "right way," but to try new avenues of expression.[20]

For example: a young boy of six, in the first grade at school, came home every day reporting his delight with school. Imagine his mother's dismay, on her first visit with the teacher, to hear, "Whatever am I going to do with your son?"

The mother's anxiety prevented her from asking the teacher what was wrong. On her arrival home, she found out. "Maybe," said the young son, "the teacher doesn't like it when I stomp on her foot."

"I should think not," the mother said, "but let's see how it happened."

Her young son showed how he waved and wagged his arm in the air to get the teacher's attention, without success. He went to the desk and pulled at her skirt but was still ignored, so he stomped on her foot.

The mother in the role of the teacher said, "Ouch. I don't think that's funny. It hurts. What did I do to you that you want to hurt me?" The mother recognized the stomp as one of the games he and his sister played when they hit each other. But they did this with each other's permission. One child would ask, "Did you get a letter today?" "No," the other child would reply. "Oh, I forgot to stamp it," the first would say, emphasizing the word *stamp* by stomping on the other's foot.

Mother and son reversed roles. He became the teacher.

MOTHER *(as boy)*	I tried to get your attention. You would not call on me.
SON *(as teacher)*	It's impossible for me to notice you whenever you raise your arm. I'll get around to you—be patient. I'm sorry, though, not to have called on you.

MOTHER *(as boy)*	I won't stomp on your foot anymore. I didn't mean to hurt you.
BOY *(as teacher)*	I didn't mean to hurt your feelings, either. Next time don't stomp. Okay?

Training through the enactment of a life situation is in contrast to the preaching and lecturing most mothers use. This type of guidance promotes the learning of gracious social behavior. And the child isn't so likely to become "mother deaf" from being "talked at" too much.

The Slow Learner

Stanley was a nine-year-old boy who was not learning to read or to make friends at school. His experiences illustrate the positive effects of the family psychodrama.[21] Stanley and his mother were being treated separately; the mother was in a mothers' therapy group and the boy was attending a group of his peers, but he never participated. This behavior reflected his school performance—he was withdrawn and dull. After a school report showed the boy's continued lack of progress, the therapists decided to invite the mother and both of her sons to a psychodramatic session. Many children behave in a way that gives the impression that they are dull and incapable of learning. It was expected that the family sessions would shed light on the child's passivity and poor performance at school. This is what happened:

Stanley, his younger brother, age six, and Stanley's mother came to the session. Stanley's participation in this family group was in marked contrast to his behavior in his peer group. He was outspoken, demanding, and fought his younger brother at every opportunity. His mother would come to the rescue of her younger child, and after each intervention, Stanley would withdraw, pouting, into sullenness. In this atmosphere of being "run off" by his mother, Stanley was painfully aware of his mother's preference for his younger brother and of his own shortcomings without coming to terms with the behavior which set the vicious circle into motion.

Stanley refused to perform in the psychodrama (displaying the same attitude as at school), so the director introduced the mirror technique. He asked the mother to play Stanley at bedtime. The director played the role of mother and assigned the younger brother to play himself. Stanley laughed to see his mother portraying a nine-year-old and became thoughtful as the director, in an exaggerated flourish, was the mother showing partiality toward the younger son. The mother, playing the son, began to realize that she was casting him as the villain. Stanley continued to resist entering into the role-playing situation. He was distrustful of the experience, fearing that perhaps he would not be able to perform as well as he wanted.

The goals of the session were to help Stanley regain his feeling of belonging to the family and to lift his discouragement about himself. With these in mind, he was asked, "What do you want to be when you are a grown man?" Without a moment's hesitation, Stanley replied, "A big-business man." In that moment, Stanley was expressing his *overambition* that was probably at the root of his dysfunction. The director dropped role playing the present difficulties and turned to the future, with Stanley as a tycoon. The three auxiliaries (the director, the mother, and the younger brother) played subordinate roles to the big-business man as he received many telephone calls, dictated to his secretary, and sat at a big desk.

The mother, to her surprise, began to enjoy interacting with her son. She saw in this situation what he was capable of doing, and this encouraged her to focus not on his inadequate present but on his future possibilities. In subsequent sessions, the mother was shown how to avoid getting in the middle of the boy's fights and how to stop blaming Stanley for all the mischief that the boys engaged in by shifting her attention to the interaction between the boys. The results were rewarding, for Stanley began to show some interest in being tutored. As his mother stopped her nagging and her overprotective attitude toward the children, Stanley's feeling toward his mother and brother changed. The role of baby, of being quiet and timid with outsiders, was dropped.

The mirror technique, in which one member reflects another's behavior, was used to include Stanley in the session and to stimulate participation. The mother was openly angry with Stan, and he refused to co-act with her in the pychodrama just as he refused to cooperate in daily life. This response gave the director an insight into the meaning of the total behavior. His attitude was, "The person I most depend on is angry at me. I prefer to think that I do the right thing. It's Mother who is unfair." It becomes clear that he is fighting back because he feels that he is a loser in the sibling battle. Encouragement for Stan came when he was given roles to play to show his performance skill. He had a pair of roles in his repertoire—dominance at home and submissiveness outside the home. After the family psychodrama, he was able to use his home experience, dominance, outside the family and his submissiveness at home.

The family diagram was shown nonverbally at the end of the session. Family members were asked to arrange themselves in a space relationship that demonstrated their behavior toward each other. The mother stood in back of the two boys, smiling lovingly at her baby as the older one made a fist at them both. The three were then asked to rearrange themselves as they wished the family to be. Would that be in a circle? Separately placed? All hugging?

The sociogram of this family was as follows: mother toward father, weak feeling; Stan toward mother, mutually rejecting; younger brother toward Stan, positive (the younger boy got lots of attention from mother because he's so lovable; also, the identification of a younger sibling with an older one is usually positive); Stan toward younger brother, rejecting.

The Schizophrenic Child

For the patient who uses unusual modes of communication, special arrangements of words, jargon that confuses the meaning, or sounds that offend people trying to relate to him, psychodramatic techniques are usually indirect enough to get the patient into the therapeutic relationship and directive enough to be of practical value to him.

For example: John, age fourteen, came to the office with his mother. She was troubled because he had been variously diagnosed as slow learner, schizophrenic, and brain damaged. Her complaint was that John "barked." He had a dog named Barney and spent a good part of his time changing roles with Barney. John followed pretty closely the old saw "Barking dogs never bite." He was never vicious, only noisy. John's mother was both confused and embarrassed by this behavior. John had attended special schools and had been in therapy. However, barking, a symptom of his loneliness and his covert hostility, continued. The director invited the mother, who was able to provide information about John's behavior, to be the auxiliary ego and play out the last time the barking had occurred. John chose to be the dog, and his mother took the role of John. The scene began with the two of them walking down the street:

MOTHER   Barney, you're a bad dog to
(as John)   go on the grass. Mr. Jones
              does not like it.

JOHN *(as dog)*	*(Barking loud.)* Arf-arf-arf.
MOTHER *(as John)*	There you go, barking very loud. Shut up! If you keep barking like that, Mr. Jones will scream at us.
JOHN *(as dog)*	*(Barking even louder.)* Woof-woof.
MOTHER *(as John)*	Now you've done it. Here comes Mr. Jones!

Identity through Role Reversal

The action was stopped, and the director checked the authenticity of the scene. The mother explained that John usually played all the roles —John, the dog, and the neighbor. John jumped up and said, "Let me show you what I do." He reenacted the situation as he had done it many times before, playing all the roles. He then took turns changing roles with both the director and his mother. When it was the director's turn to be John, she said (intuitively, expressing the meaning behind the behavior), "Barney, you're the only person I can scream at. Everyone else tells me to be quiet." Then the director began to bark. Finally she said, "Gee, this feels good, to really let them have it!" She looked at John to see if she had struck home. He began to laugh, and the next time he acted the role of John, he included this interpretation in his role playing.

John's mother began to remember that when John was two (and for a number of years) John's father had been ill, and she had had to care for her sick husband at home. During this time, she kept telling her son to be quiet. (The director guessed that she probably still did.) So John never tired of playing the role of screaming at his barking dog, or barking as the dog, or screaming as the neighbor. However, we found other situations in which John played all the roles in a situation in which people misbehaved. These included his male school teacher, the neighbor, and the barber. It seemed that the situations that caused him the greatest confusion were ones in which a male exercised his authority.

Subsequent sessions were begun and ended promptly by John, according to the contract of the therapy hour. The material or content of the session was suggested by his mother.

Acting out situations, or reality practice, seems to be beneficial for patients with serious behavior disorders; anxiety is reduced and change may be effected as patterns of interaction are presented.[22] The episodes have a beginning, a middle, and an end, which seems to meet the conditional cooperative behavior demands of this type of patient. The mother's contribution in John's case was useful in helping the director distinguish reality from fantasy, that is, in placing the event in time, for all John's monodramas were "pushed out" in the present, even though the event might have happened years ago. The mother would begin:

MOTHER	John, do you want to play barber?
JOHN	*(Getting up quickly as the barber.)* Good morning, John. You must wait your turn. I'm not ready for you.
JOHN *(as John)*	*(Shakes out a robe and assumes a barber's posture.)* That's right. I must wait my turn. How long do I have to wait?
JOHN *(as barber)*	Not long, John, not long. *(He clips away.)*
JOHN *(as self)*	Is it my turn now?

John would begin at the entrance to the barber shop and go through this scene repeatedly. John's mother explained that John asked her to go through this scene as often as she was willing to do it. The compulsive replaying of the situation was not to repair hurt feelings but to learn new modes of communication. The director suggested that at home John's father and older sister be invited to visit the simulated barber shop. It was hoped that this participation would enlarge John's relationship range to include the rest of the family. (We discovered later, much later, that he was rehearsing a hoped-for future as a barber. A child's play is often preparation for a desired role.)

The other significant episode John played was a school situation.

A male teacher, two or three pupils, and John were characters in an animated monodrama. The therapeutic intervention here, as in the other episodes, was designed to give John the experience of a dialogue, to involve him in a more personal form of communicative speech, and to help him understand that the teacher will do everything possible to keep the classroom and classmates from hurting him or each other. Although John was physically strong and large for his age, he panicked when fighting broke out or when aggressive behavior occurred among the children in the classroom, and he withdrew in terror. The director attempted to give him the experience of his strength by asking him to play the role of an aggressive boy. He refused. He preferred to keep his image of an environment too complex for him to enter and to change.

The Mother as a Resource Person

The method of treating John included his mother. With her help, a relationship problem was selected and developed. Enactments of the problem clarified the meaning of the behavior and led to improved skill in dealing with it. John attended these sessions once a week for three months and then stopped coming. His mother reported that the barking had stopped.

It came as a surprise when, fourteen years later, John's mother called and reminded me of how helpful the sessions had been. John had been in therapy of other types most of the ensuing years. He had a job, a car, and girl friends with the same disabilities, and he had a room away from home. However, he had developed a hysterical laugh, almost as loud as the barking. To his mother's amazement, John reminded her of how psychodrama had been helpful with the barking and suggested that it might help with the uncontrollable laughing. During a series of treatments for the laughing, he revealed that he was going to barber school nights, thus fulfilling his boyhood play activity.

A characteristic of John's role playing should be mentioned. He never reversed roles with any members of his family. Perhaps he was unable to separate himself from them enough to be able to do so. He did try to establish rapport with his dog, the barber, the teacher, and the neighbor.

The aspect of John's case that has implications for other patients is the ease with which a relationship was developed by entering into the imaginary world of a patient and providing an explanation of his confusing behavior. Respect for the person and his bizarre behavior results in understanding. Another important aspect is the use of a member of the family. Without the mother's presence, it would have been impossible to place in time the events that John was acting out. As important, the mother was able to change her relationship with John and live more comfortably with him as a member of her household.

Conclusion

Often, the family is the only group willing to work with grossly disturbed children, because of the bizarre and often disruptive behavior they display. It is, indeed, important for the parents and siblings of such children to get help—real life practice—as provided by the psychodramatic experience. Work with the family group is directed not only at improved adjustment for the child but simultaneously at the development of new and improved roles for the family.[23] Generally, parents show prompt relief when a behavioral situation has been resolved. The progress of the child is usually slower, but in most cases definitely observable, as with John and his barking.

The withdrawn child eventually warms up if the family acts out scenes of everyday living, such as waking up in the morning and going through the day. There is positive value in selecting the living events of the present, and the closer to the present the better. The director can become one with the child as they sit together and watch the family wake up and face what happens in a day. Or the director can become the friendly double of the patient and encourage the child to move into the drama as one of the family plays the withdrawn child. The group should work on only one current problem; a common mistake is to tackle all the problems at once. Select one difficult area and work at it until some success is achieved. Very often, changes occur in other areas as a result of resolving one problem.[24]

6

Sociometry

Once it is accepted that the role is an observable unit of social interaction, various sociometric procedures may be employed to investigate the reciprocating relationships that form as an individual interacts with the members of his group. These procedures guide a therapist into a patient's problem and are helpful in starting a psychodramatic session.

Much of a person's time is spent in groups. From infancy on, an individual seeks to find his place in the many groups that form his life situation. First comes the family, then the peer group that he joins before entering school. Schooling offers years of changing groups and group activities, and the individual's social development is reflected in the number and kinds of his group memberships. More often than not, such development is smooth, as people usually know what is expected of them and can anticipate what others will do. Most people interact with others without giving it too much thought or attention. What happens to a person as he participates in a group, however, is of deep concern to the participant and should be understood in more than an intuitive way by those who work with groups. Sociometry gives the group therapist, group leader, teacher, and psychodramatist a technique for testing the validity of the intuitive judgments he constantly makes while facing a group.

The patterns of interaction influence the development of the group and show the role each individual takes or is given. These patterns have been translated into social roles: the leader, the isolate, the rejected person, and the indifferent person. The role constellation results from social interaction and social development. Choice of associates occurs spontaneously and is based on the assessment one person makes of another[1]: "I knew the moment we met he was my type, and I hoped he would ask me out." This is an intuitive choice-making assessment that is routine in everyday living. As the two people get to know each other better, the judgment may prove to have been accurate; the underlying cues on which the response was made were correctly understood. Thus, a person's place in the group depends on the attitude others in the group have toward his behavior and on his own attitude toward belonging to the group. This negotiation may bring him recognition and reward or it may lead to rejection and isolation.

The Sociometric Test: Its Purpose

The dynamics of a group come to life, or become graphic, through a direct choice technique, a sociometric test. In the test, each member of a group is asked to choose from among the other members those with whom he would particularly like to work, to play, and to live. The administration of a sociometric test from which immediate, practical action is to be taken is important in bringing about improvement in a problem area.

Each individual, whether he is aware of it or not, is involved in groups of persons who interact with one another. The interaction may be casual, as with a bus driver who collects fares (although this may be complex when the person boarding the bus doesn't have the fare), or it may be intimate and face-to-face, as with family members. To extend the example of the bus, an individual's decision as to where he wants to sit and who he wants to sit next to may be examined and tested in a school bus setting or a hospital bus taking a group of patients on an outing. It may be discovered that a person chooses: (1) to sit next to a person of the same sex; (2) to sit next to a person of the opposite sex; (3) to sit on the aisle; (4) to sit next to the window; or (5) to stand, rejecting the people but choosing the bus as better than walking. Or the person may have (6) been rejected by many of the passengers on the bus and finds it difficult to be accepted as a seatmate.

A sociogram records these findings and identifies the role relationships existing in the group. Since this information shows the therapist what is going on in the group, it helps identify the problem. In addition, it provides the therapist with clues that may help him deal with the problem effectively; it is a technique of diagnosis and therapy. For example, on a female ward of a state hospital, a patient was observed to change her habitual speech pattern from outspoken clarity to a childlike stutter. Her gait became a mincing shuffle. She lost her tidy appearance and looked helplessly around for someone to wash and groom her. It was apparent that she was not only imitating but exaggerating the regressive features of the patient who occupied the bed next to her. The nursing staff concluded that she was using these tactics to get more nursing care, but the more attention she got, the more helpless she became. A socio-gram revealed that she rejected the patient who was sleeping next to her. She was restored to her previous adjustment as soon as her bed position in the dormitory was changed.

Sociometric testing has been reported to have been successfully applied in classrooms from kindergarten through university, and in camps, factories, offices, hospital wards, and family groups. Since man lives in groups, the area of application is as wide as his social involvement.

Description of Sociometric Testing

There are three popular forms of the sociometric test: (1) verbal choice: people are asked whom they prefer in given situations; (2) action choice: people move toward and choose each other; (3) written choice: people respond on a questionnaire.[2]

Verbal Choice

At the beginning of a psychodrama, the director carefully observes the arrangement of the group members—how they place themselves (whether individuals sit close to others or apart), the movement (if and where individuals move), the talking pattern, and so on. Since these illustrate the subjective position of each member, a sociogram of the group begins to take form in the mind of the director as he assesses the spontaneity level of the group. He shares these sociometric observations with the group. For example, he might say to one person: "I notice you sit alone. Look around. Is there anyone here you want to sit with?" The person is given the chance to choose and to act. If the psycho-drama session were taking place in a hospital, and two people were talking to each other, the director might say: "Do you know each other well? How many other people here do you know? Let's see if you know them by name. Is there anyone in the group who would like to join them?" The purpose is not to break up the pairing but to estimate the strength of the attraction, casual or intense, and to place it in relation to the acquaintanceship with the rest of the group. Each member is asked to say where and with whom he wishes to sit, and seating can be arranged according to the responses given. This direct application of verbal choosing leads into the psychodrama session as the patterns of pairs, triads, chains, or isolates become clear.

Here is another example of verbal choice. The audience, after it has assembled, may be asked to choose, not a person, but a problem. Each person stands up, faces the group, and briefly states his concern. The group votes on the problems, one by one, to discover the area of primary concern to them. Group members may vote for one, several, or all the problems. Since the purpose is to find and work on one problem that most of the group members have, the problem with the most votes is role played.

Action Choice

The director begins the psychodrama with a brief explanation of its purpose—to learn to understand and to change behavior—and suggests starting to work on this problem immediately: "Walk around and choose someone with whom you would like to work on a problem situation." Some move quickly to select one or two people; some wait to be chosen; and others refuse to choose or be chosen. The sociometric responses serve as the basis for estimating attitudes toward cooperation and opposition.

A variation of action choice is *sociometric tag*.[3] Group members are encouraged to look over the group and then walk toward the person they want to meet. After a five minute period of conversation, each partner introduces the other to the group and explains the subject that was discussed and what attraction and rejection were experienced during this encounter. Sociometric assessment, the director may point out to the group, makes one aware of the attractions and rejections existing at a moment in time and in respect to one criterion—wanting to chat with another person. It becomes clear that some people are attracted to appearance, some to the familiar, some to the forlorn or to the "higher up" or to the stranger in the group, and so on. Group members are then instructed to form units of any size they wish to complete the sociometrics of the group.

The *Indian wrestle* is an action choice technique in which a patient (perhaps as he is showing anger) is asked to choose someone in the group who arouses his competitive feelings. After the choice is made, the wrestling begins. The two competitors either stretch out on the floor or they place their elbows on a table. As each tries to force down the arm of the other, it is easy to observe the opinion each participant has of himself.

The *tight circle* is a means of graphically portraying the socio-metric problem of the role of the outsider on the stage. The group members form a circle with locked arms, leaving out one member. The outsider makes every effort, verbal and physical, to break into the group. It is up to the members of the circle to accept or not accept him into the circle. This "drama" may cause serious discomfort to the one who is not accepted and permitted to enter.[4] Perhaps this group exclusion touches the basic anxiety of a person, a need to belong, and this negative experience is not easily tolerated by a lonely person.

Written Choice

The written test is administered by asking each person in the group to choose from all those present three to join him as companions in a particular life situation in the order of preference. He also is asked to name the one person in the group he would prefer *not* to have as an associate. The choices and rejections are scored, and the results show the sociometric status of the individuals of a particular group. The resulting diagram may look like *Figure 6.1*.

Figure 6.1

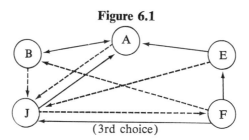

(3rd choice)

This sociogram shows the first choices (solid lines) and rejections (broken lines) among five boys, as well as one third choice for the sake of demonstration. There is one mutual choice, shown as a straight line with arrows on each end, between A and B. A received three positive choices and, in this group, is the leader. His influence is important in the functioning of the group. J received three rejections and one third choice, which, interestingly, was from the person he rejected. This diagram was developed from data in the table on page 82.

A sociometric test requires the full participation of the group. It is not a test that measures skills or capabilities; rather, it explores the number of relationships of which the individual is part, the reciprocal relations expressed by members of a group. It provides an opportunity for each person to share in the events of living in matters that are relevant to his well-being.

Planning and Using the Test

A written test works best with groups whose members know each other by name and plan to be together for a set period of time, such as a hospital ward, a school class, a family, a therapy group—any group working and/or living together. The interpersonal relationships in such groups can be explored by setting up a criterion for investigation. Knowledge of the relationships can be of therapeutic use, especially when a teacher, ward physician, therapist, or parent is interested in the growth and movement of the individuals within the group.

A test is given when the group first meets and a second test follows in six or eight weeks. The tester can then see how many pair relationships have extended to include a chain of friends, or whether an isolate has made a friend. Each person's *sociometric status* (the sum total of the choices and rejections he receives) is carefully watched, for the basic assumption is that the poorly functioning person will tend to be rejected and the well-functioning person will be chosen. The most rejected members of the group suffer from their unfavorable position.[5] When the director knows the status of an individual or the cohesiveness of the group, he can improve an unfavorable position with role playing, psychodrama, and sociodrama, that is, with some therapeutic intervention.

The test question put to the group should be relevant and in an area of active concern to the members. The director, who is familiar with the functions of the group, can select an appropriate subject. Thus, following an outbreak of stealing on a hospital ward, the question might be, "Who is your first, second, and third choice of a locker mate? Also name one person you don't want. We are getting new lockers. If it is at all possible, we will place one of your choices next to you." The question is put in such a way that the individual names a wished-for companion.

The test should tackle an existing problem. Choices of associates for leisure activities are appropriate to the school room, hospital ward, or family, but may be difficult to follow up in an industrial setting. Leisure is a broad term, so be specific and suggest such activities as playing cards or tennis, or having dinner together.

An Application: Dealing with Runaways

On three different occasions a small group (four or five boys) of twenty-five court-committed adolescents had escaped from the hospital. On the last escapade, they had tied up the aide, taken his car keys, and raided the nearby community. The community was indignant, as were the administrators of the hospital, who decided to ground all the adolescents and curtail many of their leisure-time activities. The staff working with the adolescents denounced this decision as representative of punitive custodial care and the end of the therapeutic program. The adolescents who had not run away were angry, too, at being unfairly treated. "Why do we have our privileges taken away when we didn't do anything and they did?" It was a crisis that frequently occurs when one person (the superintendent) or one member of a family or institution decides on a line of action without consulting the group. No one is satisfied or cooperative.

Procedure

The procedure that followed included (1) a group discussion (the warm-up), (2) the administration of a sociometric test (collection of data), and (3) follow-up (formulation of a sociogram and a course of action).

The discussion was heated, since the whole group was involved, and the conflict was defined. The director informed the group that an effort would be made to solve the problem through a reassignment of ward associates. It was pointed out that frequently trouble is fomented by association. Some adolescents are more suggestible than others, and often a better housing arrangement helps them settle down and follow the hospital routine.

The test followed a typical written form in which paper and pencils were handed out and each person was asked to write at the top of the page: Who would your first, second, or third choice of a ward mate be? Name one person you would prefer not to share quarters with. Sign your name at the bottom of the sheet. A staff member collected the folded sheets and assured the group that the results would be respected and acted upon. Each member of the group understood why the test was being given and was assured that the purpose of the test was to reorganize the group, if at all possible, in a way that would be helpful to all the members of the group.

The scores of the sociometric test were placed on a large sheet of paper ruled with horizontal and vertical lines. The twenty-five names were written in alphabetical order across the top of the sheet and down the side. As each person's choices were scored, they were recorded in the horizontal column beside his name and in the vertical columns under the chosen persons, indicating first, second, or third choice. The rejection was recorded in the same manner (see Table 6.1).

Table 6.1

	Al	Bob	Ed	Frank	John
Al		1	2	3	X
Bob	1		3	2	X
Ed	1	2		3	X
Frank	2	X	1		3
John	1	2	3	X	

The choices and the rejections were added up for each person. Special attention was paid to the reciprocated choices and the partially reciprocated, and to the unchosen. Reassignment of living space was made on the basis of expressed preferences. No one was assigned to live with a person he had rejected.

Follow-up

The hospital staff tried to identify from the scores an outlaw leader and the ones who followed him. The scores showed that the runaways were not selected as leaders. They had no strong feelings for each other either. They did not form a group with "ties to one another."[6] One runaway was rejected by many, and one was unchosen. The test showed that they were not liked by the leader (the person most chosen) and his followers. We concluded that the runaways had not measured up to the group values and were using daring and destructive ways to achieve group recognition.

The therapy team selected the most rejected boy from among the runaways and worked out his relationship to the group. Speculation was confirmed. His perception of the situation was inaccurate; he liked everyone in the group and thought they liked him (the mechanism of projection—when we like a person, we are prone, without supporting evidence, to project this feeling onto him[7]). It came as a shock to him when the young patients enacted scenes in which he was seen as silly, childish, unreliable, and responsible for the group's getting in trouble. This was the turning point in his hospitalization. Though the consultant had had little hope for this "infantile personality," the boy's behavior changed after the telling experience of the perception test, and within three months he returned home. This example is supportive of the work of Mary Northway, who says that "sociometric status is an indication of the individual's external social adjustment to the values of the particular group, but it doesn't reflect directly his inner psychological security."[8]

Sociometric Assignment in a Classroom

The application of sociometry is useful, too, in an educational situation, because, as mentioned earlier, learning takes place best in an environment compatible to the individual. A gym teacher came to the therapy session with the complaint that she couldn't handle a class of thirty-six high school girls that she had been asked to lecture to on hygiene. These were girls who had asked to be excused from taking gym for a variety of reasons. She was completely defeated by the group. The director recommended that she administer a sociometric test based on the most usual classroom criterion (actual knowledge of the group might have produced different criteria): "With whom do you wish to be seated?" The girls were then asked to list three choices in order of preference—one, two, and three—and were told, "If at all possible, we will place you next to your first choice." Next, they were asked, "Name one person you would prefer not to sit with."

The teacher reluctantly administered the test and showed me her findings. One young girl had received thirty-four rejections and only one first choice. It was obvious that this rejected girl was actively offensive in her behavior to have provoked so much dislike. The suggestion, which the teacher followed, was to rearrange the seating plan so that she could sit next to the person who hadn't rejected her, and to encourage the most chosen in the group to meet and act friendly toward her. This was followed by some role playing in the class where the most rejected girl gave evidence of her mistaken ideas of how to make friends. The teacher was pleased with her newfound method, for the class quieted down enough for her to give her lectures on physical hygiene (they had all had a direct experience in mental hygiene!).[9,10]

Self-Evaluation Test

You can apply sociometric theory by doing a self-evaluation test.[11] A sociogram of an individual's family provides an excellent survey of the kinds of relationships a person has formed and his attitudes toward the people who made up this group. In a clinical situation, such a test is often used to foster understanding of a person's lifestyle. Consider your own situation, and think of the way you feel about the people in your family. How do they feel about you? Begin with *early family roles.*[12]

1. Write down your father's age, occupation, education, and a one word evaluation of him as a provider. Do the same for your mother. Then list your siblings in order of birth (include yourself). Next, put down your age next to your name; after all of your siblings' names, put down their sex and the number of years older or younger than you they are (use a plus sign to indicate older and a minus sign for younger). Include in this list half-siblings and ones that are now dead. If you are an only child, use your parents as siblings.

Composition of the family

Father: age __ occupation __ education __ type of provider __
Mother: age __ occupation __ education __ type of provider __
Siblings: order   sex   age
               1 ____   ____   ____
               2 ____   ____   ____
               3 ____   ____   ____

2. Think of a situation that occurred in your family that involved you and your siblings. Describe your attitude toward your siblings within this social context. For example, the situation could be the family eating dinner together. Which sibling(s) would you choose to sit next to? Who would you sit farthest from? Write the names of the siblings under the phrase that describes your feelings.

I am close to   I am farthest from   I am indifferent to
_____   _____   _____

3. Make a sociogram of the sibling relationships in your family. Show how you feel about your siblings, and estimate how they feel about you. If possible, get feedback from your siblings on the accuracy of your perception of their responses to you. For example:

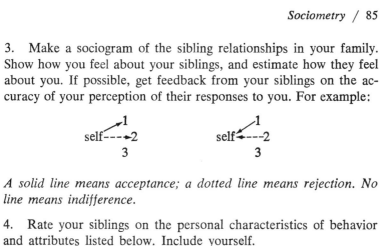

A solid line means acceptance; a dotted line means rejection. No line means indifference.

4. Rate your siblings on the personal characteristics of behavior and attributes listed below. Include yourself.

	1 (least)	2	3	4 (most)
Conforming				
Rebellious				
Tries to please				
Critical of others				
Idealistic				
Materialistic				
Sensitive				
Given to temper tantrums				
Possesses a good sense of humor				
Intelligent				
Cautious				
Analytic				
Athletic				

5. On a scale of 1 to 6, how do you rate yourself on the following traits? Rate your siblings on the same scale.

1 __ 2 __ 3 __ 4 __ 5 __ 6 __

Leader	Follower
Gregariousness	Exclusiveness
Parent	Baby
Bully	Victim

6. With which sibling did you have the most in common?
    _____   none of them   can't say

7. Which sibling did you fight with the most?
    _____   none of them   can't say

8. Who was your father's favorite?
    _____   none of them   can't say

9. Who was your mother's favorite?
    _____   none of them   can't say

10. Plot your relationship to your parents. Toward which parent did you feel closer?
    _____ mother   _____ father   _____ neither

11. Describe each of your parents.

12. What was the relationship between your mother and father?
    close   aloof   argumentative   openly affectionate

Which parent seemed to be in charge? What was the area(s) of agreement? Of disagreement?

13. From which parent was it easier for you to accept guidance?

14. Which parent seemed to have confidence in your achievements?

The relationships that you analyzed are the roles of son, daughter, brother, and sister. A sociometric self-analysis should benefit you by helping you know yourself better and crystallize your basic convictions about yourself. It is a form of self-counseling.

Conclusion

Questions concerning the choice relationships in a group, honestly answered, can clarify the social atmosphere in a group and reveal what needs an individual has for companionship. Some individuals have a telic sensitivity to others and make a large number of reciprocated choices; others make unreciprocated choices. The pattern may show that some individuals are attracted to people of a higher sociometric status than they are; others tend to choose someone of a lower status. These various patterns and relationships in the group help the therapist understand how each individual works out his social adjustment. A sociometric test doesn't offer a simple solution to a complex problem. It is more complicated than "the higher the score the better."[13] Whether one is selected as a leader or is unchosen, status is related to the individual's attitude toward the goals of the group. Either he feels a part of or attracted to the group values, or repulsed by or separated from them. Selection is not a measure of a person's personal security.

While no one is liked by everyone and few are completely unchosen, it is generally held that the unchosen and the isolate need special consideration in bringing them into a closer connection with the group.[14] It is equally important to know which person tends to reject others.

We assume that choices will change and that the younger the person, the more frequently he will change his choices. Through the effects of sociometric arrangement, and the fulfillment of the expressed needs of the individual, desirable change may take place.

7

Sociometry and Psychodrama

Sociometry provides data on the forms of an individual's roles and relationships. In order for a therapist to fully understand the meaning of the relationships depicted on a sheet of paper or as an impression in his mind, he must see the individual enter into those relationships as a role player and observe how he really performs. The role player should make gains in social competence from his experience.

The session that follows placed special emphasis on the group constellation; that is, it included all the members of the patient's family as well as the friends and relatives that formed a therapeutic group. It illustrates a friendly but firm approach in a psychodrama with an adolescent.[1]

Sociometry with an Adolescent

The psychodrama recounted here helped an adolescent; this came about because a group has therapeutic value. Members of an audience of intimately related, concerned adults may become anchor points for an individual in a crisis.[2] In contrast to other groups, the family grouping has a history of shared experience. Sociograms and role diagrams depict the effects of people living together, and the needed changes may more easily be achieved by using these tools.[3]

Adolescents frequently resist the many roles that they are expected to fill and express this hostility destructively in withdrawal.[4] When an adolescent becomes discouraged with schooling, he may give up the role of student to become an underachiever or a dropout. Usual forms of therapy often don't work, for the adolescent resists this type of role taking as well; therapy is learning, and he doesn't want to be a student. The impact of an imaginative psychodramatic session may be strong enough to revitalize the student role and shock the patient into a realistic consideration of the problem.

When a problem arises that cannot be handled by conventional methods, an emergency psychodrama meeting should be considered. This type of meeting is called to shock the group, to give urgency and importance to the situation, and to solve a specific problem. Mental health workers often think that an office and a hospital ward are the only places therapeutic intervention should take place, but a home meeting is sometimes necessary to see and work with the sociometric structure of the problem. The strategy in such a visit is to invite all the people associated with the difficulty to meet just once and present them with the contribution they may be able to make.

This case involved Barry, age sixteen, who was doing badly in high school, although he was of normal intelligence. He was the youngest in a family of four. His mother and father were well suited to each other, with a clique of friends who met regularly over the years to play cards and to take vacations together. The father had experienced some financial difficulties and had been drinking heavily for some time.

Barry's parents were called to school, and Barry's behavior was made known to them, particularly that he was truant and refused to attend any class he wasn't interested in. The battle between Barry and the school authorities took the form of a power fight: If you won't do what I want, I'll show you that I won't do what you want. Barry wanted to be on the staff of the school newspaper. The school authorities insisted, "You get a B average and then you can be on the school paper." Barry responded by finding a friend who was also truant, and together they spent most of their time away from school. This attitude, it was explained to the parents, required psychiatric attention.

The psychiatrist sent Barry to a psychodrama group made up of peers; but the peer group failed to change Barry's attitudes toward school. He said, "They don't have anything I want. I want to write for the newspaper or be a bum." He left the group, and a year later his mother called the psychodramatist to say that Barry and his friend had been expelled from high school.

The director suggested that Barry's mother call together all the people intimately associated with Barry—father, sister, brother-in-law, aunts, uncles, three couples who, as close friends of the parents, were like relatives, and the friend who also had been expelled—to have a session in Barry's home. Barry and the director were the only ones in this group who had had experience in psychodrama, a situation that pleased Barry no end.

The director began by saying to the group, "It is important for us to know each other and to like each other well enough to be able to work on a problem together. We must help Barry and his friend reach a successful decision concerning their future plans. Psychodrama is a learning method; using it we can explore areas of living without paying too high a price in real life. Experiments seem to indicate that a person can practice living and learn to act and to move.[5] Every one of us here knows that schooling is important. Barry and his friend know this too, but something blocks them. Our plan for this evening is to help Barry become free to move in any direction, to see alternate routes. Barry is perhaps the only one who knows all of you here. Let's begin by introducing ourselves."

After the introductions, the director explained to the group, "We are going to experiment with a new, perhaps different approach to help Barry arrive at a decision, since he is at a critical moment in his life. We are not here to tell Barry and his friend what to do, but to help them explore the avenues open to them. In order for all of you to catch up with the events of the past, let's begin with Barry's parents being called to school."

The director was preparing the group to solve a problem in an unaccustomed manner. It would have been presumptuous to move to the enactment of the problem without warming up the audience.

A sociometric analysis of the group suggested that the people with whom Barry had already established a good relationship were his mother, sister, brother-in-law, and friend. Barry and his father teased each other. The brother-in-law (the only college graduate in the group) had been honorably discharged from military service as an officer in World War II. The mother related positively to her friends, the three couples, having met socially with them for over twenty years. Barry's father was not as successful financially as two of the other men in his group, so he played the role of the wisecracker. Barry was viewed by the others as odd; his nonacceptance by his peers and his expulsion from school supported the general view that he was a problem child. Probably his apathy and his social isolation bewildered them.

The main goal of the psychodrama session was to help Barry become productive. A secondary goal was to show the group the ways they could support Barry's mother and father. Following is a summary of the steps taken.

1. The first step was establishing a positive attitude in the group toward psychodrama.

2. Next, a situation was enacted; a sequence of events developed naturally from the clues provided by the participants. The first scene presented a typical day when the boys cut classes; this was followed by the critical incident of Barry and his friend being expelled from school.

3. Barry's parents enacted Barry's confronting them with his expulsion. The mother turned first to her husband, who managed the crisis by becoming cynical about the school and said, "They're a bunch of dumb clucks, and they finally caught on to Barry." Then the mother turned to her best friend, Shirley, who lamented, "Oh, that's awful. What does he want to do? Go into the army? Thank goodness he needs your signature. He's too young to enlist without it." Barry's mother, who suffered from high blood pressure, was excited when she called the director, and this dramatic scene revealed her desperation as well as Barry's.

4. The director summarized by observing that the group had seen some of the emotional tensions brought on by Barry's present state of being expelled from school. Then she said, "Let's hear from Barry and his friend what their reaction is to the school's decision." The scene was a happy one. This was just what they wanted. "No more school. Let's join the army. We'll have to get permission from the folks. I don't think we'll have any trouble doing that."

5. The director asked them if this was really what they wanted. They insisted it was. The scene was then set for a recruiting station, with the brother-in-law acting as the recruiter. He concluded the interview with, "If you get your parents' permission, you're in."

6. A discussion followed this scene, in which the men in the room talked about their military experiences. (This is called audience involvement.)

7. The director, sensing the negative feeling developing in Barry and his friend toward the adults trying to restrict and prevent them from joining the army, reminded the group that its position was to help the boys be free to move in any direction they wanted. "If they want your signatures, be ready to give them," she said. Then she turned to Barry and asked, "What other ways do you see open

to you?" He answered, "Get a job." His mother countered, "Go back to school; get reinstated." "Never," said Barry and his friend. The director then negotiated a contract. The boys had a choice of action: go back to school, get a job, or join the army. The parents would not withhold their signatures if the boys decided on the army. The suggested course for the boys was *not* "Do what will make you happy," but "Do what will make you function." The parents would not financially support leisure or doing nothing. The boys had to decide on work, school, or military service.

8.   The session ended as the director advised the adults not to force their will on the boys and encouraged the boys to show their resourcefulness by exploring all the alternatives.

The results of this session were dramatic. A week later, Barry's mother telephoned the director and reported that Barry had a job in a warehouse. In time, he grew unhappy with it and asked if there were a private school he could attend. One was found. He became interested in journalism and the radio station of the school. He found his place, graduated from high school, then from college, and is presently earning his living in journalism. He had a strong future orientation; he knew what he wanted and got it. (Incidentally, the couples group gave up their weekly card games to form a psychodrama group.)

This experience points out that changes in group behavior can influence an adolescent's behavior when the group members are encouraged to give the adolescent enough latitude to feel individually responsible for what is happening to him. It wasn't necessary to probe deeply into Barry's lifestyle, but only to turn its destructive mode into a useful one, to help Barry discover his major condition for functioning (journalism) and to help him find a way to achieve it.

An initial step in developing this form of group psychotherapy begins with the external circumstance of forming the group. Those people significantly concerned with the results were invited to attend the meeting. The people forming the group had a traditional orientation that respected authoritarian parental behavior. They discovered that this attitude had lost the effectiveness it had in past generations.[6] The next step was exploring the feelings and attitudes the group members had toward each other. We saw that the primary family was devoted to their only son, but puzzled by his behavior. The son and his friend were an isolated pair, lost together in a large school which was unprepared to do more than recognize the boys' truancy and be rid of them. "They," the school personnel, were not invited to the meeting, even though they were the chief opponents. (The purpose of the meeting was not to effect reinstatement.)

The parents were supported by their friends, with one female adult expressing warmth and concern for Barry. All the adults were involved, for they had sons and daughters and felt that they, too, might someday face the same problem. They urgently wanted to understand Barry's behavior. The central issue, Barry's future, was role played. The group members observed, analyzed, and participated. Out of this, they saw a different side to Barry and began to respect his decision-making skills.

This session verified the sociometric hypothesis that an individual with a low sociometric score is a troubled person. In his peer group, Barry was an isolated person, with only one close friend outside the family. In the family, Barry was accepted warmly by some. The therapy was one of reassignment into a group where his position was altered. The method used to achieve it was an action technique, psychodrama. The case of Barry also supports the general assumption that the youngest child is in a unique position to be exceedingly pampered.[7] The commonsense and practical solutions that are characteristic of skillfully conducted psychodrama therapy were used together with current experiences to help the family and their friends solve their current dilemma.

Sociometry with Community Services

This session is an exciting demonstration of how an action method bridges the gap between the policing community (in this case, the truant officer) and the public they serve. Of equal importance to both groups is the exposure of one to the other to further understanding. This is true of an urban society and, as we found it in this case, of a society in a developing country.

When considering some of the techniques and methods of psychodrama, sociometry, and other related action techniques, it becomes clear how necessary it is to understand the family roles before trying to deal with them.

Each member of the family acts according to the way he expects things to happen. To understand a family member's action, one has to view it as a family transaction, one must see the total situation in which peers, parents, teachers, and others cooperate to give meaning to what he does.

The following sessions place side by side two forms of family counseling; one is directive or verbal, the other, action. The models for the two types are less than complete, for the psychodrama begins where the directive-verbal counseling left off. This is not of decisive significance, for even though the two forms differ, there is no direct contradiction. All theoretical approaches have certain fundamental goals in common, but each interprets and deals with issues somewhat differently. An action method is not separate from, but in addition to, these general goals.

At the invitation of the deputy chief of Children's Affairs in Jamaica, W. I., Ms. Redwin (a fellow counselor and a student of the late Alfred Adler) and I were asked to demonstrate our techniques for the truant and probation officers at one of the Friday afternoon in-service sessions at Falmouth. We met with the training committee to discuss the way in which the demonstration would be presented.

It was suggested that a family be provided for the meeting. The committee was able to do this, but concerned that the trainees (most of whom had been working for only a few months) would be embarrassed by a confrontation with a client. They were assured that an educational psychodrama is different from a therapeutically centered one in that the techniques and purposes are explained, and the trainees could be as active as they could comfortably manage. They were told that Ms. Redwin would open the meeting by interviewing the family in front of the audience. The psychodrama session would follow, focusing either on the family's problem or on the work situation of the trainees. The members of the audience could express their preference of the way they wished it to go.

A beautiful courtyard outside the building was filled with tropical foliage and flowers. Inside there was a room set aside for meetings, large enough to seat thirty or forty people. Ms. Redwin asked that chairs be placed alongside her for the children, on the right, and for the parents on her left. Seven chairs were arranged for the children and for one parent. The single parent came as no surprise to Ms. Redwin; from her earlier work in Jamaica with teachers and families, she was prepared for the "fatherless family." The case history was placed in front of her and the mother was invited in without the children being present. The family was in a low income bracket and of limited education. A few words were exchanged to explain the purpose of the interview.

Ms. Redwin   *(To mother.)* Before I meet the children, I would like to get some information from you about them, their ages, how you get along with them, what you do about the problems you have.

MOTHER	I have one daughter, seventeen, who has a baby, and I think, though she says no, she is expecting another. And six boys from fourteen to six and a half. My fourteen-year-old boy is on probation for stealing.	
MS. REDWIN	(To audience.) Let's get the names and ages of each of the children and, silently, diagram the mother's relationship to the family. (1) Who does she get along with best? (2) Who causes her the most difficulty?	*The family constellation is quickly sketched as the family roles take form through the mother's answers to the relationship questions. A quick formulation of the family pattern was explained to the mother as the interview ends.*
MS. REDWIN	(To mother.) Your favorite son is the fourteen-year-old, the one in trouble, and you can't understand why such a perfect child should be on probation for a stealing incident. Your seventeen-year-old daughter is an uncooperative member of the family who lives with you and lets you tend her and her child, while she has a good time running around. The fourth son is stubborn, for he, too, is uncooperative. One son is "born under an unlucky star" and isn't as clever as the others. The third son is the smart one and seems to be the only one who gets along with your daughter. Do I have it straight?	*The interpersonal sociogram depicts the two females in the family in a negative tele, with the boys choosing sides.*

MOTHER   *(Nods.)* Yes.

Ms. REDWIN   *(To mother.)* Now let me see
                the children. After that, I'll
                give you my impressions of
                your family.

Six neatly dressed young boys came in and seated themselves in an orderly fashion near the counselor, the youngest placing himself in the center of the group, the oldest in the first chair. (The seventeen-year-old daughter came in later carrying the infant.) A friendly relationship was established between the counselor and the boys when she playfully asked, "I wonder which one is called Randall?" They all laughed and made a game of it.

The discussion between the counselor and the boys brought up questions about the significant aspects of the family transaction. What were the roles of interaction in this family? To put it another way, What place does each child find in the family in response to the action of the others? In what ways did the "good" boy discourage the "uncooperative" boy? Did the "smart" one make it difficult for the "dull" one to function? Did they all wait on the baby boy too much? There was a lot of laughter in the group until the problem of the fourteen-year-old's goodness was focused on. He became downcast and closed up. The counselor said, "You don't have to be such a good boy. Sometimes, when a person thinks it too important to be good, it gets a person into trouble. Did that happen to you? Can you try to say no to some of the requests that are being made of you, even to mother?"

When the seventeen-year-old girl came in, she showed her displeasure the moment she saw the situation, then turned it off, smiled sweetly, and said she got along with all of the family members. The family alignment took shape—the fourteen-year-old and the mother against the "princess" and the "bright" one, with the others choosing sides. The children left, and the mother returned.

The counselor reported to the mother and gave her some suggestions about attitudes to take toward her family: "They are a fine bunch of kids. Don't nag and constantly remind the boy on probation to be a good boy. He is a good boy and seems to have gotten into trouble as an experience of being bad. Now let's hear from Mrs. Starr. I would like to see the relationship between you and your daughter. You seem to be very angry with her. This is a good place to begin the psychodrama if the group agrees."

The mother was invited to stay for the session. The group which faced the psychodramatist numbered about twenty-five, both male and female workers. They were asked what they wanted to follow up: (1) They could investigate the mother and daughter relationship. (2) They could follow the fourteen-year-old's escapade of stealing. (3) They could act out their own experiences of stealing, to understand the boy's position. (4) They could deal with the problem of getting the members of the family to talk to them.

They decided to work on the stealing episode of the eldest son, and he was asked to return to the group. The mother was called up to the stage (an open area in front of the group) and asked to *show*, not *tell*, how she learned of her son's difficulty.

MOTHER	I was returning from Montego Bay. I just got off the bus and . . .
DIRECTOR	Now who will you need to show us this? Who told you?

The mother pretends to get off a bus. Three probation officers play the parts of the young friends of her son. They gather around her and in a formal way explain to her that her son is in trouble with the police. The director stops the scene, turns to the mother, and checks its reality. The mother remembers it differently. The director says to her, "Change places with one of the boys, and show how he told you this shocking news."

MOTHER *(as boy)*	Missy Mama, K_____ is in trouble. He has run away from officers. They steal some money from girl and run. Four run away.

There was an abrupt change in the truant officers as they heard the mother fall into the local patois. They dropped the formal roles and became the excited boys of Falmouth. The mother easily switched back to being Missy Mama and continued:

MOTHER *(as self)*	I don't believe. My boy good boy. He don't steal. *(Shakes her head from side to side.)*

TRUANT OFFICERS (*as boys*)	Oh, yes, yes. He run with friends. Officers look for him.

The changing of roles, the audience is told, brings the interaction into focus and helps develop the chain of events; it helps the persons involved communicate not just the facts but also the feelings and motivations surrounding them.

When the excitement ended, the mother was invited to talk about how she felt as she walked home after hearing this bad news. One of the workers was asked to talk with her as a double; they would be "two people with one heart."

MOTHER AND DOUBLE	How could this happen to him? This is bad. The one person who is a big help to me, and now he's in big trouble! I'm ashamed too. This brings bad mark on our name. What should I do now? I'll go to the probate office and find out what happened.

The director turned to the son who was watching the enactment and asked him to come to the stage: "We all know how much you help your mother and how well you get along with her, and we wonder how it happened that you are on probation for stealing. Will you show us how it happened? Who was with you? Look around the group and select the ones you think could play these parts best." The boy selected the same people (the truant officers) he had watched enact the scene with his mother. He left the room with the three officers to discuss the stealing scene. A short time later they returned. They needed a girl victim. The girl (played by a probation officer) stood with a purse on her arm. One of the boys snatched the purse and began to run; so did the fourteen-year-old. They all met a while later in front of the movie theater, and the money was divided.

The director closed the scene with a brief discussion. "We see that you didn't do the snatching, but you shared in the profits. Now that you have thought about it, is there anything you would like to change if you could do it all over again?" The boy didn't respond.

The group was invited to try a different way of handling the situation. They were sympathetic with the boy's role of being the unfortunate victim of the mischief, so the director placed the fourteen-year-old boy in the role of the girl victim of the snatch. The scene was played again. Reality was enhanced by placing some real money in his hand as he stood reading a paper. When one of the officers snatched the bill out of his unsuspecting hand, the boy seemed to feel surprise, dismay, and hurt, and to recognize the predicament of the victim.

In this case, the roles in the family were selected and defined in an interview. A good relationship was developed between the family and the counselor. There was easy communication until the matter of one of the boys being on probation came up. This was worked through by using the positive mother-son relationship (revealed during the interview) in the psychodramatic part of the meeting. The techniques of role reversal, the double, and role training were applied to effect our understanding of the problem and to restore the young offender's self-esteem. Hopefully, the probation officers were able to see the theft as an attempt to join a peer group and to see the offender's desperate need of a stable adult relationship.

It was fortunate for the audience that the directors could talk in a meaningful way with the family. Many of the workers admitted that getting information from clients was difficult. Responses were often guarded, as were many in this session.

Action Sociogram with a Family

Since the sociogram diagrams the data on group relations, it may be demonstrated in action as well as by a paper-and-pencil test, and it may utilize psychodramatic therapy. A sociogram may be plotted directly and actively on the stage during a psychodrama session as a diagnostic technique. The responses and rejections are portrayed by the actual people or by others who represent them as they assume the position, facial expression, distance, and emotional attitudes toward the patient (protagonist) whose family constellation is drawn. This is called "tableauing" or "sculpturing," and in this way the sociogram comes to life. It facilitates history-taking and interpretation: space and, when the tableau comes to life, body movement are the important clues. However, the protagonist may be asked, if he seems ready, to reverse roles with any of the depicted figures, to double, to throw himself into the role of the most significant person on the diagram, and to deliver a brief monologue. The tableauing of the family constellation is used, then, as a warm-up to an individual's role relationships.[8]

A young veteran of Vietnam, age twenty, had been picked up by the police and placed in jail. Observing him, the police recognized a serious disorganization behind his jolly manner and referred him to a VA hospital for treatment. During the scheduled psychodrama period, the director learned that his family—mother, father, older brother, and younger sister—were visiting. They were invited to attend the session. The director offered a few words of explanation: "We want to get a true-to-life look at the family, to see them at home the way the patient does; then, perhaps, we can see how to change whatever is wrong with the picture." Then the director asked someone in the audience to take the patient's place in the family as the patient stood alongside the director.

DIRECTOR	Let's begin by imagining that this room is your house. Think of a particular time. See it in your mind. Where are you?
PATIENT	Yes. I got it. I was in the basement with my stereo on.
DIRECTOR	Arrange your "stand-in" the way you listen.
PATIENT	Music, loud, and I'm beating it out. *(Stand-in sits on the floor and begins to move rhythmically, smiling, snapping his fingers and wagging his head.)* That's it. I'm with it.
DIRECTOR	Where is your mother?
PATIENT	She just walked in and flopped out in the kitchen. *(To mother.)* Don't you? *(He arranges her as a rag doll, head down, arms limp. Mother assumes position at a table.)*

The word "stand-in" is a colloquial expression used with patients and students to minimize the difficulties of fulfilling a role.

DIRECTOR   How does she greet you?

PATIENT   She doesn't. I'm in the   *He begins to develop*
             basement—remember?   *the role of an outsider*
                                            in the family.

DIRECTOR   Now your sister. *(Patient*
             places her in the bedroom
             laughing with a group of
             friends; the friends are
             selected from the audience.)

DIRECTOR   Your brother? *(Patient takes*   *Seems to accept the*
             the brother through the   *role willingly.*
             kitchen. Mother and son pass
             an affectionate few words
             and brother goes to basement
             and joins the patient in a
             friendly hassle, waves
             goodby, and leaves to take
             his girl friend for a weekend
             in the country. Brother
             assumes position in a car
             using two chairs as the front
             seat of the car.)

DIRECTOR   Let's see your father.
             (Patient takes father's arm
             and marches him into the
             kitchen and has mother and
             father assume a fighting
             stance, like fighters in a ring.
             He laughs as he does it.)

DIRECTOR   Does that look right to you?
             Is there anything you want
             to change? Anything to say?

PATIENT   Oh, Mom came down and   *Accepts the role but*
             told me to cut the racket. The   *resents it. It is too much*
             stereo was too loud, so I   *of a hassle to change*
             split. Everybody has   *himself or others.*
             someone, but I don't. (*He*
             loses the overly affable look
             and drops the righteous
             attitude that had confused
             and annoyed the policemen.)

This subjective view of the family portrays the mode of family interaction and reflects the lines of communication. The patient is rejected or ignored. This in turn discloses the patient's isolation, his lack of intimacy with any of his family, which describes his disengaged relationships outside the family.

Action Sociogram without the Family

On the ward of a psychiatric unit, about thirty-five patients were sitting in a circle at the beginning of a psychodrama period. Ray, a middle-aged patient, announced that he had a problem: "I began pacing yesterday afternoon, and I don't know why. I was fairly comfortable until then. Now I feel restless."

This information was checked out with the group. They had noticed a change in his behavior and wondered if it had to do with the prospect of his going home on a pass the next weekend. The director accepted this hypothesis as a possibility worth investigating and explained to the patient that often a person will feel anxious before a meeting takes place. "Are you willing to show us what you expect it to be like when you go home?" the director asked.

The director helped the patient warm up to the future by remembering the past. He asked for details of the place the patient expected to go—his home—and the people in it. "How many people will be needed to show us your homecoming?" the director asked Ray. The patient selected a lovely looking nurse to be his wife, three student nurses to represent his daughters, and four young men as his sons. He explained that one daughter was married and wouldn't be there on his arrival. As he made his selection from the group, the director encouraged him to describe each one (age, personality characteristics) and to place them where he thought they might be standing or sitting on his arrival.

"This is Jane, age six, who is glad to see me and rushes to hug and kiss me. She will in all likelihood be with Margaret, my sixteen-year-old, who babysits for us. They will be happy." The two auxiliary egos showed their delight with Dad's being back from the hospital.

"Two youngsters are watching TV on the floor and will 'Hi, Dad' me. They are good boys, and when the program is over will come and sit with me." The stand-ins followed this direction and acted as much like nine- and ten-year-olds as they could.

"The fourteen-year-old girl is in her room, studying, and is a little shy. She'll come down when dinner is ready. They're a good bunch."

DIRECTOR	Where is your wife and the other two boys?
PATIENT	She's in the kitchen cooking. She'll come out and kiss me. She's a doll. My two sons, twenty and twenty-three, are hiding someplace—either in our house or at their girl friends' houses—and won't show their faces until it's time to eat.

By this time the group had gotten into the spirit of the action, and the substitute sons grabbed a couple of chairs and formed a barricade between themselves and the father, their backs to him and arms around each other.

PATIENT	They don't do that exactly, but that's the idea. Neither of them works, and that beats me down.
DIRECTOR	What does your wife do? Side with the boys, or what?
PATIENT	She calms me down.
WIFE	(Stroking the substitute patient.) That's it. Don't worry. Keep calm.

The sociogram is now complete. It vividly illustrates the positive feelings, the cooperative behavior of the younger sibling group, and the negative interaction or uncooperative attitudes of the two older boys. This investigation of the interpersonal situation in the patient's family made it easier to work on his disturbed relationship with his two sons; the rest of the session prepared him for his weekend pass.

This plotting technique made the information about the family specific by means of spontaneous development of the patient's portrayal of his family, and it gave the group a portrayal of a patient who was difficult to understand and to react to, especially since his verbal skills were poor.

Action Sociogram of the Group

A variation of the action sociogram is the group sociogram, a means whereby a patient who expresses a lack of a feeling of belonging to the group can explore with each group member the positive and negative assessments he makes in a graphic portrayal. A feedback occurs when the patient's conclusions are checked for accuracy in a confrontation or a role reversal. Since the goal of the session is to achieve emotional involvement which will lead to a change in attitude, the physical and verbal contact of "sculpturing," estimating, and switching roles proves stimulating and helpful.[9]

Sociometry In Situ

This is the case history of Janet, a troubled young woman in her mid-thirties. Janet was the younger of two children and had been placed in therapy with a schizophrenic diagnosis at an early age. Later she married and had children who were developing without any marked difficulties. The marriage was very difficult. Janet was under the complete and often sadistic domination of her husband. She was willing to stay in this situation, but he wasn't. He divorced her, and at thirty-four she was alone, since he received custody of the children. She was allowed to keep the house. Soon she was inviting unhappy "strays" to come and live with her. The effort to replace her lost family was a good one, but the choices she made were not.

Someone reported to the police that Janet's friends were using the house for prostitution. It all came to a sad end when the "friends" carried away her furniture, and in a helpless fury, she attacked them violently. This behavior brought the police, and she was placed in jail with serious charges against her. Her parents rescued her and brought in a psychiatrist, who placed her in a private hospital.

After a sodium amytal interview and other diagnostic procedures, the psychiatrist revised the diagnosis to serious mental retardation and began to participate actively in reorganizing Janet's life. During a six-week hospitalization, a psychodramatist was introduced into the treatment to become her auxiliary ego, to help restore her confidence by becoming a friend. She was helped to find an apartment, to direct her activity toward realistic goals. The therapeutic procedure was supportive and direct as a double, in situ, correcting any distorted image she carried as she met with other people.[10] Group psychodrama was begun but soon dropped as too upsetting in favor of brief individual sessions that dealt with answers to practical questions. With the psychiatrist's continued help and counseling, Janet was able within a year to replace her lost husband with another who was more understanding, a disabled man who needed care and companionship as much as she needed to care for someone.

The significance of this case is in the application of the sociometric principle of improving a person's predicament through knowing that (1) loss produces agitation, and the observable behavior may not be a reliable index of the nature and extent of a patient's mental status, and (2) loss needs replacement and, often, needs outside intervention to be given the opportunity to participate in repairing the loss.[11] Jules Masserman noted the importance, in the treatment of mental deficiency, of "a special emphasis on the need for sympathy and patience in dealing with the defective, sympathy, sincerity, and directness in communicating with him, and wisdom in arranging and supervising his occupational and social milieu."[12]

8

Setting the Stage and the Warm-Up

The stage can be any open space with room enough for a few subjects to be watched by an audience. Chairs are arranged in a circle or a U with the center designated as the acting area. This arrangement seems to foster interaction, as each member of the audience may be seen by every other member. It is a familiar setting associated with group therapy and theater-in-the-round. The stage in psychodrama is the vehicle of therapy; a person may move from a position in the audience to a place on the stage, from listening to acting.

The director of psychodrama is an initiator of the warming-up activities of the group. He or she searches out the problems and helps reproduce them on the stage. He may give a short talk, show a film, or use a situation or a relationship that someone in the group suggests. In general, the director begins the session, helps define the problem, selects the players, chooses the first scene, develops and guides the action, interrupts and prompts, and closes with a group discussion.[1]

The Session

As a director faces the audience, he assesses the immediate behavior of the group, and the group evaluates him. The director may be seated on the stage or standing as he delivers a short talk about the meaning of the session. He is offering help as he raises expectations in the minds of the audience. This is a general warm-up.[2]

The goal is now vague. The audience knows that something is going to happen, that someone is expected to respond, to come out of the group. Tension mounts as the members wait to see who will respond to the director. Usually the director searches out the problem and asks, "Does anyone in the group have a problem to work on?" When someone volunteers, he is invited to take his place beside the director and, in a friendly, unhurried dialogue, the director puts him at ease by saying, "Tell us what problem brought you to the group."

Defining the Problem

The interview between the volunteer and the therapist is a direct warm-up; now the goal is known to both and leads to the action on the stage. As the director determines the area of investigation most productive for the patient, he also elicits cues with which to begin the first scene. This interview may be brief as the patient moves quickly into the problem, or it may take a careful sorting through of events that the patient will reproduce on the stage.

To help the patient give an account of the problem, the director asks him to show a situation in which the problem occurred. Out of the many, many interpersonal experiences, the patient selects one as an index to his pattern of behavior. The precipitating circumstance—loss of employment, the death of a loved one, family conflict, money problems, sexual difficulties—is put into an action situation. In this enactment we see how the patient responds to the difficult events in his environment. This may or may not demonstrate the cause of his problem, but it shows how he comes to terms with his reality.

A young woman lies outstretched on a sofa, face down, as the session begins. The director invites her to sit up and become acquainted with the group. The patient is quick to comply and explains that she's tired, she didn't sleep well the night before. "I woke up and found worms crawling all over the pillows," she said. Although it is unlikely that this private hospital would have worms or bugs in the bed linen, the patient is encouraged to go into more detail until the complaint is clearly stated. "Were you having a nightmare?" asks the director. "What did you do when you discovered worms crawling around? Can you show us how this happened to you and what you did about it?"

Selecting the Players

The director asks the patient to choose from the staff of trained auxiliary egos, or from the audience, those people needed to act out the situation. (Sometimes the patient takes the auxiliary ego aside and orients him to the problem. This isn't always necessary.) The director helps set the scene by asking the patient to describe the place in which the action will take place. As the patient talks, the director reminds her to keep the dialogue in the present tense. The director then takes himself out of the set, but stands ready to prompt the players, to introduce role-playing techniques, and to stop the scene when important aspects of the relationship have been made.

Choosing the First Scene

The first scene begins with an evening ward party (enacted by a few members of the group). There is a game of bingo and some dancing. The patient smiles softly at the recollection of a happy time with the other patients. She goes to bed but wakes up to see worms crawling around on her pillow. She quietly goes to the dayroom to report the incident to the night nurse. The night nurse checks but can't find any worms. The patient stays with the night nurse in the dayroom—face down on the sofa.

Developing and Guiding the Action

The director is interested in similar occurrences and asks, "When did this happen before?" A second scene is enacted. The patient places herself in the kitchen at home playing on the floor with her two-year-old daughter. She is having a good time, but when she gets up from the floor and goes to the sink to wash the dishes, worms begin to crawl out of the drain and all over the sink. A person playing her double ego stands beside her. Speaking as the patient, the double says, "I hate to wash dishes. Worms crawling all over the dishes—ugh! I'd wash them, but I can't." (The hallucination is accepted, but the double must guess at the motive of the symptom.)

The enactment continues. The patient goes to the phone, calls her aunt, and asks for permission to visit and bring her child. The mother and child go to the aunt's house.

Interrupting and Prompting

The patient explains the worms to her aunt, asks if the child can stay with her for a while, then goes to the telephone and calls the doctor. The director interrupts the action to ask, "Why did you call a doctor and not the Board of Health?" "I had gotten sick before and I knew I was sick again," she responded.

From the patient's verbal and nonverbal behavior, the gravity of her emotional state was recognized by the other patients and the patient apparently recognized it too. She then enacted the incident prior to her present hospitalization. The patient and her seven-year-old daughter were sitting on the floor. She brushed a worm off her daughter's face. The daughter reprimanded her mother gently, "That's not a worm, Mother. You know better than that." The patient ended the scene abruptly with, "The doctor told me whenever I'm happy I can't stand it, and then this happens to me. Happiness is not for me."

Closing with a Group Discussion

In these vignettes, we were able to see what the patient was unable to say: "I'm unable to function as a mother and as a worker." She had relinquished dishwashing, household duties, all social activities. The daughter assumed the mother's role during these periods of withdrawal. The recurrent episodes after hospitalization provided enough information to see the patient's withdrawal from society.

The group members became acquainted with one another, surprisingly, as they admitted to "seeing" people or things when they felt guilty or worried. The spontaneous statements of the patients seemed to point out that hallucinations can occur even when there is no serious sickness. Hallucinations may be a signal of real distress.

We see, then, that the behavior of one human being becomes a key to understanding our own behavior. Almost all of us have had "dream-like phenomena occurring in a half waking state, usually concerned with worries of the hallucinator. All such experiences can be brought on by auto-suggestion. Most of us learn to ignore private sensations; some build hysterical symptoms on them. In the schizophrenic, they provide a source of hallucinations."[3]

The Warm-Up

The last example showed how the director became acquainted with a patient. The acquaintance took form as the patient's chief complaint was dramatically shown. The precipitating stress or burden introduced the patient's reality—her environmental background.

The director has to have, besides a sensitivity to the warm-up rate of a patient, a working knowledge of all the techniques that will enable patients to confront and work on special problems. Following are warm-up activities for individuals and groups.

The Indirect Warm-Up

For an indirect warm-up,[4] the director may briefly interview one member in the group at a time, asking such questions as, "Who would you like to know in the group?" or "What do you want to know about someone in the group?" When the discussion reaches an individual with a problem that seems urgent or whose problem represents that of most of the group's membership, he becomes the protagonist. The group is mobilized to become a part of the action that will take place on the stage. A variation of this is to have group members interview each other to find the relationships that are troubling them.

The Undirected Warm-Up

Another kind of warm-up is the undirected one.[5] A person enters the group; his tension is visible as he reacts with acute awareness to the words and movements of others. He might make an indiscriminate verbal attack on the director or someone else in the group. The reason for this is unknown. Some hospitalized patients come to a session resenting the intrusion, but they really do want help. Others may feel that being hospitalized is like getting a ticket for drunken driving and feel that they are going before a judge; the outcome is unknown and provokes anxiety. The director must respond to this chaotic behavior. The following case is an example.

Ed, a twenty-five-year-old veteran of Vietnam, broke out of his usual quiet reserve and silence as he opened a psychodrama session by glancing quickly around the room and announcing to the director, "I don't want to be called on today. What are your qualifications? Are you supposed to run a psychodrama session? Do you ever help anyone? Or do you just hurt people?"

He continued to lash out verbally as his eyes darted from patient to patient to staff members, challenging the validity of the therapy. The director invited him to come to the center and discuss the issues he had raised. After some persuasion, he revealed that his agitation was caused by his fear of keeping an appointment with his psychiatrist. He also felt unable to report accurately on his condition and thought perhaps the doctor would misunderstand and give him the wrong medication.

The Chain Warm-Up

In the chain warm-up,[6] the director interviews one person who then warms up the rest of the group. The patient may talk of a dream; others in the group respond by thinking of their dreams. The director may return to the first person and begin there. It may happen that the director walks in as an issue is being discussed by the group. He may begin the session with this issue.

The Immediate Warm-Up

An emergency situation usually requires an immediate warm-up[7] in order to deal with the emergency. (An example is given, in Chapter 17, involving a patient who engaged in a kissing-struggling match with a student nurse.) The director and the group are expected to react with whatever spontaneity they can muster. There isn't time to do more.

Physical Starters

So far we have discussed the mental influences of the warm-up process, the interpersonal starters (tele). Moreno has further divided starters into psychochemical or artificial stimulants (food, coffee, alcohol, other depressants, and amphetamines) and bodily processes (singing, rhythmic movements). The mental starters are related to the physical; one reinforces the other.[8] An example of a physical starter is when the director requests the group to mill around (walking is a physical starter). He may say, "Find a person you want to know better," and the group members' choices may reveal the problem.

Some groups respond more readily to a physical warm-up—walking around and visiting informally—where the director gives some definition to the exercise, some goal of interaction. Otherwise, moving around may create more anxiety than the group can handle. The enacted scenes, as a result of the director's encouragement and of the group's momentum, represent fantasies related to the patient's current reality problems. If the patient blocks in this production, there are techniques (reversing roles, providing a double, using the mirror technique) to help him continue.

This chapter has outlined the action of the director as he discovers and works through the problem of a member in the group. The warm-up signals prompt the director to make decisions that lead to the emergence of situations. The following chapter will offer more group warm-up techniques.

9

Group Warm-Up Techniques

In order to begin a session, a director needs to know something about the group: how often it meets, how long it has been meeting, and the kinds of people in it. Moreno observes: "The younger the members, the more important is the age of the individual; the older the members, the more important is the age of the group."[1] In any session, there is the question not only of how to start, but of what can motivate the members to reveal themselves. The initial phase of a psychodrama session challenges the resourcefulness of the director and the group as they prepare for the events to follow.

While most directors use a spontaneous interview of the group to uncover its structure and to bring out problems, as described in the chapters on sociometry, there are times when the director needs action techniques that will reach the spontaneity level of the group. Regressed, chronic patients in a hospital setting certainly respond to a highly structured warm-up, while games, exercises, and fantasy are good with adolescents and often with professional workers who want to have some fun. All types of groups can profit from a fun session—one in which there is nonpersonal involvement and a light mood.[2] Many male adults, however, particularly alcoholics and drug users, are preoccupied with defensive isolation, and the more directly the warm-up leads into a relationship and a problem, the more easily the resistance is lessened. Group warm-ups differ in what the individuals are being aroused toward

113

—a view of problem relationships, an introspective view of the self, physical activity, or relaxation. It was pointed out earlier that a warm-up phase precedes each act. This is a natural process that is holistic and takes place without conscious awareness.

Warming up a group is much like warming up the fans at a football game. There, the band music, the cheerleaders, and the players arouse an emotional and behavioral response in the audience that helps them maintain an interest in the game. All these factors arouse involvement. Homework given by a teacher is a guided warm-up, since it prepares for learning the next day at school.

An auxiliary ego warms up to a role, and the patient responds by accepting the relationship. These two, the patient and the auxiliary ego, warm up the audience by portraying what the audience and the patient may have in common. Because it is difficult to know exactly how little or how much structure is necessary for achieving individual and group participation, the director has at hand a number of group warm-up techniques, some of which will be described.

Walter Bromberg, working at Mendocino State Hospital, presented pictures from detective magazines and tabloids that implied sexual or criminal activities to a group of court-committed sexual deviates in the early phase of warming them up to psychodramatic treatment.[3] The patients were asked to develop dramatic situations about these or any subjects. It took more than ten sessions for the patients to feel secure enough to do this. Resistance to personal involvement is consistently reported with this type of group (the prison population).

Chair Techniques

The auxiliary chair[4] is one of the techniques used by all action therapists as a warm-up to evoke a feeling or an image, or to direct a feeling toward an individual. When an auxiliary ego is unavailable, or the patient is more comfortable without an auxiliary ego, an empty chair is substituted. It is placed in the acting area, and the audience is invited to imagine that a person is seated there, an absentee to whom they would like to say something, for example, a husband who is at home with the children or a doctor who is on vacation. They are given time to warm up to an image. The director encourages them to visualize the person and comments, "Did anyone find it difficult to place a person in the chair? This is not easy for some people to do." Usually, someone who is able to project a role onto the chair speaks out, for example, a woman might say, "I'd like to talk to my boyfriend." The director asks the volunteer to describe him. "He's a big slob," she says. She is reminded to say what is on her mind to the chair. The patient itemizes a list of complaints—all the things the absent boyfriend does that she objects to. When she has exhausted her anger, she is asked to move into the empty chair and answer in the role of the boyfriend. As the patient becomes the absentee, she is being introduced to role playing.

The chair can provide an outlet for the expression of warm, tender feelings as well as angry ones, since a chair may be embraced, pushed, or hit. When this technique is used with children, as Rosemary Lippitt introduced it, or with withdrawn patients, the director can stand in back of the chair and respond as the absentee. This warm-up sometimes occupies the entire session, as other volunteers take a turn at addressing the empty chair. It frequently is used during the session to help the patient complete an idea or a feeling that seems blocked by the counterspontaneity of the auxiliary ego or by internal excitement. The mood of the session is influenced by the image projected onto the chair, as absurdities in the shape of animals, machines, or trees may lead the way into a fun session.

The High Chair

In the high chair technique, a chair is placed on a high spot on the stage or acting area, or the director may use a stool that is higher than the chairs in the room. The director then asks what the patients would like to say to the person placed in this elevated chair. This usually stimulates projection of figures of authority and enables group members to be expressive toward them. This technique is especially valuable with hospitalized patients that are angry with the staff.

Multiple Chairs

In the multiple chairs technique several empty chairs are placed in a circle on the stage. All the patients in the group who are able to project a character onto the chairs are invited to come up and take a place in the circle. One empty chair is placed in the center of the group. Each patient takes a turn at "identifying" the "person" in the empty chair. This becomes the basis for a psychodramatic production.[5] Alternatively, new patients in the group are invited to occupy all but one of the chairs and to name a person they like very much to sit in the empty one. Or, each member may be asked to name an aspect of himself, then shift to the empty chair and show how this part of the self operates. In this way, the others may get to know who he is.

In a hospital session, the chair is often filled by patients representing mother, father, siblings, and so on who would mourn the loss of a suicidal patient. This is called a "death scene." As members from the group express the grief and disappointment they would feel at the death of the patient, the suicidal person reverses roles with the mourners and frequently finds, in assuming these new roles, a reason for living.[6] A more realistic solution to the unhappy situation may then be explored.

Multiple chairs may be arranged back-to-back or with three facing each other and one facing away. The group is asked to fantasize, to say whatever the organization of the chairs calls to mind. Regressed patients and those withdrawn into depression are often helped to function and participate by being asked, "What does this arrangement of chairs remind you of?" Their associations become the basis of a scene. Whatever activity is recalled is promptly put into practice. Such fantasizing may become the basis for a whole session as one after another the patients describe a railway station, a lunchroom counter, a doctor's waiting room, and so on.

Milling

Schizophrenic patients on a ward are usually vague, aimless, and isolated. The director may suggest to them that they are walking through the forest preserve and that when a patient makes a remark, all the others should act on it immediately. "I'm cold" is followed by huddling together for warmth. "I'm tired" is followed by sitting or lying down. The value in this is that the whole group cooperates in movement.

Another technique has the group arranged in a circle. Movements are initiated by the director or a helper. He may start clapping and everyone claps, as in follow the leader. Then the next person may tap his feet, and the whole group taps their feet. Each person in the circle takes his turn initiating a movement or a sound. Next, group members are asked by the director to form duos, then quartets. Members of each of these subgroups are now able to talk to each other at the readiness level of the group.

Patients in better contact with reality may consider this warm-up childish and resist it. They may prefer wandering about and welcome the selection of partners through milling. But it is helpful to give the activity some structure—a theme to work out—after they are in subgroups. Have the members verbalize their preoccupations: "I'm thinking about my job" or "I didn't want to come here today." The go-around can last as long as it produces meaningful attitudes or until one person seems to be in serious need of help and the other group members are interested in following up.

Other times, a director may ask the group to walk around silently and associate to words called out by the director, such as *mother, job, sex,* and *dating.* This continues until someone reacts to a word; one member might say, "I'm a loser on a date." Then the milling stops, and the actors are selected to work on the problem.

Adolescents delight in milling. They also like the fun of the "blind walk" and the touching that accompanies it. One person becomes "blind" by tightly closing his eyes and is guided around the area by a seeing person. This is sometimes called the "trust walk," since the discussion at the end of the walk usually is about being able to follow another in these circumstances and the amount of trust or lack of it that is present.

Milling ends with patients in twos, standing face-to-face. They are instructed to stare at each other, then to hold hands as they speak first as friends in a social situation, then in conflict. The verbalization can be done in unison or pair by pair. This format gives the patients control over the areas they plan to explore. A variation is to have the pair sit face-to-face with eye contact, or back-to-back, and invite a discussion of the problems that brought them to the group. This leads into role playing a problem.

These exercises and games are good ways to establish rapport with an adolescent group and to further group influence. The antagonism that usually builds up between an adolescent group and the staff lessens as the adolescents feel they are gaining respect and running their own session. If all goes smoothly, the exercises lead into an enactment of values. Peer group influence is strongest at the time of adolescence. Often it exercises a dictatorship over attitudes and behavior. Loyalty to the peer group is often stronger than that to the family.[7]

Music

Regressed or confused patients can be motivated by music when the spoken word is too threatening. Jules Masserman writes that all people respond to the rhythms and sounds that are the basic ingredients of all types of music.[8] For the regressed patient, music may be the technique that works when other forms of communication fail. A dramatic response to music described later involves a psychotic woman who responded to a love song sung by a patient playing her imaginary lover.

"Music permits communication without awakening defenses and

at the same time implies a nonobjectionable order, primarily through rhythm, but also in its other aspects of regularity, harmony, and melody. In this sense being exposed to music, either as a listener or a participant increases communication and evokes a subtle acceptance of order so essential in therapeutic endeavors with psychotic children." In this way, he may warm up "to participation in his real life roles, without being forced to abandon at once his fantasy life."[9] Participating in a band, or drawing as one listens, may provide clues to the many situational difficulties that the person is unable to bring out in the open.

Improvised music, called psychomusic[10] by Moreno, is particularly helpful. It is a combination of music and psychodrama. The patient is asked to compose music describing a person or a feeling. An instrument may be used. For example, the patient may play a few notes on a piano. The therapist discusses with the patient the images evoked by the notes and invites him to create a story from the music. These stories are projections of the patient's dilemma. A variation of this technique is to use a recording.

When there are no instruments, the body becomes the producer of musical rhythms and sounds. An imaginary band may be formed. Group members are invited to come to the stage and play an imaginary instrument, one they are familiar with or one they always wished they could play. The rest of the group joins in by humming or whistling along with the band. When the director knows that someone in the group is a musician, he may ask him to perform during a session. This may stimulate associations to early experiences with music teachers, overambitious parents, siblings, or family values.

A musical play is an active use of music that is especially helpful in warming up a group of patients with speech disorders. The roles are taken by different members in the group. Following is an improvisation that resulted from the director's suggestion that the theme of the musical play would be: How can I get a date?

DIRECTOR   (Sings out as he faces the group.) I am alone and unhappy. Why can't I find someone to admire and love me? (Glances around, discovers someone, and walks toward her, singing.) Do you mind if I ask you a personal question?

PATIENT	No, no. What is it?	*If she doesn't respond with song, she is prompted by the director to sing.*
DIRECTOR	*(Singing.)* My friend who stands over at the bar wants to know if you recognize him?	

In people with speech disorders, the blocking often associated with words is reduced as the focus of attention becomes the production of a melody. The rhythm of breathing necessary in singing also helps free the inhibited speech patterns.

Music as a warm-up to relaxation is furnished in another format called the *crib*.[11] A recording of a lullaby is played or the lullaby is sung by a participant ego. Group members are invited to arrange themselves on the floor and curl up as if they were babies in a crib. In a soothing, appealing voice, the director instructs the patients to feel that they are a few months old, to relax, to know that someone is watching over them, caring for them. The director as mother walks from patient to patient and pats and reassures each one as the lullaby serves as background music. This regression induces introspection and finally relaxation. The director guides the imagery of the group, encouraging them to become older and older as he continues to caress and reassure them. The final phase is reached when the director asks the patients to return to the present and share with each other the imagery and feelings elicited by the experience.

Acceptance Exercises

In another kind of warm-up, the whole group is prepared to become acquainted with one another nonverbally by means of acceptance exercises. These exercises break up rigid patterns of body movement.

The patients are asked to arrange themselves in two groups facing each other from opposite ends of the room. One group stands waiting to be approached. The other group approaches them with friendly feelings; they meet and interact. They disengage themselves and go through the exercise again with more intense feelings, perhaps as if they were friends meeting after a long absence.

The groups are then given roles: one side are mothers; the other side, children. The children are asked to run toward the mothers as if they were meeting after being away at camp for two weeks. This is reversed as the mothers move toward the children to pick them up after a long absence.

Each group is asked to work out a real or imagined experience of meeting or being met and to show, without words, what happened after the initial encounter. They may make sounds but use no real words. They may grunt, exclaim, use nonsense words, or whistle.

Part of acceptance is admiration and/or imitation. The group members are invited to look around and decide on one person in the group they like. They are to focus on the whole person, the characteristic head position, shoulders, chin (pointed to chest or ceiling), eyes, walk (a swagger or a shuffle). Once the selection and observations are made, each person walks around as if he were the person he chose. One by one the members perform. When anyone recognizes himself in a portrayal, he acknowledges it; otherwise the imitator finishes by standing in front of the imitated. (They are selecting and responding to each other.)

Another acceptance exercise is to direct two group members to move toward each other slowly, keeping eye contact. When they meet, each performs an act that shows how he sees the other. (When enemies in the group meet, it is wise to watch the warming up to assaultive behavior and guard against it.)

The next exercise involves pairs and deals with the notion that surrender is part of acceptance. One member is seated on a park bench. The other approaches, makes a request that must be shown in action—to walk, swim, make love, dance, and so on. The first member responds. The two then discuss with each other the availability each recognized in the other and the way each one felt.

After one such beginning, a man in the group nonverbally invited a woman on the bench to share his lunch with him. She refused. As she began to move her head from left to right, in a gesture of refusal, she began to cry. It recalled a painful experience of early childhood when her grandfather insisted that she eat an apple. When she was too slow in responding (surrendering), he forcibly fed her a red pepper. The nonverbal exercise led the way to a situation that revealed the origin of her lifelong stance against people.

The exercises lead easily into a discussion of the comfort or lack of it that each person felt in executing the exercises, and can show the director what psychodramatic techniques to use next. These exercises help the members in the group stop for a moment and react to some of the simple, everyday situations in life.[12]

The Intermediary Object

The use of a puppet as an intermediary object[13] can speed the warming up process when working with a hallucinating patient in the group. If, when the session begins, the patient is unresponsive to the usual forms of communication, an auxiliary ego puppet player is asked to address a monologue to the patient. At the close of the monologue, the puppet player calls the patient by name. If the patient responds he is led into a dialogue with the puppet.

The value of the puppet, it would seem, is that it protects the privacy that the patient guards. The puppet is outside the society from which the patient has withdrawn. He doesn't give up his basic notions of withdrawal by talking to another symbol of nonexistence. Once the spontaneity level of the patient is found, therapeutic interaction can begin.

Building Self-Esteem

Warm-ups that build self-esteem[14] are appropriate to all groups. Each patient is encouraged to take a hopeful look at himself and to decrease his defensive maneuvers.

The director says, "Here is a time and a place to learn something about yourself. There are many things in your life that are well organized and satisfying. Let's start with them and try to balance them against your troubles."

As each member identifies himself by name and something about himself that is of positive value, the group begins to relax and feel the acceptance and concern of the group. The director can then ask each member to consider a time when this positive attribute led to a happy solution or an unfortunate one. The situations are then enacted.

Constructive Feedback

After a group has had several meetings, a storehouse of experiences has accumulated, and it is time to begin a session with feedback. One member is selected to sit in the center of the group (called the "hot seat" by some patients) and receive the good impressions of others—

not a verbal assault, but a playback of positive qualities. This may develop into projection if the discussants discover that the traits they see in the person in the hot seat are their own.[15]

The Two Circle Warm-Up

In a hospital situation, when the director knows that a problem exists in the group, he can announce to the patients and staff: "We are faced with a problem that can probably be worked out here and now. Will the staff come to the acting area and sit in a circle?" The staff complies, and the patients sit around and behind them. The problem is discussed honestly by the inner circle of staff members as though the others were not in the room. The outer circle of patients has the right to interrupt and ask for more information. After all the factual material has been elicited, the inner circle is asked to come to a conclusion; then the outer circle becomes the inner circle and closes the meeting. This is a way of lowering the barriers between staff and patients. It can also be used with students and teachers, parents and children, and other similar groups.

A variation of this technique is to have the inner circle (staff members) be played by patients, with the outer circle composed of staff role playing the patients. Airing differences this way can be a revealing experience.

The inner and outer circle technique is also effective in a large therapy group. The persons ready or willing to participate are invited to sit in the inner circle, close together, and the ones whose warm-up takes longer place themselves on the outside, still close to each other and to the inner circle. Those in the outer circle are reminded that whenever they want to, they may move to the inner circle. This is a non-threatening warm-up suitable for any group whose members need to look before they leap into action.

10

Improvisation: A Sociodramatic Test

The use of the term *improvisation* in the field of psychology is relatively recent. It is more frequently used in the language of the theater. Chapter 1 describes how impromptu acting came to be called sociodrama, that is, how role playing came to be used to portray the problems of the group. Since improvisation is a procedure most generally used when clinical procedures are inappropriate, for example, in the classroom or in industry and in professional training workshops, it is important that the psychodramatist knows something about it.

Improvisation is a technique for personality assessment. Although the procedure is seemingly a test, it has therapeutic as well as diagnostic values. Helen Hall Jennings, who worked with school children, says that "sociodrama offers a method which in vital ways aids the individual to mobilize his personality resources for communication."[1] Moreno points to its training value: "Improvisations are the royal road to spontaneity training."[2]

An improvisation is designed to tap one aspect of a person's behavior. An individual may test his role in relation to other players in an extemporaneous production. For example, the director might point out to the group something they are probably not aware of, that many in the group came from another part of the country. The problem of being a stranger is common to the group. With sixth grade students in a classroom, the parent-child relationship is a common concern, as is the pal relationship. The director might explore aspects of behavior in these relationships that need analysis and training.

When the director uncovers a problem that the group is ready to work on, he selects three people as representative of the problem. The group members examine and discuss the behavior as it relates to the situation and to themselves. Some directors have a repertoire of standard situations, and when they assign the roles, they hand out printed instructions to the role players. Other directors prefer to influence the warm-up with a series of verbal instructions, giving a sense of spontaneity, of urgency and excitement, to the situation.[3]

Improvisations are nonthreatening productions that protect the individual from feeling attacked but still show the inadequacies of his behavior. Putting a patient in a realistic situation in which he has to respond to the counterspontaneity of another tends to reveal well-established patterns of behavior. This is helpful for diagnosis. As a rule, an individual is more comfortable holding on to old patterns of behavior than trying new and improved modes of communication until change finally seems necessary, practical, and possible.

Improvisations for personality assessment are projective tests. In order that the improvisation be a reliable test, it is important that the situation be relatively free of structuring. This requires the individual to create a solution spontaneously. An improvisation situation should be developed out of basic conflicts common to all people: parent-child relationships; authority relationships; relationships with the opposite sex.[4] The roles in these main categories are dramatized as husband vs. wife, sibling vs. sibling, employer vs. employee, teacher vs. student, boy vs. girl, and black vs. white.

The following test provides a conflict situation involving authority. The subject or subjects (usually three people) are asked to leave the room and return one at a time on call. The tester (auxiliary ego) is told to play the part of a policeman who stops a speeding car. The subject is called in and warmed up to the role of being a speeding driver. He is asked, "What kind of car are you driving?" and told, "As you sit in your car, feel that you are speeding along toward your destination."

The police lights flash, the siren screams, and the speeding car is stopped. Arguing begins. (The police officer has been advised he is on his own and can give a ticket or not.) All the subjects play out the situation. Then what has occurred is discussed and clarified. The audience evaluates each driver's management of formal authority.

Here are three examples that indicate the usefulness of this technique as an interpretation of role behavior.

1. A young boy of nine, when stopped for speeding, jumps out of the car, refuses to accept the ticket, pulls a pretend gun, captures the policeman, and hauls him off to jail.

Interpretation: The boy, a "soiler" (he has defied toilet training), is a severe discipline problem both at home and in school. He defines his behavior problem in this fantasy role as "I overpower authority in order that I may become the authority."

2. A young, hospitalized female patient, when stopped for speeding, explains to the policeman that she has a dead body in the trunk of the car and asks him to please not delay her any longer.

Interpretation: The patient's attempts to deal with authority are distorted and indicate her life pattern; she arranges to make things go from bad to worse.

3. A young male student, after a big hassle with the officer, offers him a bribe.

Interpretation: The patient feels that a policeman is corruptible and is not above subverting him if it serves his purpose.

The significance here is in the way a person presents his own role and that of the tester. In the interaction, the patient may be dominant or submissive, extroverted or introverted, or sadistic or suffering as he meets a figure of authority, a person of the opposite sex, or a parental figure. The way a person talks to the other people in the situation is representative of his characteristic attitudes toward himself and others. He may see himself as the victim of the other person's misbehavior, or he may refer to others as essentially stupid and easily duped by his superior skills. Or he may have idealized the other person and expect that person to rescue him when he is in trouble. As he talks about others he is saying something significantly important about himself.

Situation Test

Other improvisations that are realistic and interactive and require a spontaneous solution can be used as a projective technique.[5] Three people are asked to volunteer to leave the group and wait out of hearing until they are called. They are told that a situation is going to be set up and that they may respond to it in the way they have in the past or in the way they hope to in the future. After they leave, the group members are asked to think of a situation they would like to see worked out. When the group reaches a decision on what the test is to be, the individuals return one at a time. As they complete the test, they join the audience to watch how the others handle the problem. Each group designs its own test out of its chief preoccupations. The following situations have been presented:

1.   A mother (auxiliary ego) walks into the family room and discovers her teen-age daughter giving her girl friend a lovely, expensive piece of antique jewelry that the mother had given her as a birthday present. The mother has noticed, during the past months, a change in her daughter's attention to dress, indifference to the mother's standards. The mother has decided to talk to her daughter. The situation between mother and daughter was spontaneously acted in different ways: (1) the daughter was indifferent to the mother's dismay; (2) the daughter was argumentative with the mother; and (3) the daughter consoled the mother and asked the friend to give back the jewelry.

2.   After two weeks of working on a construction job, a long-haired, bearded youth is given his check and advised by the foreman that if he wants another check, he must get rid of the beard and the long hair. The three subjects who met this situation demonstrated a conflict with an authority figure. Their various solutions were to try to persuade the authority to give up his prejudice against the length of hair, to explode in fury that such a prejudice exists, and to take the check without a murmur of protest and simply not return to work.

Usually a single incident with three approaches is presented to a group during a given meeting. At its conclusion, the whole group discusses the behavior of the tested subjects and is requested to generalize on the situation:

1.   What kind of conflict was portrayed?
2.   What was the basic theme of the conflict? What value was at stake?
3.   How was the conflict resolved by each of the subjects?
4.   Was anyone surprised by the way someone handled the conflict?

Projective Action Techniques

Projective techniques are used extensively in psychodrama. In projective action tests the auxiliary ego is a stand-in who responds as the protagonist expresses himself. The protagonist is asked to submit to a series of projective action tests.[6] The instructions are given one at a time. As each is completed, another test is requested. Here are examples of test situations:

1. Select a political figure, anyone you'd like to talk to. Throw yourself into the feeling mood and start talking to the figure of your choice. You have complete freedom to say what you like.
2. You are at the airport meeting a friend. Show us who it is you are meeting and how you feel as you meet.
3. You are angry at someone. Show us who it is and how you express this feeling.
4. You are wherever you wish to be. Be there. Fill in the details. Are you alone? Where? What are you doing?
5. Here are three items—an umbrella, a cigarette lighter, and a statue. Use these items with words and action.
6. You have the magical power to become anyone you choose. Be that person.

An individual's reactions to these instructions provide a capsule profile of his relationship to people and to fantasy. They also show whether a person has organizing skill and the strength of his orientation to the future.

The nine-year-old boy, mentioned earlier as driving the speeding car, used the umbrella, cigarette lighter, and the statue as follows: He came in out of the rain, closed the umbrella, placed it in the fireplace, ignited it with the lighter, and became the statue of Hitler in a "Heil Hitler" salute. His responses indicated his above-average intelligence and also the destructive goals of his behavior.

An imaginary telephone call, letter, or cable involving a threat, a sexual insult, or a notice of termination of employment may be used to give the subject a chance to respond spontaneously to a message. Since these improvisations relate closely to everyday experiences, they give accurate impressions of a person's characteristic methods of dealing with others and reveal social attitudes that often are missing in paper-and-pencil testing. The chief purpose for introducing improvisations in a clinical setting as an assessment method, however, is to indicate to the psychodramatist the patient's basic error in living and to locate specific areas in need of treatment.

11

Techniques for Training

Psychodramatic therapy makes inroads into behavioral change by starting with the external behavior and working inward. The techniques that are basic to the development of a psychodramatic session have been defined as the mirror, the soliloquy, role reversal, and the double. These are the basic techniques with which to integrate observable behavior with the probable subjective state—the private world—of the protagonist. Such extensions and intensification of roles give the patient an opportunity for a more adequate and interpretive reenactment of his conflicts than he has been permitted to express in life situations. Scenes may be extended beyond the patient's experience, too, to move into the future, to recreate the past, to provide satisfactions that the protagonist was unable to have in life, or to explore his fantasies, hallucinations, and delusions. In playing roles, the protagonist condenses events. An interview may be a self-presentation as the patient enacts all the roles himself—his mother, his father, his employer—and ties together his attitudes toward others and his ideas about himself.

Behind-Your-Back Technique

Role-playing therapy provides many ways to clarify the protagonist's perception of himself and his behavior. For example, in the *behind-*

your-back technique the protagonist leaves the room psychologically by turning his back to the group. For all intents and purposes he is out of the room and overhearing the group discuss him. The group's involvement is heightened as they are asked to change from listening to talking. This technique provides the protagonist with feedback. It may be used effectively at the end of a portrayal of a life situation or during a presentation if a patient seems to be uncomfortable and looking for signs of approval or is suspicious that he has lost group support.[1]

A young male homosexual in his early twenties was in bitter despair that his lover had left him. He had begged his lover to stay—not to hustle the street—and was deeply hurt that his lover preferred making money soliciting to staying with him. In the reenactment, he stood outside a gay bar watching for his lover when a policeman approached, called him a "queer," and threatened to run him in if he didn't watch his step. After a few more insults from the policeman, the patient stopped role playing and looked around, wondering, it seemed, if he hadn't been careful enough here, if he had talked too much. The director asked if he wanted feedback, and he replied that he did. The patient was asked to turn his back while a selected group of patients addressed themselves to a specific aspect of his behavior. Each made one statement. The patient was asked to return to the group by turning his chair around and responding to the group's feedback; he picked up on one person's comment, "excuse me for living," as reflecting the way he experienced himself. This moved the direction of the session toward restoring the man's self-esteem. The encounter with the policeman was replayed until the feeling of being alone and victimized was resolved. By becoming aware of his own behavior in the interaction with the policeman, through repetition of the scene, he increased the possibility that he would be able to handle his feelings toward the rejecting lover.

The behind-your-back technique can also be reversed. The audience is asked to turn their backs to the patient, to act as if they were really out of the room. This method, like the previous one, is based on the idea that freedom of expression may come from an absence of visual stimulation. It is a form of confrontation for it gives the protagonist a chance to tell each member of the group how he feels about them; the members of the group see themselves as the patient sees them. They are instructed not to respond, only to overhear what is being said. A patient's fear of giving feedback may be overcome through communicating how others encourage or discourage him, how hyperdependent he may be.

Fantasy Scenes

Fantasy scenes range from wishful thinking and normal daydreams to the irrational convictions and misinterpretations of psychotic delusions and hallucinations. This section will describe the production techniques of the normal day and night dreams.

Dreams

When a person reenacts a dream, he reexperiences it. Each image in the dream event is realized. The analysis of the dream takes place as the person progresses through the dream and discovers its meaning.[2]

During the beginning warm-up the patient is asked to assume sleep position, eyes closed and relaxed. Before the reenactment takes place, the patient is asked to get in his mind a clear image of the dream—its plot and the locale of its beginning. When he is ready, the director asks, "Where are you in your dream? Do you see yourself? Are you sitting, reading, running?" Here is an example involving a female patient:

PATIENT	I am at the seashore.
DIRECTOR	Get out of bed and place yourself as you are at the seashore.
PATIENT	I am walking through a group of people who are not sunbathers; they are dressed up.
DIRECTOR	*(Signals some people from the audience to form a group for the patient to walk through.)* Are they talking?
PATIENT	Yes, but not to me. *(The group begins a soft chatter.)* Then I went into a room— maybe a hotel; I can't figure it out, but there are a lot of people there. *(The group forms again.)*

DIRECTOR　　What kind of group is it? Arrange them as you remember them in the dream.

PATIENT　　I know some of the people and we greet each other— men and women—but I walk away. I'm looking for someone. *(The group follows the dreamer's directions, greets her and visits as she walks away.)* Dear God, I'm looking for Bill. I said this in my dream. I woke up disgusted with myself.

DIRECTOR　　Who is Bill?

PATIENT　　An old boyfriend from years back.

DIRECTOR　　You said you awakened disgusted. Why?

The emotion produced by the dream is an important clue to follow.

PATIENT　　It's such a futile thing to do, to look back so much.

The dreamer was asked to role reverse with each element of the dream in order to further understand the problem being elaborated. After this reenactment, there was a sudden clarification of the problem.[3]

DIRECTOR　　When did you see Bill last? In psychodrama you can extend the dream experience. After all, you produced the first dream. Now go back to the dream position and find Bill.

PATIENT　　I don't want to find Bill. I want to quit looking for Bill.

DIRECTOR   Fine. Fine. It may be
                        helpful to train yourself in
                        the dream. Change your role
                        in the dream. Be what you'd
                        like to be.

This procedure is based on the idea that by changing the dream, the patient can change the attitudes that produced the dream.[4]

A Festival Fantasy

At Christmas time, a legend can be turned into an improvisation. The patients on a hospital ward are readied for the presentation in this way: Three or four male patients are taken out of the room by a trained auxiliary ego and told that they are to play the parts of members of a gang of jewel thieves. Rumor has it that at the top of the hill outside a small town in Switzerland live three maidens who have a fortune in jewels that they have saved for years to give to the Christmas angels. But the angels have never visited them. The director says, "Your part in this play, men, is to get the jewels. In the first scene, you plot the deed. In the second scene, you break into the house. Wait out here for your cue."

Three patients are chosen to play the maidens. The three are instructed to trim the tree and play the role of the maidens hoping the Christmas angels will visit this year. They place the jewel box at the foot of the tree and go to sleep. When the men break in, the maidens wake up, mistake them for the Christmas angels, hug them, and give them the box of jewels (a spontaneity test).

The thieves creep into the house, and the maidens awaken. With howls of joy they hug and kiss the thieves and give away the jewels. Everyone starts singing "We Wish You a Merry Christmas." After the merriment dies down, the director asks each man, "Do you feel like a thief or an angel?"

Fantasy scenes are usually used to end a session, for they provide the director with a diagnostic evaluation of the patient's perception of himself. It is important that a session end on an "up" note for the patient, and fantasy is a nonthreatening way to do this.

The Magic Shop

One of the most popular of the fantasy scenes is the magic shop. It is often used as a warm-up with groups who are slow to become involved (it is especially useful with children and regressed patients). The director explains to the group that he is setting up a magic shop, a shop filled with things of value. The items in this shop cannot be bought for money, but they can be bargained for and traded for other things. All the patients in the group are invited to come and barter. The director or a skillful member who knows the group becomes the shopkeeper.

In order to get what he wants, a shopper first must really want it. Second, he must be willing to leave something he no longer can use. The shopkeeper must ask the shopper what he wants to give, what price he is willing to pay, for his dream, his ambition. The shopkeeper may play the role in any way he feels comfortable.

With children the director explains that a magic shop is open for business. At this shop, a person pretends to buy whatever he wants. But in order to get it, he must show (enact) what he plans to do with it. "Who is my first customer?" says the director. This engages the whole group in an animated interaction with "things." This technique gives the group a feeling of success, as the time spent in fantasizing a desire is translated into action.

Judgment Day

Ever since Dante visited Hell in the *Divine Comedy*, Hell has been used in fantasy trips by many writers. Through psychodrama, we can travel to Hell too. The scene is usually played in dim, red light. Mephisto sits high in the acting area and interrogates the people who are brought before him.

MEPHISTO	What brought you to Hell?
PATIENT	I drank, beat the wife and kids, and brought them to shame and poverty.
MEPHISTO	You are a dissolute man, full of conceit. What else did you do?
PATIENT	I shacked up with anyone who was around.

MEPHISTO   That caused others a lot of
pain and places you in Hell.
But no one has to stay here
unless they choose to or want
to. Do you think you belong
in Heaven or in Hell? I give
you the choice.

Patients who see no possibility of changing will elect to stay in Hell; others who are more optimistic about themselves will leave, and will feel encouraged about their decision to change. The session ends when each member in the group has had a visit in Hell. Robert Siroka approaches this with an emphasis on the death and rebirth of man[5]; James Sacks stresses the judgmental aspects of the episode with God, not Satan, as the judge.[6] The scene ends as each man becomes his own judge in a role reversal with God.

Future-Projection Techniques

Future projection helps the patient prepare for the various tasks he must face in the immediate or distant future—going to a job interview, asking for a raise, or meeting an estranged spouse. The enactment helps the patient formulate his objectives in the situation as it brings out the different angles for him to explore. It is a rehearsal for living.

Future projection also may be used as an exit test to determine a patient's readiness to leave the hospital. The three roles of worker on the job, member of the community, and family member—all necessary to adjustment—are put into short scenes, and the patient's behavior is evaluated by the group.[7] An exit test may be personalized by asking the subject to select a situation in which there was a problem before hospitalization and to show what he plans to do about it on his return to the community. A patient portrays what he expects to be a few years in the future—a happy person or a sad one, a success or a failure; that is, he expresses a sense of fulfillment or disappointment. This is usually done in a monologue.

Paradoxical Intention

·   The paradoxical intention is an interesting therapeutic technique in which a patient practices exactly what he fears. An example of this principle, and of the director's going along with the patient and even intensifying what he fears, is illustrated in this application in a hospital ward psychodrama group.

A thin, middle-aged woman (with little education and no familiarity with psychological language or dynamics) complained repeatedly, "I can't sleep. That's the reason I'm in the hospital. The pills don't help." It was not possible to get her to talk about what was bothering her. The director arranged the patients in small groups and told them how a seal sleeps—with the eyes open, moving its head from right to left as far as the neck can be extended. The eyes close only when centered directly in front. The director explains that the seal thinks to itself as its head revolves, "I'm on the lookout for danger." In this exercise not only do the eyes scan the field, but the head rotates like a beacon.

After the exercise had been done a few times, it was suggested to the patient who complained of sleeplessness that she try it before she retired. The following week she reported great success. "The exercise made me drowsy and I slept fine," she said. She was shown how to go along with her sleeplessness and not to *try* to sleep.

This technique of antisuggestion usually brings only temporary relief, but, as O'Connell[8] points out, it demonstrates to the patient that he can exert control over his behavior when he understands the principles by which his symptoms and his personality operate. The principle underlying this technique is that such "nervous" symptoms are aggravated when the individual tries to fight them; tension is generated in this struggle and diminished as he accepts the symptoms: "So what if I don't sleep!"

Unfinished Business

The unfinished business technique deals with the past and is a frustration test.[9] The goal of the training is to help the patient become assertive. It works well with many types of groups, since unfinished business is common to all. The way the technique is introduced, of course, depends on the age, sophistication, and tolerance of the group's membership. The director may say to hospitalized patients, "All of you have some experiences that you file under 'Unfinished Business.' It may be something that happened a long time ago, but you keep thinking to yourself that you mismanaged it. Let's think about it." He waits, then says, "Has anyone in the group thought of a situation?"

These problems are easily transformed into scenes of action and may lead into a full session devoted to one patient. Example: A young man had been working for his older brother in a retail store. The brother, a successful businessman, called the patient into his office one evening and fired him for being a thief. The young man denied the accusation, but feebly. Over and over, obsessively, he defended his honesty, but not to the brother. The situation was played out, first as it actually happened, then as the patient wished it had turned out.

It is important not to let the patient tell the whole story before he enacts it, since this lessens the interest of the audience as well as the patient. It is like knowing how a mystery story turns out before reading the book. The director may comment on the difference between the actual happening and the way the unfinished business was finished in the second reenactment. The difference between the two indicates the amount of inadequacy experienced by the patient. Acting out the second version may restore his sense of effectiveness, for it extends the patient's role beyond the real life situation and serves as an action catharsis. It may indeed become action learning as the "new" man becomes a part of the "old" one.

Embarrassing Situations

In another technique, patients are asked to tell of a frequently experienced embarrassing situation.[10] What seems to be a minor problem is often worth looking at, for it may be expressive of a basic pattern in the lifestyle of a person. The scene may help the person become aware of his own behavior by tying the embarrassment to a particular role.

One person in the group mentions an embarrassing incident, such as making an appointment with a stranger, calling in sick to the office, returning a purchase to a store, talking to a stranger, inviting a friend to a party. The embarrassing situation is acted out with other actors selected from the group. After the portrayal, another group member is asked to role play the same situation. But this time he shows how he meets and feels comfortable with the situation. Closure is effected as the individual who had the problem interprets it in terms of his basic mistaken idea of self. He tells the group whether he learned anything about the problem and what he learned about himself as he watched his incident being enacted by someone else.

The Obstacle

The obstacle technique is often called the pressure circle.[11] The members of the group encircle a patient. Each stands for an item of dif-

ficulty that cuts him off from the world of others, such as perfection-
istic striving, no sense of humor, or fear of directly expressing feelings.
Or a patient's progress may be obstructed by people, worker, boss, and
so on. After the people who represent the obstacle have surrounded him,
he is told to be rid of them by dismissing them verbally or physically.

Closure Techniques

The following techniques provide closure. They sensitize the total
group to the relevance of the psychodrama session and help them relate other people's behavior to their own.

The Antagonist's Chair

At the end of a session, when the patient has defined one person
or several as the chief obstacles (the villain or villains) in life, an empty
chair or chairs are placed in the acting area and the group is invited to
tell the absent opponents how they feel about them. The group telling
the bad guys "a thing or two" helps the patient dismiss the past scenes
that were unhappy.[12] The strengths shown by the patient may be itemized at this time.

The Comfort Circle

The comfort circle is a technique in which the group members
form a circle around the patient and respond in a loving way to his
predicament. Or they may simply express joy at his successful fulfillment of a difficult task. The scene becomes one of hugging, handclasp-
ing, and physical movement. This technique may be entirely nonverbal.

The Close-Up (Spectrum)

In the close-up, or spectrum, the director picks a characteristic
of the patient's behavior that was developed in the patient's acting on
the stage. The director asks each person in the group to rate himself
as being most like or least like the patient. For instance, one patient,
a young man, showed himself to be overly compliant, pleasant, vagrant:
another patient says of him, "He's like a puppy dog wagging its tail
when it is stroked." The patients are invited to place themselves on an
imaginary line drawn across the room; one end of the line is friendly,

the other aloof. After the patients have placed themselves on the line, each one ranking his own behavior, they check their self-rating by comparing it with the opinions of others in the group. This completes the working through of identification (the state of finding a similarity of purpose, use, attitude with another) with the actor and corrects whatever distortions may have occurred.[13]

Discussion and Evaluation

Most discussions at the end of a session need to be handled with tact and understanding. In educational and industrial settings, the discussion should be kept objective and impersonal. Even in clinical sessions, the director often closes the psychodrama with the comment, "Why don't you think it over?" A "rubbed in" interpretation may make the therapist feel better, but it doesn't always help the patient.

In educational sessions, one may wish to alert the audience at the outset to watch for special points. As soon as a role-playing situation is completed, observations of these points can be discussed or the situation replayed for skill practice. After group members have observed the role playing of a kind of behavior they find difficult to understand, they may ask themselves:

1. How is the individual feeling?
2. What did he want from the group?
3. Why was he acting that way?
4. What can the group, or anyone in the group, do to help the situation? (*This may be acted out to test its suitability.*)

Many psychodramatic sessions lose impact if the audience is not encouraged to individualize and then generalize about the episode. It sometimes helps to ask group members to sit silently with eyes closed and think how the insight may be applied in their own situations. Sharing these ideas helps each member generalize.

Sharing

Sharing is a special form of closing a session.[14] As the patient ends the action part of the psychodrama and is ready for some feedback, the members of the audience are encouraged to move toward him and speak, one at a time, recalling personal incidents that listening caused each to remember. To reinforce this effort and serve as an example, the director may disclose an appropriate incident from his own life. To do this, a director must believe in the value of setting aside his professional attitude and making contact with other human beings through a common experience. This message goes out to the group and awakens them to participate, not with analytic musings but with expressions of personal concern and sharing.

12

Psychodrama as Marital Therapy

Marriage, that ancient institution, is under considerable stress. Many of the rules and regulations that once gave consistency to the marriage tradition no longer exist. Industrialism destroyed feudalism and thus ended the rights and privileges of nobility and led to greater promotion of individual rights. As men improved their economic position, freedom of thought turned into freedom of action. Man's relationship to woman was set by social custom; the male was dominant, and the female had to obey. Around the middle of the last century, all this began to change. The status of women slowly but constantly improved. After each war, the place of women in relation to men changed. Women's rights to vote, to work, to enjoy sexual freedom finally were realized.

These radical changes have not made the male-female relationship easier or more satisfying to either sex. One would have been justified in assuming that when women were "liberated" and given rights, tension between the sexes would lessen, for discord could be understood in terms of revolt against oppression and tyranny. This is not the case. When women had to obey, they had no choice and more or less accepted this humiliation as their fate. The man was "supposed" to rule. If he didn't, he lost face in the community.[1] The idea persists that a man must demonstrate his masculinity. Although his sex is not of his own making, his masculinity is. While a feeling of masculinity is important to his self-respect, achieving it is often difficult.

141

He may choose to find it in accomplishments—a profession, a trade, the military. In the absence of accomplishments, he may adopt a pattern of behavior—tough guy; strong, silent male; cool outlaw—that demonstrates his manly traits. Constant anxiety accompanies supporting the masculine role.[2] Consequently, and ironically, the relationship between the sexes has become more tense as women fight against submission. A woman demands rights, and her increased activity arouses the man's anxieties, for he is insecure about his place. Each views the other more as an enemy and less as a companion. A man's goals are more specifically defined than a woman's, although the man's goals may not be as easily attainable. The woman's predicament is that among many choices and many alternatives, she must find a role satisfying enough to give her a sense of self-esteem.

As each partner in a marriage seeks a way out of the dilemma, the discord between them can reach a state that threatens to disrupt all cooperation and understanding. It seems that there are now no rules or regulations, that marriage is lawless. The old regulations held the couple in a manageable relationship to one another. Now, each partner must discover for himself his relationship to persons of the other sex.

Every social change is accompanied by extremes that caricature the problem. In the case of marriage, some choose to return to the "good old days" when women were submissive and men dominant. At the other extreme are those who find an evolutionary change impossible and declare that marriage is outmoded, that its age is evidence of its uselessness. Both of these attitudes are translated into action, culminating in an escalating divorce rate and avoidance of marriage—a fear of committing oneself to the dangers of the marriage relationship. Dreikurs predicts that "the end of the struggle cannot be expected until mankind has finished the process of establishing equality for all its members. True equality has not yet been reached, but the progress toward it is rapid."[3] As part of that movement toward equality, couples seek help in resolving the conflict and achieving more cooperative relationships.

Considerations in Treatment

The husband-wife dyad with which the marriage begins offers the potential for great variation in marital harmony and disharmony, satisfaction and conflict. Attempts to solve marital problems have resulted in an equally varied collection of individual and group techniques. Therapy may be *intensive*, as in individual psychotherapy; *supportive*, as in marriage counseling; or one of the six C's of therapeutic techniques—

counseling, collaboration, concurrent, conjoint, combined, or classical—as Bernard L. Greene classifies the various approaches.[4]

In any case, therapeutic treatment has come to include exploring in action how the partners get along in the various roles they play in a marriage relationship. The focus is on the here and now; the historical events of the marriage are enacted as if they were taking place in the present. Each person's role conflict may be explored and self-discovery achieved through the psychodynamics of role playing, role reversal, and mirroring. This does not exclude the findings and insights of dynamic psychiatry, but rather is a direct outgrowth of them.[5] Psychodrama as a form of treatment moves into the life drama of the partners, into the reality context of their world, and includes all the significant people involved in the situation, singly or together.

The first concern in the treatment of a married couple is to ascertain the nature of their interpersonal relationship—the kind and degree of each partner's participation and the strength of their attraction (tele) to each other. As the partners role play the ordinary events in their life together and the crucial challenges in the marital situation, well-established patterns of relating to each other become apparent. The form of the interaction is put in motion.

Once the focus is on the relationship, the psychodramatist has his role cut out for him—to become a participating actor who calls attention to the difficult interactional issues through co-action. Most persons come to therapy pointing a finger at the other spouse, expecting that a change will take place in their mate, not in themselves. The director must guard against concentrating on one individual as the source and cause of the conflict.

The marital therapy session begins with a private interview with each person. This may be conducted by the psychodramatist or the referring therapist.

Interaction Patterns in Marriage

An examination of the pattern of interaction in a functioning, healthy marriage reveals that each marriage partner appreciates and understands the role of the other and that there is an attitude of co-operation in working toward mutually beneficial goals.[6] When both partners feel equal in a marriage, then both feel motivated to seek constructive solutions to problems. They can effectively manage day-to-day patterns of behavior, stress, problems of verbal and nonverbal communication and interchange, and questions of agreement or disagreement on roles, values, and goals. They move toward each other, and the intensity of participation in the marriage is not diverted by their individual personal goals, since the "willingness to cooperate overcomes many obstacles."[7]

The pattern of interaction in a conflict-ridden marriage may take many forms. The intensity of participation of the partners may be unequal; one may be fully invested in the other but be met with only indifference or arrogance. One partner may fail to meet the role expectations of the other. The marriage partners may be rejecting each other as they struggle for dominance and fail to give each other the satisfactions of a wholesome relationship. They may fail to help each other separate themselves psychologically from their respective parents. The couple may be unable to extend their past role of singleness to act as a team. They may fail to satisfy in the sexual sphere. Sexual interaction typifies the couple's problem of relating to one another. Each spouse acts as a physical starter for the other and monitors the warming-up process, and this process is in turn influenced by previous experiences. The patterns of behavior may be tested in action situations to bring into focus the responses of the couple to crucial life situations.[8]

Major Challenges in Marriage

Movement and change occur in the formation of every marital relationship. The developmental tasks of this relationship are a gold mine for role playing. First, there are the tasks found in the beginning of the relationship; the length of time spent between the meeting of the pair and the decision to marry suggests the strength of the reciprocal attraction of the pair. Lack of social acceptance and the difficulties encountered in finalizing the marriage are examples of the kinds of problems individuals must deal with in this critical period in the relationship. In some instances, it takes years for the decision to marry to be reached, which may be a recurring annoyance to one or the other; on the other hand, some marriages are formed precipitously, and not enough time is allowed to test the relationship. The former reveals a cautious warm-up to the roles of marriage; the latter, impulsiveness. Another aspect involving time is the amount of time two people spend together before and after they are married. The task of reorganizing work and play time is usually regarded as independent action versus togetherness.

Another category of tasks involves relationships that extend outside the marriage. Two people do not live alone; they are connected to their original families. A person marries into a complicated chain of relationships. Another string of relationships feeding into the marital system is made up of the acquaintances that interact with the couple during work and during such leisure activities as sports, church, and politics.

The degree of involvement with the members of the extended group either integrates or disturbs the couple, depending on the strength of the attraction of the pair to each other. In a unified marriage, partners tend to exclude those relationships that isolate the mate and to include the outside relationships that are mutually inclusive. When either the husband or the wife indulges in independent activity, the other member of the pair may have the feeling of abandonment, even though this may not be intended. An example is professional business meetings that absorb interest and time and may cause marital discord. Also, most people enjoy being alone for certain periods, and such persons as scientists, philosophers, and creative artists seem to need more isolation than others. The spouse is expected to adapt to this special need.

The intuitive level of interaction determines the response to real problems and their solutions. No member of a dyad knows everything about the other, but each knows more than either one often acknowledges. These dynamics are subtle, yet they exist in a positive way in a deep and enduring relationship. The reactions of the couple will be based on a common effort to reach agreement or disagreement.

The sexual functioning of the husband and wife, a fourth aspect of marriage, is the most intimate expression of their attitudes toward cooperative behavior. Frigidity and impotence are the organs' expressions of a lack of effective and affectionate responses in the nonsexual areas of marriage. The difficulty is not localized in the genital organs but is an expression of one aspect of the individual's behavior pattern: evasion, revenge, sabotage. A fear of not performing adequately, skillfully, or consistently evokes images that interrupt the sexual function. Equally disturbing to a satisfying sexual union is setting standards. Partners expecting each other to reach an orgasm simultaneously may be the source of a feeling of failure or triumph. As in the other areas of life, each person brings to the sexual act his own definition of intimacy. "It is the will which makes the way."[9]

Marital Choice

The fact that a person is attracted to certain people but not to others has been explored by social scientists. Similarity in a number of characteristics—social and economic background, religion, attitudes, and values—is predictive of a successful marital relationship. But dissimilarity, too, has been proposed as a source of marital success. These investigations are interesting, but they tell us little of an individual's basic motivation in his dealings with people. They fall short in revealing outside influences on the individual such as the pressures of the group and the individual's position in the emotional field of attracting and rejecting others.

It is left to the therapist to discover the setting in which the choice of marital partner is made and the circumstances that led to the two people choosing each other. The choice may have been based on an attraction to appearances—money, sex, or a gentle, kind nature. Some persons are attracted to daring and adventurousness, to the aggressive display of knowledge, or to a helplessness that invites protection. Some are too cautious and timid to choose another (receiving few attractions and many rejections), but respond to being chosen as an escape from loneliness, a means to independence, or an exit from an unpleasant situation at home or a dull, monotonous one at work. The question arises, then, of what "attracted" one person to another. Most people in love do not look at this question too closely for fear of interfering with the magic of love, and they may resist the confrontation of reality issues.

As a relationship begins, the two people hope that their reciprocal love will be fulfilling; one person has what the other feels he lacks and needs. The bonds that reinforce or improve the self-concept of each partner tie the two together as well as draw them into conflict. At first they are two with the same attitude toward life—together they are able to face the world. Later, in conflict, they see each other as part of "that" world, the opposition.[10]

This theme is readily seen in a review of couples who have sought help: A doctor, overly conforming and rigidly organized to the most essential detail of behavior, married an impulsive artist, whose spontaneity was precariously close to sociopathy. He was stimulated by her zest for living, and she needed the safety his overconformity presented. An ex-nun married a marine sergeant with a demanding attitude toward sex. The trouble began when he became so sexually insistent that he wanted sex all the time, even with the children present or when friends were visiting. What at first had been a liberation from her own inhibitions became a loathsome, humiliating effort. The more she withdrew from him, the more demanding he became.

A less dramatic and more common situation involves a woman

who marries a sweet, tender, obliging man and is sorely tried when he extends this obliging quality to the neighbors, all his friends, and especially his mother. Being married to a man with benevolent qualities does not cause conflict, but the wife's feeling of desertion does, as the husband mends the neighbor's fence while his own needs repair—or so the wife thinks.

The Patients and the Setting

The examples in this chapter come from my experience as a psychodrama consultant to a group of Adlerian therapists in private practice. Since Adlerian therapists are particularly interested in the interactional aspects of a person's life, psychodrama is an effective method for their purposes. Consequently, many families who came for counseling were placed in psychodrama groups. Family interactions often showed that the conflict between the parents was so intense that marital therapy—either individual or joint—was indicated to repair the damaged relationships. The psychodramatic sessions became adjunctive therapy in an overall treatment plan.

When a married person came for individual therapy, the marriage relationship naturally came under close scrutiny. The patient sometimes had individual sessions with the psychodrama therapist. A couple who came for counseling was either placed in a group or treated separately, and psychodrama was used for diagnosing the pattern of interaction and for practicing the skills needed for resolving the conflict.

Persons with all sorts of marital conflicts have been referred into psychodrama. Some came for a few consecutive sessions; others I worked with regularly four times a month, with every fourth visit in joint session with the referring therapist. Usually the referral to psychodrama is made at a point when an understanding of the pattern of interaction needs to be clarified, either for the therapist or the couple, or when the interaction needs to be experienced by the couple. Psychodrama is added to accelerate the learning process. When one member of a marital pair needs to have his lifestyle tested, the conjectures of the interpretation can be corrected or revised with the help of the evidence of the action. Often what a patient tells the therapist about his relationships is at variance with what comes out in the enactment.

The office space for my psychodrama sessions was somewhat larger than usual, with a desk, chairs, and ashtrays to accommodate a group of ten or twelve patients. There was no stage or special lighting; a circular bentwood cocktail table in the center of the room could be used to sit, stand, or pounce on. The table was used to represent levels of interaction as well as to define the area of performance.

Case One: Connie

The following case has been selected to illustrate how the director became a participating actor in a session without an auxiliary ego and with only one marriage partner present. The referring therapist joined the sessions after a prescribed time and became a participant observer who could become an auxiliary ego if needed.

The therapeutic goals in this marriage of a domineering husband and a submissive, frightened wife were to strengthen the wife's self-image by making her sensitive to the situations in which the uncomfortable feelings would arise and to help her recognize the husband's motivation in order to change her projective image of the "indomitable other."

Connie, a good-looking woman in her late forties, had been married for fifteen years to her second husband, Joe; this was his second marriage, too. Both of their former mates had died, and each had brought children to the union. Joe's children had made reasonably good adjustments to school and marriage. Connie felt that her daughter, who was still at home, played the same submissive role as Connie played in her own marriage. She was worried about the daughter.

Joe was a successful supervisor in a factory. The ability to show and tell everyone the right way to do something made him an efficient supervisor but a terrifying person to his wife, who was sure she couldn't do anything right. Her response to a simple homecoming greeting of "Hello, Honey. What's new?" had been to start to say what was new. But he would turn away from her, saying, "Can't you wait until I catch my breath?" The husband found something wrong with any response she made to his stereotyped "Hello. What's new?" She was unable to offset his role of dominance with any self-satisfying strategy. She began to feel uneasy, and when he was ready to listen to what was new, she couldn't or wouldn't think of anything to say. (How could she change her role of subservience when she was convinced that whatever she did was wrong?)

The referring doctor had suggested that she be trained to fight back, not with tears and trembling as she had reconstructed her role from childhood toward her domineering mother, but with a more satisfying response pattern to her husband's role of constant domination.

The only occasion, the doctor explained, on which Connie recalled fighting her husband was to defend her daughter. We began the psychodrama sessions with the enactment of this situation.

When a married person has a problem, it indicates a disturbed relationship, so both partners must be in the psychodrama therapy, either in person or by means of a substitute who plays the role of the absent mate. The substitute ego acts as a physical starter for the mate who is present; feelings and images are often suggested by the presence of the alternate ego. Following is an example of self-presentation with one patient with one therapist (dyadic).

Session with One Therapist

Three roles are required to present the interaction among the husband, wife, and daughter, but only two persons were present in the office. The director decided to encourage the patient to act out all the roles as the events of the situation emerged. The director became the other person needed to complete the interaction.

The scene began with the husband and wife reading in the family room. The daughter enters; she is waiting to be picked up to go to a dance.

CONNIE
(as daughter)   How do I look, mom?

CONNIE
(as self)   Smashing. I'm glad we
                        decided on that dress. What
                        time do you expect to be
                        picked up?

CONNIE   Any minute now. *(She starts*   *The director assumes*
(as daughter)   *to go out of the room.)*   *Connie's space and*
                                                          feeling. As Connie
                                                          plays the roles of
                                                          husband and daughter,
                                                          the director moves to
                                                          other positions in the
                                                          room to take the space
                                                          of the daughter and of
                                                          the husband when the
                                                          need arises.

CONNIE *(as husband)*	You're not going anywhere, at least not tonight. Go to your room.	
CONNIE *(as daughter)*	Why can't I go? It's date night.	
CONNIE *(as husband)*	Because I said no; that's why.	
CONNIE *(as daughter)*	But my date is on the way. *(She starts to cry and removes her earrings, a first step to compliance.)*	
CONNIE *(as self)*	Oh, but she is going! You are being unfair to her. You would never in a million years treat your own daughters this way. Please, please go with Tom. *(Begins to cry and pushes her daughter out of the room; the bell rings, and the daughter goes to the dance.)*	*As the climax of the feeling is reached, the director stands as an observer.*
CONNIE *(as husband)*	I hope you realize what you are doing. *(He retires in silent fury to the study.)*	
CONNIE *(as self)*	Now what have I done? *(She cries harder and begins trembling. She says that his silent fury lasted for several days. He resisted all her attempts to open the subject to discussion. She cried in recollection of the event.)*	*A situation is completed before the retraining phase begins.*

Next, Connie was carefully questioned about her feelings as she played the roles. Did she feel a sense of victory or defeat as her daughter left for the dance? At what point did her self-esteem seem adequate to the situation?

Connie and the director concluded that she was able to act in a strong role when her daughter seemed unable to deal with the domination of the father. She was able to feel that she was doing the right thing in relation to the daughter, but this left her feeling, "I didn't handle my husband properly, look how furious he is." Her "dis-ease" came from the concluding conviction: "See, I'm wrong again. I just can't win." Observation of her role playing revealed that her greatest sense of self-esteem (productivity) came in the role of her husband. She was able in his role to be loud, vindictive, and verbal, whereas when she played herself, she cried easily and had difficulty presenting the sequence of events in her private reaction to the situation. She identified with the aggressor but had chosen to be the victim.

Session with Multiple Therapists

After several psychodramatic sessions in which Connie played out arguments with her husband, the director felt that she had practiced the role of assertiveness (in the guise of the husband) enough to be able to enact it as herself. It was suggested that an appointment be made with the referring doctor and the three work together. Connie demurred, "Dear God, you don't expect me to perform for him, do you! It was hard enough for me to talk to him, much less show him what happens. He makes me feel like my husband does. He knows everything, and I never know what is expected of me." The following is, in brief, what happened during the interview:

CONNIE (to doctor)	I'm supposed to tell you that you make me feel as inadequate as my husband does.
DOCTOR	It sounds as if I do, since you are bringing in heavy artillery to defend your position.
CONNIE	You see, that's what I mean. Whatever I do, it's wrong. You sounded just like Joe.
DOCTOR	I was agreeing with you.

CONNIE *(to director)*	I feel just like I'm with Joe. I can't think of what to do except cry.
DIRECTOR	Hold the tears and express it in words. What do you want to tell the doctor?
CONNIE	I can't.

At this point, the director rescues Connie by becoming her double and castigating the doctor.

DIRECTOR *(as Connie)*	You know everything! You're arrogant and make me feel like a washed out rag. *(The director drops the role of Connie.)* Did I say anything that you would have liked to say? Don't answer. Instead, you be the doctor and tell Connie how you feel about her. Doctor, you be Connie. *(They change seats, and with a little prompting from the doctor as Connie, Connie as the doctor begins.)*
CONNIE *(as doctor)*	You worm. You dumb, dumb woman! If you can't do what you're supposed to do, don't come crying to me. I told you not to let him get away with all that crap. Why do you stay in the marriage just to complain? You know you have a choice. You can stay with it and like it, or stay with it and complain, or get out. Make up your mind. Why do you stay in the marriage?

DOCTOR *(as Connie)*	I don't know. I don't know. Why do I stay in it? *(Crying.)*	
CONNIE *(as doctor)*	That's the answer? Because you don't know?	
DIRECTOR	Switch roles and go on from where you are.	
CONNIE *(as self)*	Tell me—why do I stay in this marriage?	
DOCTOR *(as self)*	Because you love Joe. He is difficult, but you love him. You are learning how to live with the kind of person you feel attracted to.	
CONNIE	No one ever said that before. I feel better. I can understand that.	*She had, at this moment, put aside her erroneous conviction about herself, that she never did the right thing. This recognition enhanced her feeling about herself since it restored her self-esteem.*

The next session was devoted to a clarification of Connie's daughter's submissiveness, since Connie and her husband were getting along without any arguments. The following episode seemed a crucial experience in changing Connie's relationship with her husband. Connie began to recognize that her daughter's obedience to Joe was different from hers. Though the external action might be the same, the feeling behind the daughter's obedience was not fear but aloofness.

Next, Connie was asked to play all the roles in a situation involving her husband, Joe, and her daughter, Jane.

CONNIE *(as daughter Jane)*	*(Stands facing a wall to simulate talking on the telephone to a friend.)* It sounds like a good plan. I think I can come to you.

CONNIE *(as father)*	*(Moves to desk and bellows.)* Jane, where the hell is the package you were supposed to have ready for me to deliver? When I call you, come! I'm late.
CONNIE *(as daughter)*	*(Drops the phone and goes to father.)* Sorry, I didn't hear you calling. I was on the phone. *(Gets the package and gives it to him.)*
CONNIE *(as father)*	You are really stupid. You knew I had to deliver this present, and you hid it. Why couldn't you put it where I could see it? You never do anything the easy way. Dumb, that's it. God, you're dumb.
CONNIE *(as self)*	*(Meekly, weakly.)* You ought not talk that way to Jane. *(She begins to cry as Jane goes back to the phone. The mother cringes as though she were attacked, rushes upstairs to Jane, and lectures her on showing more spirit.)*

The rest of the session was spent responding in alternate ways to Joe's outrageous behavior. Family roles were selected to play out the unique and different ways each had of communicating with the father. It became apparent that the daughter had selected the model of compliance as the one she managed most comfortably. Perhaps she saw strength in weakness. The more he raged, the greater her moral satisfaction.

Connie was advised to study and analyze the characteristics of this interaction at home—that is, to become a spectator of the performance and to report her reaction at our next meeting. In distancing herself from the problem, she discovered that she was married to a computer, which, unlike the real thing, screamed when he was fed the wrong information. She came to better terms with what could be realistically expected of him, that her need to be in the wrong activated negative aspects of his need to control through being right. This enabled her to yield without giving up her self-esteem. While conflict was always imminent, it was easily resolved. There probably was little change in Connie's basic personality, but she was able to see her husband differently and this led to a more satisfying relationship.

Case Two: The Jealous Husband

A man in his late thirties came to the session with his wife. Her reluctance to be in therapy was obvious. She sat, arms together, slightly turned away from her husband. The goal of the session was to help the wife develop a constructive and understanding attitude toward her husband's jealous behavior.

During the preliminary interviews, the doctor discovered that the precipitating factor of the man's excessive jealousy was his being passed over for a promotion with his firm. A close friend got the job he felt should have been his. He quit and found another position, but it was not particularly satisfying. During this period, his wife turned to the pastor of the church for counsel and help. The pastor became a friend of the family and began to visit the home regularly. The pastor became the suspected "other man" but still was regarded as a reliable advisor. The husband went into therapy at the pastor's insistence. The wife was angry that the husband threatened her friendship with the pastor. She had few outside interests or friends.

The first step in such a case is to discover the kind of jealous feelings the patient actually goes through during an experience of jealousy, for jealousy is a common emotion ranging from a sudden feeling of competitiveness to a persistent and overwhelming pain, usually a symptom of a severe mental disorder.[11]

Behind every problem of jealousy is another problem, that of hostility—a desire to attack and hurt the loved one, to make someone suffer as the jealous person suffers. Hostility is compensation for a deep lack of self-esteem. The unhappy person usually recognizes and acknowledges the feeling of insecurity that is aroused in the provoking situation, but fails to see what he does with the feeling. Discomfort is real, and what is done with it, as we shall see in the following case, is destructive to relationships.

The plan in this case was to make the patient sensitive not only to his own hostility, but also to the behavior in the other (his wife) that stimulated feelings of inadequacy. It was expected that the pattern of behavior revealed in playing out situations would do several things. First, it would show the purpose of the husband's socially disturbing behavior—the accusations and blaming. (For some, the purpose is to excuse their own shortcomings: "It's your fault; I'm not good enough." For some, it may be a way to get the undivided attention of the spouse in order to exert the power "ownership" carries with it. For others, it may be to express revenge: "You had better watch out; I'm stronger than you are.") Second, it would help the wife gain some insight into the marital transaction and work out a new role for herself, to lessen the conflict. Third, alternative transactions would provide a setting for practice in social behavior.

At the beginning of the session, a couple is asked to look at and talk to each other, to ignore the director as much as possible. This defines the session as a period of relating to one another rather than reporting to the director. Most couples have difficulty doing this, so it is best for the director to explain that he will join in when there is a lull: "What shall we talk about? Your present problem?"

At times a couple is overheated, and charges and countercharges are made furiously; sometimes one spouse is reserved and the other points to this as the major difficulty, usually identifying the problem as no communication. At that, the director could say something like this: "It is hoped that you will learn during these meetings that there is no such thing as no communication. The silence may develop because you feel irritated and are not able to say so; or it may come from a fear of saying the wrong thing. Each person has his own way of concealing or being unable to say what is happening to him. Let's work on one situation and see how far you can go at this meeting in understanding each other better."

With two spouses and a director, a conflict is easily portrayed; a lifestyle can be viewed, a dream enacted. A current problem becomes the current relationship. The possibilities of interaction are varied:

1. The partners role play an angry situation. It usually is more completely felt and more revealing when it is played out than when it is reported as an incident. Some couples refuse to act; this refusal must be worked through, as it may be especially indicative of the relationship. Is it possible that they haven't learned to act together in a common activity? Encouragement at this time is important.

2. The partners reverse roles. This is a most practical and effective method, for it enables one partner to hear how he sounds to

the other. Usually only one side of the dialogue is recalled. The roles are reversed, back and forth, until the dialogue is completely agreed upon—not word for word, which is impossible, but in terms of the feelings, facts, and movements. Repeated role reversing breaks up rigid patterns of behavior.

3. The members of the group become alter egos to each other. This is accomplished by having one spouse be the double to the other spouse while the director acts as the protagonist. This is usually done situationally—that is, to clarify a feeling response to a situation. This increases the guessing skill (intuition), a very important development in the bogged down marital relationship.

4. The director substitutes for one of the partners, while the other sits and watches. The director has the opportunity to show the observing spouse his behavior and attitudes. Since it is entirely within the mirror technique to exaggerate and intensify the role, the spouse may benefit and decide to alter the situation.

Development of the Session

In the case of the jealous husband, the husband-wife interchange made it clear that the husband was not able to see his jealousy as anything other than a reasonable reaction to a fact of life—he believed his wife would do anything if she thought she could get away with it.

The situation they selected was a recent one. They were at a dance, and a friend came to the table and asked the wife to dance. She accepted. The husband waited for her at the table. When she returned, the accusations began and lasted the rest of the evening. She tried to explain that the friend just wanted to dance; he loved dancing, and his wife had a sprained ankle. This added fuel to the fire: "What else doesn't his wife do that he wants you to fill in on?" She wasn't sure what he wanted her to do—apologize, promise never to dance again, admit that it was the start of a flirtation. She groped for the right way to respond, and, not knowing what to do, became angered and started screaming, "I'm going to leave you! I can't take it any more!" He then interpreted this as proof of her guilt.

The director stepped into the role of the wife, continued the anger, but started accusing him, almost word for word, in a counterattack. She blasted him with a series of questions as accusatory as his, using a female co-worker of his as the dangerous rival. He dropped his jaw and turned toward his wife as he began to realize the sadistic role he had been playing. There was no way to answer, and he realized this. The wife exclaimed, "You see now just what it's like."

The role, as played by the director, was not intended to encourage the wife to express anger for anger's sake, but to make it absolutely clear to the husband and the wife that a dialogue on this subject was impossible. He had based his script on the assumption that blaming, accusing, and being furious would deter his wife from sexual acting out.

The task of psychodrama in marital therapy is to use a current problem—money, religion, children, sex—as the way to pinpoint the role conflicts expressed in these situations. The example shows how the director can avoid wasting time on the issue of fidelity and work on a consideration of alternatives.

Second Session

The next session concentrated on the jealous feelings of the husband. The aim was to show him how he arranged his self-torture before he lashed out at his wife. The wife selected a recent event that led to an outburst (we could call it an inburst, for he closed up like a clam; his wife was aware of his discomfort).

DIRECTOR	(*To the husband.*) For this to be helpful, you must talk about your thoughts out loud. Let's begin by talking in the present tense, as if the event were happening now. Please don't just describe your actions; talk as you feel.
HUSBAND	I walk in the apartment from work, and the first thing I notice is that this house smells like a whorehouse, all perfumed up.
DIRECTOR (*as the double*)	My nose tells me that there's something going on that's different; no cooking smells. How come no food?
WIFE	He's always angry when dinner isn't ready when he comes home.

HUSBAND	What's wrong with that? What else do you have to do all day?
DIRECTOR *(as double)*	See how she picks at me. I can't even expect dinner from that bitch.
HUSBAND	You hit the nail on the head. I walk into the bathroom. *(He runs his hand over an imaginary bathtub.)* She took a bath; there's talcum on the tub. She must be going out with some man. Why else talc? She usually cleans up like that before sex. I run to the bedroom. Maybe she's in there with him *(Mounting excitement.)* No one is there and the bed is made. That doesn't mean a thing. Maybe they fucked off and left. I throw the covers back and smell around. Maybe she went to a motel. She's getting away with making a sucker out of me. *(He turns to his wife.)* Who was it?
WIFE	Nobody. I've told you a million times. Nobody. Are you some kind of nut or something?

(To the right of the WIFE's line:) *The fight circle begins.*

The husband's excitement increased. He was like a bloodhound following a trail that leads to his prey. The clues have to mean something, and he is forcing them to fall into place so he can express his domination by anger. His fantasy is stronger than reality. This trick of reading infidelity into all clues enables the husband, in this case, to move from a minus position to a plus, from a feeling of being neglected to one of being a smart detective and a judge. The depreciated position of no-wife-at-home-to-greet-him becomes transformed as he becomes gloriously and self-righteously angry.

The director talks to the couple and reviews what was revealed by the action: "Feelings are like gasoline in an engine; they take you where you want to go. You went in the direction of antagonism. Let's go back to the moment where you entered the house. Your wife and I will become the clues, the odors that led to your mounting suspicions. Wife, you be the sweet-smelling odor and I'll be an odor, too. You speak to us as the odors."

The couple resisted continuing, perhaps because they were still warmed up to the role-playing episode in which typical responses occurred: one felt bullied and the other angry. After a hassle, they finally agreed to try it. The husband sniffed and commented on the odor.

DIRECTOR *(as an odor)*	I was sprayed with air freshener to cover up cigar smoke.
WIFE *(as an odor)*	She burnt the cabbage, opened the windows. It didn't help so she sprayed me. Then she went out to buy some more cabbage.
HUSBAND	*(Warming up to the idea.)* I still smell trouble. She's not home. Where the hell is she? Out screwing around?
WIFE *(as an odor)*	She isn't. She's out shopping. Why don't you believe me? I was here in the room all the time. I'm telling the truth!
HUSBAND	You're a liar!
DIRECTOR *(as an odor)*	That's the idea. You believe what your nose tells you; it's the cigar smell that is hard to get rid of.
WIFE *(as an odor)*	So is burnt cabbage.
HUSBAND	I don't believe the burnt cabbage bit. If I let this pass things will get worse. She has to realize that she can't put anything over on me.

DIRECTOR *(as an odor)*	Go to it, man. Think the worst. It's smarter that way.
HUSBAND	You're damn right. Give her an inch and she'll take a mile.
WIFE *(as herself)*	Or run a mile. I can't take any more of your ranting and raving. You keep me up, sometimes until two in the morning, with your checking and double checking.

The husband and wife began again to scream at each other, blaming and accusing. The director interrupted after a few seconds by asking them to reverse roles and continue the argument. It was hoped that the lack of respect each had for the other would be recognized and felt.

| HUSBAND
(as wife) | You're very tight with money. I have to ask for a dollar at a time. You never consult me even about my own money. Remember the wedding present of a thousand dollars I got from my folks? You put it in the market. I wanted to buy a rug with it. And the stock went down from fifty to seventeen. |
| WIFE
(as husband) | You weren't sore about it until the market went down. Now we both know it wasn't such a good idea. But you throw money away on junk—cosmetics, records, and a whole lot of unnecessary things. When you know the meaning of a dollar, you'll get more. And besides that, you're a cold potato. Who's getting the goodies? I'm not. You either say you're too tired or lay there like a dead ass. |

HUSBAND *(as wife)*	I find you unattractive. You don't turn me on. You've gotten too fat and jealous.
WIFE *(as herself)*	It's true. I don't feel the urge for sex anymore.
DIRECTOR	(*To the husband.*) How do you feel when she calls you unattractive, fat, and jealous?
HUSBAND	Like nothing. Shit, maybe. Put down. Do you really want a divorce?
WIFE	I'm not sure. I still haven't decided. I have to think about it.
DIRECTOR	The fight circle has ended, I think. Who won?
HUSBAND	She did.
WIFE	He did.
DIRECTOR	It's a deadlock. Since you are both losers, there will have to be a return fight. But it's a discouraging round of charges and countercharges. Not a single issue was settled. Is the fighting a way to get out of not doing anything to improve the relationship? Now, in the role of the other, say what you want.

Role reversal was continued until each was able to be explicit and reasonable. This changed the form of the conflict since the two were in a direct bargaining situation.

The issues revolved around giving: one was willing to give sex but not money; the other was willing to give money but not sex. The sexual roles were in conflict, and the working (budget and management) roles were at odds.

Goals and Progress of the Therapy

These scenes show that both partners were lacking the ability to yield to the other. Therapy would focus on a variety of attitudes, strengthening their ability to give in without feeling defeated by it. The jealousy of the husband was overheated, and it could be expected that the wife, who suffered less, might be able to change this condition when she learned what to do. The director hoped that, through psychodrama, the wife's sympathetic feelings could be released so that she could move toward her husband with warmth and understanding.

Change does not take place, as a rule, from repeating situations that preserve the social behavior that didn't work in the first place. However, this situation differed from the usual reality or true-to-life situation. The impact of reexperiencing the marital drama provides an opening for therapeutic intervention: diagnosis and therapy occur simultaneously. Correction takes place by verifying what was experienced in as many details as can be produced.

The technique of organizing the husband's imaginings was to make the fantasy seem like reality, almost as if it really happened. He could then begin to understand the excitement, the ideas that kept coming, as momentary responses to anxiety. These ideas are not undirected or fantastic but represent the goal of the behavior. There didn't seem to be an effort to solve the problems in the relationship, but rather to bring about an unpleasant or unhappy state of mind, which may have been the disguised motive.

The psychodrama director asked the husband to describe what he thought the wife did when he left. The wife and director prepared to take the roles necessary to portray his description. The husband talked and the auxiliaries followed his directions, as in the technique of the dream. In the fantasy, a man circled the apartment house, waiting until the husband left for work. He did not recognize the man or the car. His wife joined her lover and they rode off together, laughing and happy with each other. He did not visualize them in bed together or in the sexual act, just as having fun, swimming, walking hand-in-hand, or touching and holding one another.

Training in Sex. The director pointed out in the discussion that followed that the husband's attitude toward the sexual act was interrupted even in his suspicious musings about his wife. Was he, as well as she, avoiding sexual performance? A scene was arranged between husband and wife to portray a typical warm-up to the sexual act. The warm-up to sexual activity is accompanied by auxiliary images: a slow or fast warm-up progresses in line with the images accompanying the activity.[12]

The couple was asked to relive a situation in which they made love. They were to act as they usually did, only this time, add the thoughts, the images that come to mind and say them in an aside. The time is before retiring, as the two are watching a TV wrestling match. He goes to the icebox and brings a can of beer for her and one for himself.

It could be seen how the sexual situation was avoided. The ideas referred to distortions in self-image, or painful recollections of the past as a form of punishment, or any number of hostile attitudes that interrupted the sexual warm-up. A sexual adjustment could result when the partners learned to avoid using the sexual situation for negatively expressed interpersonal issues and developed images appropriate to the sexual act instead.[12,13]

Training in Empathy. The husband was asked to enact any situation with his mother, father, or important people in his original family.[14] The early recollections were used to show the patient his current attitude toward other people and toward himself. The wife, since she knew the family members, played these roles as he recalled the incident. He selected an early one, when he was seven or eight. On his return from school, his mother met him outside the door and said, "Don't go in. Dad's on the war path, drunk. You know what he's like when he drinks. Let's go hide under the stairwell until he's asleep." They did this, huddling together in terror as the sounds of dishes and furniture breaking and profanity resounded through the walls. The husband's association to this was a feeling of terror of the father and one of anger at the mother's ineffective management of the father. "Wait until I get big. There's nothing to be done about this injustice now, but later I'll be able to handle it."

Training through Role Identification. Next, the husband played his father. Then the husband became the mother, and his wife played the role of the son. The wife was able to enact a warm, protective mother to a scared and frightened son, but she refused to be the screaming father (she couldn't act like that). The mood between the couple shifted from smoldering anger to a more warm consideration of each other.

Then the wife was asked to show one of her earliest recollections. She placed herself in a stroller at the age of four, being pushed along the street by one of her older sisters (the director played this role), laughing and waving at the passing people. A strange man stopped and tried to engage her attention. He patted her on the head, and she began to cry. Her sister tried to console her, but she couldn't stop crying until she got home. And she couldn't understand why she was so frightened.

The couple, getting acquainted with each other as children, talked about the kind of little people they recognized in the scenes they enacted. The director summarized with, "Both of you showed fear as a response to external events that took a turn you didn't like. You [to the husband] didn't expect to be able to change the discomfort, and you [to the wife] expected someone else to take you to safety. What events can you think of in which you showed that you were able to untangle yourself from an uncomfortable situation? This can be any time, either in the immediate present or the past."

Inferences

The patterns of interpersonal relationship brought out during this session were the social roles involving the husband and wife, mother and father. The crucial problem of the husband's jealousy was experienced in the enactment of the distrust. During this last session it seemed to be related to his feeling of being neglected. The early recollections of the husband helped him become less defensive and allowed his fear of being neglected and humiliated to be seen. The wife in the mother role responded to the frightened child.

It has frequently been observed that changing the mother role of a wife, if it is weakly conceived, distorted, or inadequately developed, is crucial to changing the nature of the relationship. When the mother role is sufficiently strong, the escalating of an accusation into a battle royal is circumvented, because the mother role becomes ascendant over the competitive aspects of a sibling role. This is important in restoring a feeling of adequacy to a jealous person.

The husband's suspicions came from within; they grew out of his belief that he didn't measure up to other people. The director became a voice at the husband's ear that expressed the idea that what comes from within, if it is verified by outside circumstances, may seem to be imposed from without. The situation of being passed over at work made the imaginings within seem real, which might not have happened if rewards at work had been forthcoming.

Jealousy arises out of the conviction that one is not able to keep what one has, be it sexual love, esteem, or a dominant position in relation to another. The husband's jealousy and the wife's anger were intertwined aspects of the relationship. The connection between coming home to an empty house and having had an unsatisfying day at work was not stated, but it was apparent. The jealousy angered the wife and her anger was resonated in the husband. We can understand the tension as it developed between them when we know that the husband and wife acted as a team: the husband accused and the wife became angry. When the spouses identified these roles, it was easier for them to hold discussions concerning marital problems. After the situation that demonstrated jealousy had been played, various other aspects of the experience were introduced in succession.

Role reversing was one of the techniques used to help the couple humanize their relationship. The wife's recollections offered the husband the clue that his wife runs back to mamma, not to men, for comfort. The two became better acquainted with each other. Each situation placed them in a new relationship that reflected another possibility for interacting, a new design for living. The husband's recollection of his childhood, it was hoped, would arouse in the wife a sympathetic view of her husband's jealous ravings. At the same instant, the husband may see how he incorporated his father's terrifying behavior into his own acts and modify them so that his wife need not feel toward him as he felt toward his father.

Case Three: The Aloof Husband

In addition to the generally used techniques of role reversal, mirror, and soliloquy, there are others designed to be used in various combinations to help a patient experience feelings of tenderness and concern that for one reason or another have not developed. People with this type of narrowed or limited social concern display callous and destructive behavioral responses. They frequently maintain a detachment that insulates them against involving relationships. Even when such a person acknowledges that his spouse is a concerned friend, the meaning of this is lost in the greater urgency of a personal striving for independence. What the person wants from others is service and compliance, not warmth and love; the spouse does not understand this and fights the conditions that are the basis of the disturbed relationship. Striving for independence becomes "raw egoism" as the individual's fear of dependency becomes more and more pronounced. It is considered therapeutic to overcome the exaggerated need for independence by breaking through this defense mechanism and having the person experience weakness, a need for protection and love. The following example is an interesting exposition of the dynamics of failure; this couple ultimately was unable to keep their marriage intact.

When the couple came for treatment, the problem presented was the husband's aloofness, expressed as sexual indifference. The marriage was three years old, but the relationship went back many years. The wife became frightened when she realized she was pregnant. She quit work and secluded herself. The husband began to use marijuana compulsively as he found himself pressured by his wife's increasing demands for closeness. The more she wanted from him, the less he would give. Each request became a demand that he countered by passively withdrawing from her. Both came from homes of little and careless parenting. The couple first had marital counseling with a therapist, who then referred the husband to a psychiatrist for individual therapy. He had been in treatment for some months when it was considered advisable to place the couple in psychodrama.

It is helpful to the director and the couple to map the emotional expansiveness of the individuals who make up a marriage. A diagram identifying all the significant individuals in a person's life situation, with their attitudes of acceptance or rejection, increases the therapist's chances of selecting the life situations in need of change and the types of changes needed. (In a large group, this is acted out as an action sociogram.)

Profile of the Couple

The husband, David, was an only child raised by a mother who had worked since he was an infant. She worked out of boredom, since she had married a businessman who was seldom at home. The little boy began day nursery at an early age and spent summers at camp. His parents' marriage ended in divorce. The boy's relationship to his father was periodic; they spent occasional days together. He looked forward to these events, but was also glad to return home.

David's mother was a scrupulous housekeeper who worked hard and who tried, in their short periods together, to be loving to her son. But he rejected her touch. She had a few close friends and dated men after the divorce. There were no other male relationships, no extended family system.

The boy played rough and tumble games with his friends. He was only moderately successful in school and with friends. As an adolescent he took jobs after school and exhibited interest and skill in whatever job he undertook. He dated a few girls, then formed a close relationship with the girl he finally married.

The wife, Jane, was the firstborn child of a woman who compensated for her loneliness by dating men other than her husband. When the husband discovered her infidelity, he divorced her. She remarried an ambitious man who worked hard and spent most of his time away from home. Her loneliness continued, and she turned to alcohol. The little girl tried unsuccessfully to win the love of her mother. She was more effective in capturing her stepfather's love, although she was soon to feel the pressure of an enlarging family as her mother had more children. Her ability to please her stepfather formed her modus operandi—pleasing men. Her sense of well-being first came from feeling that she was pleasing men; then she extended this attitude to her siblings, girl friends, and finally her baby.

Jane's and David's attitudes were diagramed. The results were:

David	Jane
Wife—vacillating, negative	Husband—positive
Mother—negative	Mother—negative
Infant—indifferent	Mother-in-law—negative
Father-in-law—indifferent, negative	Father—positive
Partner—negative	Infant—positive
Male companion—positive	Sibling—negative
Employees—positive	Girl friends—positive
Housework—negative	Employers (men)—positive
Business management—positive, industrious	Work outside the home—positive
Money—positive, careful	Housework—negative
Sex—indifferent, passive	Money—positive, careless
Interests—good restaurants, photography, swimming	Sex—positive, active
	Interests—reading, movies, TV, photography
(He seems to cooperate with only those people whose position is subordinate to his authority, except in occasional encounters with his drinking buddies and girl friends who support his position against the expectations of his wife, partner, and mother.)	(The choices show a wide range of positive feelings, especially toward authority figures and people she must trust, and a rejection of unimportant and uninfluential people—the alcoholic mother, the mother-in-law, and siblings. She also rejects housework.)

The diagram of David, the husband, showed a limited number of positive feelings outside the home situation and negative and indifferent attitudes directed toward the members of his intimate circle—his wife, mother, infant, and business associates. His emotional interest was transferred to the casual group. Motivations of his negative feelings can be studied in psychodrama and by interview.

The wife's chart, by contrast, showed her positive feeling toward her husband in spite of his negative feeling toward her, of which she was aware. The large number of positive choices she made again showed, but didn't explain, the motivation for her preferences. To say that the husband was angry at his wife is an external description of an attitude. It does not explain what motivated his behavior. Knowing that the wife was jealous reveals to us the reciprocal influence; he was meeting her angry feelings. It is hard to understand the husband's negativity and the wife's warmth without considering these to be dynamic movement aspects of interaction. Following is a description of the breakdown of a complementary marriage relationship in which a new life situation had disturbed the harmony. The new roles of parenthood would have to be worked through or the marriage would dissolve.

The Psychodrama Session

All the roles and relationships surrounding the roles were developed by Jane and David, who played the auxiliary roles. We began in the present with the vacillating flow of affection from the husband to the wife. While David lacked verbal expressiveness (he was very guarded about giving an account of the smallest details of his daily life), the techniques of psychodrama warmed him to greater freedom.

Jane complained that David was critical of everything she did. His quick response to this was a countercharge; she criticized him. The director hoped that two doubles would involve David enough so that he could be less defensive and more spontaneous. One double was played by his wife; the other was the director. One stood on either side of him; Jane voiced all the negative thoughts that crossed his mind as he walked into the dirty apartment; the director spoke all the positive thoughts.

POSITIVE DOUBLE   It's great to be home. I'm glad to be here.

NEGATIVE DOUBLE   Now what? I don't have anything to do—I wish I were back at work or

someplace else. If there was
someplace else to be, I'd
be there.

Positive Double   There's the wife. She's glad
to see me.

Negative Double   God, she's a slob, didn't take
the dogs out. The house is
full of dog shit.

Positive Double   The baby is so cute. I think
I'll play with her.

David rejected the positive double as not expressing the way he felt. He objected to defining the negative double as being critical. There were no visible signs of warming up.

The next scene utilized an actual situation; David walked into the apartment and described its condition as he recalled it. Recall is important both for what is remembered and for what is forgotten. It helps show the accumulation of data that support the personal bias. Jane and David could not agree on the appearance of the apartment. She expected him to overlook some of her carelessness in housekeeping because of the baby, and he was obsessively concerned every time he saw any dirt. Her vulnerability to his rebuff caused her to explode in outrage. In contrast to her husband, she appeared to be letting herself express her feelings completely. "That baby is four months old and you've never even changed a diaper, given her a bottle, or taken the dogs out for a walk. You haven't washed a dish, dusted, or taken the garbage out—nothing, nothing, nothing. It's like living alone. I ask if you want to go to a movie. You never say, 'Yes, I'd like to.' You only say, 'If that's what you want.' I want *you* to want to. It's the same with sex— I do all the trying." Her attempts to please were not being rewarded, and she began to cry convulsively.

An extreme coldness was evident in David as he drifted emotionally away from her. The director was baffled by his indifference to his wife's outburst and pressured him to show how he was feeling inside. David responded, "How should I feel? I'm bored. She's always crying." The director made an observation that David accepted as positive and that could have been taken as censuring: "You looked happy when she was upset and sad." David said, "That's true. I want to stay in charge of this marriage." Then he was able to lean toward his wife and pat her forearm awkwardly. He rigidly defended against any closeness or concern.

Before attempting any educational changes (training), the director must get a clear picture of the reciprocal behavior patterns of the couple by developing a series of challenging situations that the couple acts out. Such situations give an impression of what the oppositional feelings protect: weakness, ambition, power, and so on. In this instance, the husband appeared to be defending his fear of being obedient; he reacted by appearing bored. He was asked to change roles and be Jane at the moment of the tirade. While he played her role, she became an army sergeant issuing orders. David's refusal to cooperate included caring for the baby. His behavior seemed to indicate that he considered activities such as caring for the baby to be tasks in which he was submitting to the authority of a superior, his wife; and Jane's pleas were viewed as continuous commands. He was unwilling or unable to translate her negative nagging for attention into a positive appeal for love.[15]

The director was puzzled by Jane's complaint about her husband's lack of contact with the baby. He was asked to imagine the baby in the crib, his wife, the furniture, the mess—all without talking. As he was warming up to this, the director placed a book on the floor, explaining, "I'm a pile of dog shit." Two chairs were pulled together to become a crib; a pillow became the baby; and the wife stretched out with a book. "There should be more crap on the floor," said David. Quickly more books were placed on the floor. The wife objected, but not much, and volunteered to be the dogs. She ran to meet him, barking. He quieted the dogs and looked around the room, walking carefully to avoid the mess. One pile (the director) spoke: "Pick me up." The husband was startled as one after the other, the piles made the same request: "Pick me up. Clean me up." The baby also cooed, "Pick me up. Hug me. Change my diaper—it's dirty." The wife chimed in with, "Help me. Love me."

The husband continued his walk through the living room into the bedroom and threw himself on the bed, reflecting, "I do my job from A.M. to P.M.—why can't she get off her butt and do hers?" This re-enactment of the problem helped David define his situation and partially removed some of his inhibitions.

He continued in soliloquy, "It's an obstacle course without any reward. She'll climb into bed and wonder why I'm asleep. I won't lift a finger to help her." He quickly corrected that hostile withdrawal; he said simply "I am really tired."

The director closed the scene with, "This is a new situation in your lives, which, if your marriage is to prosper, must be met with new responses. Let's go back to before the baby came. Is there any period you recall as being especially pleasant? The husband and wife got into a huddle and presented a life situation in which they shared an apartment with other friends—both were working, and entertaining was easy. Cooking and cleaning were easily managed without rancor by the wife. "I waited on him hand and foot. I guess I spoiled him," Jane said.

"And what did you argue over?" asked the director.

David laughed. "She was really wild with money. I had to keep a check on her." He was obviously attracted to her pre-motherhood attitudes.

The session ended with a contract between husband and wife to change the existing conditions of the homecoming. It is always a calculated risk to ask a couple to practice cooperative behavior, since this may escalate into open rebellion: The cleaner the apartment becomes, the more appreciation the wife will want from her husband; the more he helps her, the more he will feel continuous pressure. The mutually destructive interaction became the subject of discussion.

This session resulted in a lessening of the conflict. The fighting over the messy house stopped as each began to consider other issues. The relationship to the baby improved; David still refused to feed or diaper the infant, but he was able to pick her up and play with her. He continued to withhold affection from his wife.

For a time, the couple felt that David's attraction to the baby would keep the marriage intact. But eventually, the marriage ended in divorce. David satisfied his emotional goal of no entangling alliances as the intimate family group exerted emotional pressures that he was unwilling to meet. His sensitivity to the kind of person he married was accurately estimated—Jane was an affectionate, manipulative person who was concerned with David's welfare, but her perception of him was inaccurate—she was attracted to his detachment, which she felt as strength. This caused profound interpersonal conflict.

Case Four: A Couple in a Group

Married couples' groups are as varied as the needs of the individuals. For instance, it is now considered helpful to work with parents of delinquent adolescents, parents of schizophrenic children, spouses of alcoholics, and so forth. The list is as long as the ills of the community.

A marital couples' group may grow out of a therapist's private practice, on the theory that the stimulation of other couples provides a healthy setting for change. Or, a group may form spontaneously as a result of experiencing a crisis together, as described in the chapter "Psychodrama with an Adolescent." A group of married couples, who had been social friends for many years, became a therapeutic agent for the son of one of the couples, felt the value of the experience, and met thereafter once a week for over two years. The size of the group changed; at times it became too large and the original five couples lost a sense of intimacy. A sociometric questionnaire was used to break the group into compatible couples, and the marital groups continued working on the relationship problems of husbands and wives to each other, to their children, to work situations, and to the members of the group.

Married couples also may be placed with a group of patients who are working on general problems of maladjusted behavior. One couple that joined a psychodrama group had been married for ten years and had three children. This was not their first group therapy experience. They had used the time before the meeting to enjoy dinner and a short museum tour. As they entered the room, there were visible signs of feuding.

The First Session

The group warm-up began with the request that everyone close their eyes, relax, and drift—let the mind wander wherever it wished to go. After a time the invitation for sharing brought out the husband's concern over conflicts with his wife. "The interminable fighting, there's no end to it. It just keeps going on and on." He sounded tired and drawn.

The wife, Sue, reflected, "I wish I were home with the children." A patient picked up on the rebuke and withdrawal pattern and wanted to hear more of what was going on between them. The couple began with the situation that preceded coming to the group.

As they left the parking lot, Fred, the husband, asked Sue where she'd like to eat: "At an ethnic restaurant or grab a hamburger?" If it was to be ethnic, he preferred Italian. "Greek," she said. Fred followed up with a suggestion that they go shopping. It would have to be done before the stores closed. She suggested the museum. They finally walked over to the museum and wandered about holding hands. The husband dropped her hand and went to look at a picture alone. Said the wife: "I didn't come here to look at the pictures. I could come by myself. I want to share the looking with you, but, no, you start off in a thousand different directions without me. That's the way it is with everything. You go off without me. That's why I wish I were at home with the children. They like to have me around. They want me to be with them."

Sue seemed to be getting satisfaction from expressing her conviction that her husband was shortchanging her while denying her participation in the proof. The husband warmed up to his feelings of being injured and began, "This was to be a special evening out, and as usual it turned into an argument. I did something wrong. You keep a book on what I do wrong. You are too much. I went to the museum; we ate Greek food; and still I have to hold hands with you all the way or you feel neglected. I can't, can't, can't do it." The volume increased. They stood facing each other and screamed. The anxiety and anger broke so fiercely that they ignored both the director's interference and the group's. It was open warfare. The director had to separate them physically. Then the director asked for a role reversal to demonstrate that neither had heard the other. In the role reversal, the two stood silent at first but soon fell back into the accusations and blaming. The director requested another reversal.

DIRECTOR	Do you argue like this often?
SUE	No. I don't usually see him long enough to have a knock-down, drag-out fight.
FRED	She usually waits for an audience—like a therapy group.
SUE	And this is just the kind of interpretation that infuriates me. You know everything, and I don't. At least that's the way you come across to me.

They went at it again; this time it was, if possible, even more furious. This couple's difficulty in attempting to break the deadlock in the marital conflict was that their method of resolving it began another fight. In a case like this, it is often easier to help the spouses find a more satisfying relationship by working with an auxiliary ego for one of the spouses until the established patterns are interrupted and understood.

Anger expressed in the group (or between intimate enemies) is constructive when catharsis results in learning, in an experience of integration, a clarification of what the antagonist wants from others or what the angry couple want from each other. The verbal attack can magnify the goal of the behavior—to hurt someone, to be hurt, or without intention to hurt, to demand appreciation and wonder why it is withheld. The verbal attack can also show the distancing effect of repetitive expressions of anger based on distortions and misunderstandings.

The expression of anger can be therapeutic when it helps the patient become aware of his movement. When a dependent patient challenges the strong one in a relationship, this can give a feeling of courage and help round out the picture of the opponent as a human being subject to the same laws of living as other people. This is an example of how the hostile attack of one spouse on the other escalates into overheated confusion and how it may be resolved.

The intensity of the warm-up to anger as Sue and Fred faced each other suggested examining the way in which anger was produced with other significant people in the couple's social atom—mother, father, siblings, children. Each relationship was presented as a separate situation, and the feeling produced toward the opposite partner—sympathy, fear, dominance, anger—was observed and commented upon. In the first scene, Sue chose a member of the group to play her sick father, and she chose her husband to demonstrate her complex relationship to her older sister and mother. The scenes developed quickly and briefly and showed how Sue felt rejection and withdrew. As Fred and Sue faced each other when they played the scenes, they directed no vindictive anger toward each other. They warmed up responsibly to the situation and plotted it accurately. They were able to show that Sue reacted with fear to the dominance of her mother and sister and found security in her room, alone, away from the family. Fred could see how others abused Sue, but disclaimed doing so himself.

Fred selected a member from the group to play his anger with the significant people in his social atom. After a few attempts, he gave up. The family was too big and the relationships were complex and, besides, he was exhausted. "Another time, maybe," he said. The director, with the group's agreement, accepted his refusal.

The responsibility of the director and the group is to show the couple what they are doing, but what they want to do with this knowledge is up to them. Although emotional release and self-reflection are therapeutic, the patient often responds better when his interaction, not his subconscious psyche, is analyzed. Fred and Sue's overheated relationship suggested the use of a mirror technique, a time to sit back and observe what each partner is doing to the other. The role challenge was diminished, and it became easier for them to decide if they want to generate excitement with a fight or not.

Ending the Session

The mirror technique was used to end the session. The couple was asked to sit with their backs to the group, as if they were out of the room, and listen as the group talked about them. The first question to be answered in a go-around was, "Who seems to be more empathic to the needs of the other?" The second question was, "Did either know what the other wanted?" The third question was, "What was the most revealing piece of interaction in the role playing scenes?" The couple faced the group and responded, not to each other, but to the group.

FRED	I hear that you are impressed with my playing what you call auxiliary roles to my wife. We didn't fight then.
SUE	I hear that I distrust what you do for me.
FRED	And I do it.
SUE	We get from each other what we expect. I object to that.
DIRECTOR	We are no longer discussing, just reflecting on what we heard.
FRED	I'm a good guy, but not good enough—I give just enough to keep that image, but not enough to complete it.
SUE	I know what I want from my husband and he knows too, but he won't give it. I want his undivided attention. I object to that, too.

FRED (*Laughs.*) Somebody said I upstage her and she walks on my best line. There it is in a nutshell! Siblings fighting each other.

The thoughtful reaction of the couple showed some lessening of the tension between them as the effects of the quarreling were being corrected, as the competitive roles were being realized. "We can train to become sensitive, not to our emotions, but to the situation and the motivation of others."[16]

Empathy Training in Role Reversal

Sue and Fred presented a natural life experience; there was no make-believe in the encounter between husband and wife. Some critics have reservations about the two-way role playing situation. They think it artificial and prefer a direct life experience, as Pitirim Sorokin[17] calls it: to place the poor man in the rich man's shoes, to ask the stockbroker to be a newspaper vendor, to trade for a time the anxieties and worries of one person for those of another, in this way to live through the trials of the other and to learn through the direct experiencing of the other. This, however, becomes a game; it can be stopped at will and is no more real than role playing.

For a few moments, the couple's anger was at fever pitch and all attempts at action strategies were ignored. They finally responded to a role reversal, which provided each of them with another perspective of the projected image, like a mirror being held before them. As the reversal was completed, Sue became silent; when Fred became the wife, he was silent. The silence communicated the difficulty: neither one had been listening to what the other had been saying. When they returned to the original position of husband to wife, the quarreling began again. Another reversal of roles was tried; this time each showed a little movement toward understanding the other person's position and reaction in the situation.

The role reversal technique has the effect of augmenting the spontaneity of the couple by shifting each of them from rigidly held positions. The reversals continue until they are able to hear each other and there is some indication that they are communicating the other's role without distortion. Repeating the role reversal is a way for patients to break up a repetitive pattern of destructive responses and makes useful exchange possible.

The preceding case of a wife who had set honeymoon standards for a visit to the museum and a husband who saw the visit as a chance to look at the pictures was one in which reversing roles is clearly indicated. It is difficult to take the role of the other without broadening one's sympathetic range of behavior. Knowing more about how it feels to be the other is an effective way to develop empathy, an ability to "reach beyond one's self" into a social feeling for the other.

We are expected to be sensitive to the feelings of the person with whom we are interacting. Too often life becomes an empty series of day-by-day events that dull one partner's sensitivity to the interactional expectations of the other, and this lack of sensitivity results in conflicts. It becomes hard to restore the intimacy that existed between them.

Conclusion: Mirror Technique
and Body Language

An important point in the growth of the child is the moment when he sees his image in the mirror and discovers that the image is of *himself*. As the child makes this discovery, he reaches for the image; he may touch it, kiss it, or hit it. This action, immortalized in the myth of Narcissus, is translated into an action technique in which the looking-glass image reflects the self as seen by another. This method draws on the world of images. In role reversal, the image is one of intimate exchange: I see myself as you see me, and you see yourself as I see you. In the behind-your-back technique, the people who form the audience hold the mirror to the couple. They study the couple's problem and say honestly whether or not what they have seen and heard is believable and point out the moments that were most convincing to them. This frankness is often sufficient to break the intensity of negative emotion.

For certain types of patients it is better to move away from reality problems, such as the argument at breakfast or the dismay of sexual rejection, and move into either the future or the past. In the session involving Sue and Fred, where strong competitive feelings were aroused, we observed interactional patterns from the past.

Listen to the tone of voice of each spouse, for this is an indication of the nature of the relationship. A harsh, firm inflection usually arises from a fixed position of authority; this person's words end abruptly and the message is sharply direct. The voice of submission or obedience is soft and hesitant, with many pauses as opposition is being held in reserve; compulsive obedience is frequently caricatured by a quick, sharp "yes, yes" response. A soft, friendly voice with lifting inflections emanates from a sense of well-being, a feeling of adequately meeting the other.

An indication of the relationship can be observed in body carriage. The way a person walks may show a cautious, fearful attitude. Arms hanging limply clearly evidence a lack of desire to touch or to hold the other. Courageous persons show a free and easy gait; they are open in their desire to touch and to make contact with others. Sometimes the relationship between two people is immediately recognized in the way they stand or sit together. (As one is able to view a drawing by James Thurber and see in a moment that it describes a recognizable male-female relationship, one can mentally put a frame around the couple and get a picture of the interaction.) Every psychological act has a physical element; a conviction of the self is revealed by the action. A basic consideration in all marriages is the degree of intimacy and close-ness each partner in the marriage seeks and how each partner tolerates these expectations. An ability to tolerate the intimacy demanded is shown in a partner's posture, in his facial expression of self-preoccupation or boredom when others are talking, or in his looking only to the thera-pist and ignoring the spouse. Most marital couples want to work on their real-life problems and need little urging. The foregoing techniques are especially helpful in reaching the more aloof and reticent individuals.

13

Psychodrama with Children

This chapter describes the way children enrolled in a child guidance center participated in a series of role-playing sessions, while the parents were being counseled in a separate room.[1] The center offered practical training in understanding and dealing with children. These sessions were open to parents, teachers, and, of course, children, as well as the concerned public. The center's approach was an application of the psychology of Alfred Adler, who demonstrated his theories to his colleagues in Vienna in 1920. He used group techniques, especially discussion groups, to bring to the surface the interpersonal conflicts that arise in school and in the home. To accomplish this, he brought children and their teachers, parents, and siblings together to be interviewed before a group of professional people. These demonstrations were held in schools and, according to Rudolf Dreikurs, were the first breakthrough for group therapy.[2] Before this, therapy was carried on in seclusion. Group procedures were eventually open to observers as Adler moved into the community. Before the Austrian Fascists closed the centers, there were almost thirty of them operating in Vienna.

Two of Alfred Adler's former colleagues and students, Rudolf Dreikurs and Eleanor Redwin, established the Chicago Child Guidance Centers (now called the Family Education Association), which used Adler's method of treating the problem child as well as his classroom procedures for educating the child toward social living. The Chicago centers are not intended to provide psychiatric services; rather, they are

181

educational, instructional facilities that seek to engender harmony in the family and to enrich family living.

The procedure of the center followed that of the Vienna clinics, with a counselor interviewing first the parents, then the children. While the parents attended a counseling session with other parents, the children were worked with and observed in a playroom prior to their interview. One or two presentations were made at weekly meetings before a spectator attendance. The problems that brought a child to the center were normal behavioral ones, as evidenced in school difficulties such as failure to learn to read or in other symptoms of evasion of a life task such as overt aggression expressed toward siblings or others; laziness; temper tantrums; bed-wetting; tics; lying; stealing; and negative attitudes toward family participation—all the problems that parents need help with in their daily living with children.

There was no psychodrama in the Viennese playroom. Psychodrama was innovated by Dreikurs. The children's playroom, in addition to keeping the children busy while the parents were in session, provided a time for the children to interact without too many limits being placed upon them in order that pertinent observations could be made and later presented to the counselor and parents for interpretation. In addition, playroom activities were a form of treatment for the children.

The following discussion indicates how psychodrama, which in this situation may more properly be called role playing, is modified to deal with the problems of the emerging roles of childhood. Children show established patterns of behavior at an early age, and the theme of the behavior, as evidenced in their roles, is more readily available to diagnosis and to education than is the case with adults. More often than not, the psychodramatic session moves the child toward new patterns of relationships rather than, as with adults, repairing the old entrenched ones.

Role playing at the centers was designed to give the child a new understanding or insight into his behavior and to help him learn other, more acceptable, roles for meeting social situations. It focused on training in the essential skills of childhood—crossing the street, taking a bus, preparing for a new experience, working constructively with other children, improving sibling relationships, and, most important, having fun with other children.[3]

Facilities

It is not always possible to obtain the right kind of physical facilities for a playroom and a separate room for role playing. Counseling sessions can be held in churches, settlement houses, school buildings, and libraries. Since the buildings were not originally designed for counseling sessions, the difficulties are varied and, in some cases, seemingly impossible to deal with. A large room, such as a gymnasium, gives the children a feeling of space and encourages outdoor activity like throwing things and running wildly about. It is difficult to pull the children into a unified group for role playing under such environmental handicaps. In a smaller space, the playroom can be divided into areas for music, art, and toys, and one part can be converted into an area for acting. Chalk marks define the dimensions of the stage area and show the position of the audience in two semicircles. However, a separate room should be made available for special meetings with the children, a sibling group, and one or more of the other staff members. At times, an individual child may be worked with in a separate room, since most of the children will not act as an audience when one child is the protagonist.

Structuring a Children's Group

The role of the audience is omitted for the children who come to the playroom. After a series of experiments, it was found that unlike a schoolroom group, which is constrained by a formal or informal authority, the group at the playroom didn't serve as an effective audience because anarchy and explosive behavior resulted. It takes from eight to ten sessions of active participation in psychodrama before the children are willing to serve as an audience to the other players. If six children are referred to psychodrama, all participate in some part of the action. So the group must be structured in such a way that the children are free to enact and develop the roles they are eager to try out and to increase their spontaneity in accepting other roles.

Wide age range and differences of race and economic background present interesting challenges to the psychodramatist. The variety of symptoms shown by the children, sibling and peer relationships, the fact that contact among the children is limited to the weekly session, and the facilities available for working out the drama must all be taken into account. Yet the group must be structured in such a way that the children are able to role play solutions to show how a problem could be handled.

Sibling Groups

Groups may be structured on the basis of sibling relationships. In psychodrama strong sibling rivalry prevents the acting out of new social roles, so siblings are permitted to reproduce the roles they have accepted in life. The first action scenes retain the sibling relationship for purposes of diagnosis—to determine the role the child has assumed. Later sessions will permit the child to experience a group which is more encouraging to him.

Symptom Groups

Similarity of symptoms is not a sound basis upon which to form a group for psychodrama. A group made up exclusively of children with speech difficulties, for example, slows the action of the group. Having too many children who have been referred because of destructive aggressiveness in one group results in fights and does not permit group cohesion. Forming a group of only overly dependent or timid children results in their being unable to warm up to action, and the director is compelled to assume the role of actor and to be extremely directive in the acting warm-up.

Same-Sex Groups

No hard and fast rule can be observed in terms of grouping by sex. However, boys from seven to ten years of age are usually not interested in playing house, while girls of this age are. Boys at this time choose dynamic roles: outlaw, policeman, engineer, pilot, Indian, or cowboy. As the action progresses, girls of similar age find it too rough. Even girls with a strong desire to be boys, after the first enjoyable experience of tussling with the boys, usually will refuse to be in psychodrama with boys of this age range. Boys who are afraid to compete with other boys in this situation will play domestic scenes with girls younger than themselves until they are ready to assume their place in a group of peers. Boys and girls from twelve to fourteen are usually receptive to working in psychodrama together.

Sociometrically Determined Groups

The action sociometric test serves as one means for assignment into role-playing groups. The child in therapy is given an opportunity to select the children he prefers to have as auxiliary egos. At the start of each session the child is asked, "With whom do you wish to go into the psychodrama room and act?" If he is not ready to choose, the director helps form the group for him. Boys from the age of five to eleven often choose a fighting partner, someone with whom they can compete in physical skill.

The choice test is an aid in determining changes in the child's status as well as in locating the chosen and rejected children in his range of relationships in the playroom and in his family. The kind of children and the number selected are reported to the counselor who is working with the child. At first the choices seem to be exclusively family ones. Siblings choose each other, and this may be less conducive to growth than an outside-the-family choice. It reflects a tendency to prefer the familiar situation to the unknown. Thus, a good criterion for change is the increasing ability to establish a constructive relationship with someone outside the family, and finally with at least one member of the family.

Children in the Playroom

The attendance of the children at the center was not stable. The irregularity may have been due to illness, moving, changes in the family plans, or resistance to coming. The size of the group varied from five to thirty with the age range equally wide, from two-and-a-half to twelve. Fourteen-year-olds were usually placed in adolescent groups, although there were times when a fourteen-year-old was asked to attend with his siblings. It is of positive value to have a wide age range when siblings are involved, for this provides the director an opportunity to observe the interaction of the siblings and to work with them over an extended period of time.

Children who came to the center exhibited behavior that, in a general way, could be divided into two types—aggressive and docile—the degree of activity or passivity as distinguishing traits. (All the children, however, had some positive traits upon which social behavior could be built and structured.) The difficulty each had, whether at home, in the classroom, or at the center, and the dismay of the adults who interacted with them, is familiar to all of us. Role playing helped teach them to handle one another. Both the aggressive child and the docile one wanted to belong to the group and have friends. Both wanted to be accepted, but both had mistaken ideas of how to achieve acceptance. Episodes designed to help the child rearrange his pattern of behavior were fun, but had enough structure to insure learning.

There may be many different types of behavior shown by the children in the playroom:

1. The boss of the barnyard, who must be in complete control of everyone and everything in order to function.
2. The very withdrawn or discouraged child, who has given up attempts to solve his problems.
3. The disorganized child, who has poor concentration and attention span.
4. The lone wolf (or isolate), who sits far from the group and trusts no one.
5. The charmer, who manipulates others to serve his special needs.
6. The detective, who spends his time reporting on the misbehavior of the other children.
7. The whiner, who complains, nags, and keeps reminding the group of his boredom.
8. The baby, who makes demands upon others since he is too weak or inadequate to do anything on his own.
9. The bully or physically aggressive child, who is revengeful and by his action hurts other children.
10. The hyperactive child (or moving target), who flits from one thing to another, never pausing long enough to associate with another person or to an object.[4]

Following is a description of the way role playing was used at the centers. The psychodramatist invites some children, including those to be interviewed by the counselor during the week, to come into the psychodrama room. The director has a plan to help the bossy child learn to make suggestions and win the cooperation of the other children. He may say, "Let's play going to the zoo," and assigns roles to the children. Since acting is a form of playing for children, it is rarely difficult to get something started. The choice of roles, the way in which roles are conceived, the measure of spontaneity, and the responses each child makes to the counterspontaneity of the other children in the group are all observed and noted.

Reports to the Counselor

Out of the production, the director makes deductions and reports them later to the counselor. The counselor and the psychodramatist work together. The psychodramatist reveals through role playing the normal interaction of the child while the counselor uncovers the lifestyle and purpose the action serves. By using role playing, the psychodramatist can measure the amount of learning that has taken place. Here is an example of a psychodrama group and the resulting action by the counselor:

Three siblings had been enrolled at the center for three months. Alice was nine years old, Bert was six, and Chris was three. The children at first were unable to develop roles that would lead to a drama, or structured situation. Alice wanted to be the boss of the production (she was aloof in family participation) and was eager to tell the others what to do. Bert wanted to be the leading man but was unable to sustain the role and resorted to hitting his three-year-old brother in the stomach or turning his attention to the molding on the wall and ripping it off. Chris wanted Bert's role and cried when he wasn't given it. As he cried, both Alice and Bert rushed to comfort him. The session ended in disorder as soon as Bert couldn't have the action move the way he wanted it.

By the eighth session, in which the group was structured around Bert without his sister Alice, Bert's behavior change was shown by his being able to play the supporting role of Tonto to another person's Lone Ranger and to stay with the role playing long enough for the episode's completion. Alice progressed from the role of boss to playing animal roles. She refused to be the princess in any situation because she didn't consider herself pretty enough. She preferred to be a horse. She balked at a mother role and frequently wouldn't participate. Chris no longer played the baby but took the part of a messenger. Bert showed the greatest amount of role development. The counselor integrated these psychodramatic data in the interpretation of the case and suggested future role-playing situations to help make each child's goal apparent to him. Through systematic psychodramatic action, new responses may be learned. In any case, the episodes were designed to help the child adjust his disturbing behavior and find positive ways of solving problems and of behaving.

Creating Roles

A child's role learning is reflected in his play activity. Through play with his peers, the child learns by putting himself imaginatively and realistically in the various roles he pretends to assume and begins to see things from a different viewpoint. These play activities not only reflect role development but directly contribute to it by helping the child learn to shift from one role to another. This is apparent in any role-playing situation as a child shifts easily back and forth from getting instructions on what the next step of a psychodramatic incident should be to moving directly back into the psychodrama as if it were a living experience. There is little or no loss of spontaneity as the child becomes completely absorbed with the "play."

Childhood is the period of greatest spontaneity; the ease of the warm-up led Moreno to conclude that all childhood is a warm-up period during which each person and object is seen as an auxiliary ego and acts as a mental and physical starter.[5] This explains the many novel and often inappropriate responses of children and indicates the need for the director to explain cause and effect in interpersonal behavior. It also influences the direction the psychodramatist takes in working with children.

A child does not initiate the search for help, either in coming to the center or in the psychodrama session. Rarely will a child say, "I need help," although he may know that something is wrong, and he usually quickly makes the connection when there is a clear demonstration of the consequences of certain types of behavior. The director creates a session from the problem area as defined in the child's activity in the playroom and from the reports received from parents and teachers, not from a warm-up session with the group of young children.

For example, siblings fight, and they are encouraged to fight more when the parents feel inclined to play umpire and make decisions to separate the fighters or call timeouts or fouls. This approach is unproductive, for it doesn't stop the fighting; in fact, the weaker child will often provoke the stronger so that the parent will come to his rescue. Such a response thwarts the child's ability to resolve his own fight problem.

While the parents are being counseled not to interfere in children's fighting, the director is working with the children on the fight scene on the psychodrama stage: "How would you like to play two kids who are having a good time together, maybe playing catch? Along comes Jim on a two-wheeler. He offers one of the boys a ride on the bike. They both want to ride. You get the idea? You and Tom can play the two friends who are having fun together. We'll give you time to do that. Let's pretend this chair is a two-wheeler. Charles, do you want to stand over there and wait for your entrance? The rest of us are sitting on the sidewalk watching what is going on." Everyone has a part. There is usually no trouble getting it started; when there is a lapse, the director prompts, corrects, and is active in keeping the action moving toward the discovery that a good time together turns into pain when a fight over the possession of the bike takes place, and someone or something gets hurt.

At the end of the play, the director makes a summary. (If the children are old enough, the director helps them comment briefly.) The director then asks for a different way to play the scene. Usually the children call out, "Take turns."

"That's a good idea," says the director, "but what if one of the boys won't take turns? Then what?" The children might suggest that both ride, one pedaling and the other on the back. Each solution coming from the children is carried out as a role-playing episode.

Since there is less emphasis on learning than on playing, these incidents should offer a solution in which there is fun but from which the competitive aspects of the interaction are removed.

DIRECTOR	Let's begin with the argument over the bike. You ask to go first, and he says no. This time say okay and turn away from the bike and look at us. What can you do with us to have some fun until it's your turn?
CHILD	Play ball. (*An imaginary baseball game ends the scene as the bike rider joins the baseball players.*)

Roles should be freely and spontaneously developed. Effort is directed toward creating a new response and encouraging the development of a new role. This format with many variations may be used with an older group of children. For example, the director and one of the staff workers may take the parts of the two who fought over the bike. They will exaggerate the movements of having a good time together until it suddenly turns into a fight.

When a child needs to play a role of independence (this is the child who usually runs to an adult for help), this problem situation is played as it happened. Afterward, the director leads off a short discussion of the scene and clarifies the meanings of the behaviors by saying, "This actor in the play acted too weak, as if he couldn't handle the situation himself without help. Who can you think of that is strong and independent enough to ask for a turn without running for help?" The child says, "The Cisco Kid." The scene changes as the Cisco Kid selects a Poncho and the two begin having fun together. A third person interrupts, and the weak, dependent child is given an opportunity to improvise freely in the role of the Cisco Kid.

Sessions with children are short, usually lasting about twenty minutes or, at the most, half an hour. Meetings are held weekly, and a real effort is made to include in the role-playing episodes the children who are scheduled to be interviewed by the counselor. This is not always possible. Refusal to participate is included in the report to the counselor as part of the behavioral development of the child. When a child resists coming into the psychodrama or the counseling room, the psychodramatist respects his right to make this decision but reminds him that he could be having fun with the other children if he changed his mind.

Role Acting

While the goal of the director is to help a child form better relationships through acting out the problems of everyday living, young children warm-up negatively to roles within the actual area of their difficulties. Psychodrama with adults and adolescents differs considerably in this respect. Children seem to work more readily in fantasy or symbolic roles. Therefore, the director needs to know the child and the goal of his behavior and plan the session with them in mind. Here are some fantasy and symbolic roles that can be effective.

Dreams

Children, like adults, can profit from acting out their dreams. Dreams provide a bird's eye view of a developing personality, similar to an adult's early recollections. The acting out of dreams can give a child who is reluctant to interact with other children a chance to have a "successful" role, since one child narrates and the other children act out the dream in pantomime.

Pantomime

It is difficult for many children to coordinate words and acts, and pantomime gets the child to "flow" from spontaneous movement into verbalization. All scenes can be done in pantomime. At first, an adult does the narrating. Later on, one of the children may become the narrator.

Puppets

Puppets provide a worthwhile experience for children of all ages. A child will confide in a puppet, telling his hurts, angers, admirations, and other things he might not be able to release in a more direct way.

Assumed Adult Roles

Children can enact scenes on the playground, at home, and in the school by trying such roles as the following:

Policeman. The child under study selects other children who are to act as pedestrians, law-breakers, truck drivers, or children going to school. The child's age and temperament determine the drama. The action that the child plans is a clue to the child's attitude toward formal authority.

Doctor. The child selects a patient and a nurse from the group. The director and cast discuss the doctor's role playing of helpfulness.

Teacher. Role reversing the behavior of a naughty, noisy child in the classroom often helps such a child learn how to hold and experiment with a new role.

Playing house. Children love to play and pretend, but they often do not want to learn what the adult is trying to teach them. Picking up toys and putting clothes away is a sugarcoated training in a playlet. The child plays a parent who comes home to a messy room. This is a clue to the perception of the mother and father as felt by the child. The behavior of the child always reflects some facet of the parent's attitudes and values and in the role playing, the child shows his response to them.

Fairy Tales. Enacting fairy tales explores the self-concept of the child. A "good" girl with high standards may select the role of Snow White, or she may take the part if she feels abused or tormented. Also, in the story "The Three Bears," the choice of the role of the baby bear is of interest to the therapist. The director doesn't insist that the story material be followed, since it is important that the children do what they wish with the role.

TV heroes. Older boys who scorn fairy tales can make up a story around a TV hero and act it out.

Episodes. Episodes that have been reported to the director by the counselor, parents, or playroom worker—such as fighting over a TV program or meeting a situation for the first time—can be reenacted.

Problems. Older children prefer to work out a problem that faces them, while younger children either are unable to know what the problem is or prefer to disguise it.

The Role-Playing Session

At the start of a session, the director seats the children in a semi-circle and sits in a position from which he can see each member easily. In a friendly way, the director explains what is expected of each child and what the group can do. It is best to have a few situations ready to role play. The scene should be simple so that the children aren't intimidated by the method. With older children, a group discussion follows the playing of the scene. With younger children, this is omitted, since spontaneous development of the act is more important than intellectual analysis. It is sometimes difficult to get younger children to talk about a role or a scene. Frequently, discussion is hindered by a lack of social integration, which may develop, in part, if the therapy is effective. The director notes and comments on the good qualities each child shows in the role playing.

The atmosphere should be friendly and encouraging. The director may begin the first session with, "We [a volunteer worker and the director] are going to act a scene for you. Try to guess what we are pretending to be." The volunteer places two chairs together to indicate a bed and curls up on them as if asleep. The director calls out, "Mary, hurry. Breakfast is ready." No answer from Mary. The director calls out again, "Get up. You'll be late." A child guesses: "It's a mother getting her child up."

"You were right," the director replies. "Do you want to try one with me? We'll let others guess." The director takes the child to the side, and they plan a scene. They may decide to show a bus driver who has to answer a lot of questions. The group has more difficulty figuring this one out, but the episodes are beginning to capture the imagination of the children. One child becomes a bus driver who calls out the names of the streets and another is a passenger who didn't get off at the proper stop. The following are plans for short episodes, or scenes, that hold the interest of children.[6]

1. A person trying to find the way to school alone for the first time. A policeman comes along to help her.

2. A teacher meeting the students for the first time.

3. A boy who wants to change the TV station. Have someone else in the group lying on the floor watching the TV, too.

4. A person going boating with a friend. Invent some emergency.

5. Someone going to a friend's house for lunch. Have a mother meet and greet the guest.

Many episodes are possible; the children can supply and suggest ideas after they know what is expected of them. After one person plays a scene, invite another to show his version of the same role. While these scenes seem to the children to be for enjoyment only, many are planned to give them the experience they need to do a future task or training for a current one. A scene that deals with going somewhere on a bus alone is especially helpful for a slow learner, while making a request for something is a good role-playing episode for a shy and awkward child.

Sample Scene: Boating

It is not usual for the counselor to request that the mother join her child in the role playing, but, in the case used next as an example, the mother was asked to participate. The goal of the session was to break through the fixed interaction between a mother and her stout, preadolescent son, Tom. The son smiled his way through thick and thin. He was failing academically, although he was of normal intelligence. In the role playing, he had chosen to play only animals that slithered on the ground, such as a snake or a crocodile. The advantages of this position for satisfying sexual curiosity were obvious, but the rest of the message was obscure. There was a contradiction between his smiling behavior and his self-concept as a crawling thing.

Chairs were arranged to symbolize a rowboat. Tom placed himself at the front of the boat with his mother facing him. He took the position of an oarsman and pretended to row. The mother said, with a patronizing, sweet smile, "My, you do that well, I'm surprised. This is really fun." Tom didn't answer or stop smiling. The mother's monologue continued for a while. Then:

DIRECTOR   A big wind sweeps the boat
       around and mother falls into
       the water.

MOTHER   Help, help! (*Falls to the floor and continues in role.*) Help, I'm drowning.

TOM   (*Still smiling and rowing.*) Let her drown.

When the situation was reviewed, the mother was willing to stop pampering and infantilizing her son. It had been suggested that her son ruled her with his school failure and that it was necessary for her to liberate herself from his determination to maintain this disability. She saw in this brief episode the discrepancy between Tom's smiling behavior and his contempt for her. He wanted to conceal the way he felt. He made a pretense of being affable; he was a snake-in-the-grass. She realized the part she played in nursing his egotism and made an about-face.

Sample Scene: Future Projection

After the group is comfortable with role playing, the director asks, "What would you like to be when you grow up?" This is always a good question to ask children, since it reminds them of roles in which they will be functioning later in life.

In the next case, sadistic behavior evidenced in a boy of ten was an attempt to express feelings in the socially accepted role of surgeon. The boy's two older brothers expressed their antisocial behavior in reality and were spending time in a training school for wayward boys.

DIRECTOR   What do you want to be when you grow up?

KEVIN   I want to be a doctor, just like my uncle.

DIRECTOR   Fine. Come up here and show us how you are going to be a doctor.

KEVIN   Old sawbones, that's me. I need a patient and a nurse. (*He grabs Janice for the nurse and Jerry for the patient.*) There, you get on the table; I have to operate on you. (*He starts to make sawing gestures and gurgling and sawing sounds.*) There goes your heart! There goes your liver! You don't need your stomach, either. (*He pretends to throw each organ on the floor vigorously.*) I guess I'll sew you up! (*He throws the patient off the table and lunges for another patient.*) Just keep my sister, that little angel, out of my way. Come on, Peter. (*Peter runs out of the room, and the others follow, leaving Kevin alone.*)

The volunteer worker brought the cast back to finish the session. Kevin was then discussed by the children who played the scene with him.

DIRECTOR	How did Kevin play the role of the doctor?
JANICE	A doctor doesn't throw his patient off the table, and a nurse is supposed to help the doctor. He didn't let me.
PETER	He acted like a butcher cleaning a chicken.
DIRECTOR	I wonder what kind of doctor would show so little concern for his patient.
KEVIN	A bigshot who wants to push other guys around.

The scene was played again, with explicit directions on how a doctor shows concern for his patients and staff.

The Staff

A word about the experience and training of the staff is necessary at this point. The director of the role playing, the psychodramatist, needs to have (1) a good understanding of the dynamics of interaction and an ability to use this knowledge as a therapeutic tool or as a training method, depending upon his or her experience; (2) sufficient information about the problems of the children and their parents to play out characteristic situations to meet the individual or group needs; (3) a satisfactory relationship with children and the ability to stimulate them without pressure or threats, to redirect a child's mistaken goals without resorting to preaching or the common mistakes of adult-child interaction; and, of course, (4) professional training as a psychodramatist, since this type of action therapy is a specialized form of group therapy.

At the center, some people considered that role playing and psychodrama could be too difficult for the inexperienced, so all the staff workers attached to the playroom had an opportunity to practice the method. Those in charge of the playroom met in a series of staff meetings to discuss their opinions about role playing and to define the goals of the next psychodrama session. Each had an opportunity to "feel" role playing as a typical playroom experience was played out with the staff. It was not always possible to follow the plan as set out for the children, but planning made the staff aware of their needs. Plans were flexible enough to accommodate the spontaneous development of the group—staff and children.

Training through Psychodrama

During the center's early use of psychodrama, work was centered exclusively around children in the playroom. Later, as psychodrama became an integral part of the center's functioning, it was felt that mothers in therapy groups (as well as playroom workers) could profit from periodic "action" sessions. Playroom volunteers were invited to a series of role-playing sessions in which the director attempted to recreate a playroom atmosphere. Instead of discussing how to deal with children in the game room, the workers were encouraged to act out relationships and to deal with the problems they had experienced there. Part of the rationale for this procedure was that it might be more profitable for them to experience in action the conflicts that arose in a playroom. This program seemed to help the playroom workers become more perceptive of group processes and interactions.

The first task for the worker was to observe the overt action of the child and define the child's behavior as he perceived it. To add information to the verbal report, the worker was asked to think of a particular child in the playroom: "Become the child and enter the room as he does. Show his energy. What choices does he make? Does he move toward things or people? What kind of people does he approach? What does he do with the things and the people? Or does he isolate himself? Is he unwilling to make a choice of activities? Be the child as you remember him in an encounter with you and with a child-member in the group. Show how he solved a problem. Show an episode in which you observed his discouragement, his courage, his destructive behavior, his constructive behavior."[7]

Since all the playroom workers knew the children, they joined in and supplied situations that gave a profile in action of a particular child. The worker had an opportunity to be the observed as well as the observer, and in this way he learned to distinguish between nonverbal and verbal behavior. The discrepancy between what the child said and what he did was experienced and made explicit as the staff worker became the child.

A discussion of the action profile followed and dealt with such questions as: What did you see as the child's response when limits were set on him? Under what conditions does he seem to feel adequate? Does failure have a special meaning to him? What does the child do when responsibility for making a choice is thrown back to him? These in-service training sessions ended with approaches that might encourage the child and the staff worker to have a healthy interaction.

14

Alcoholism and Psychodrama

MacDuff: What three things does drink especially
provoke?
Porter: Marry, sir, nose-painting, sleep, and urine.
Lechery, sir, it provokes and unprovokes; it provokes
the desire, but it takes away the performance.
—Wm. Shakespeare, *Macbeth*, Act II, Scene 3

Long before Shakespeare commented on the deleterious effects
of alcohol, and "connected drink to sexual anxieties"[1] there were reports of the wanton, often cruel behavior that resulted from its inges-
tion. The ancients told the story of Bacchus, who discovered the "culture of the vine and the mode of extracting its precious juice, but Juno
struck him with madness and drove him forth a wanderer through various parts of the world. In Phrygia, the goddess Rhea cured him, taught
him her religious rites, and he set out on a progress through Asia teaching people the cultivation of the vine. . . . He undertook to introduce
his worship into Greece, but was opposed by some princes who dreaded
its introduction on account of the disorder and madness it brought with
it."[2] When Bacchus's arrival was announced, throngs of people, principally women, joined his processional. Pentheus, king of Thebes, went
to the mountain where the crowd had gathered and where an orgy was
in process. He tried to stop Bacchus, but his mother, blinded by Bacchus, mistook her son for a wild boar, and directed his aunts to tear him
limb from limb. And so the worship of Bacchus was established in
Greece. This may be the first reference to the state of being "blind"
drunk.

Despite the poisoning effects of alcohol, destruction of physiological powers and gradual deterioration of mental abilities, men and
women risk addiction to gain solace for their feelings of deficiency and

to rebel against the demands of life. Alcohol is probably the major means of adult withdrawal. One of the attractive effects of alcohol is loss of inhibitions; one's censor is lulled and one forgets the anxieties of daily living in abandon and oblivion.

The goal of psychodramatic therapy is to raise the lowered self-esteem of the alcoholic, to move him (or her) from a negative to a positive estimation of his ability to function without alcohol. Alcoholics seem to be less antagonistic to understanding why they drink than drug users, or "addicts," are to learning why they are drug addicts. Alcoholics are prone to view the treatment program with the same discouragement as they view managing their own lives, discouragement mixed with rebellion. It is important that the director keep this in mind, for often the actions of the alcoholic are provocative and confusing not only to the director of a session but also to the people with whom he is in close contact—his family, the people at work, and the community.

It is essential to define the psychodrama session as an educational process. This communicates to the group that their status is that of students who want to learn what personally held attitudes resulted in behavior that led to hospitalization. As students, they are in a position of equality to the director and respected as active participants in this learning process. In addition to getting help, the members of the group are expected to help others by joining the director as auxiliary egos.

"There are few of us who do not know the satisfaction of losing themselves in some great feeling, whether it be love, nature, music, enthusiasm for a cause, or sexual abandon."[3] Nature has provided man with many ways of finding release from the stark realities of living. W. Beren Wolfe calls these solving devices sleep, dreaming, forgetting, crying, laughing, and sex. Man also has the cultural activities of listening to music and poetry and of creating these arts. Or he may read, write, paint, act, or engage in other creative activities. But, for many, these satisfactions are too hard to come by or outside their experience. Some are not content with these "emergency exits" and search for fast relief in alcohol or drugs. Some drink to escape responsibility; being drunk is an almost universally accepted excuse for any action: "You mustn't mind what I said or did to you—I was drunk!" It is helpful when entering an alcoholic treatment program to keep in mind how deeply imbued in the societies of man the use of alcohol is.[4]

The victims of alcohol and drug addiction must examine their life patterns and face their problems with greater courage. A constructive scheme of living is within the reach of everyone. Psychodrama provides a fertile ground for developing such a constructive scheme for a new life; it may serve as the excitement for experiencing, feeling, and learning to *live* life. A director in an alcoholic program, therefore, can act to resolve the resistance, to correct some of the false expectations, and to modify anticipatory fears of the clients.

A group is usually made up of middle-aged males and females, with a scattering of young adults, male and female. This predominance of the middle aged may change as the public, industry, and the military become better informed on the danger signals of alcoholism and more willing to refer young adults to rehabilitation programs. The alcoholic when he is sober can communicate with the nonalcoholic director or therapist, and he responds well to treatment. All treatment programs report a high rate of success with the highly motivated alcoholic, that is, the person who has achieved a place in the scheme of living, a good job, a family. The skid-row derelict is not a good candidate for treatment. The problem is to get the alcoholic into treatment and keep him there.

A drug addiction group, on the other hand, can immobilize the therapeutic efforts of a session by the cohesive force of hostility expressed in apathy or sarcasm. A therapist must face his own rejection of the group and resolve it. The drug user seems to feel that the fault lies not in himself but in the system, a system he turns his back on—as a schizophrenic turns away from society. While there is ample evidence to support this point of view, the essence of the problem is what the individual does about the adverse situation. The alcoholic seems willing to consider that the healing must begin with himself. This does not imply a difference in motivation for taking drugs, for "the mental disorder is more alike than different—all efforts to find adequacy and security."[5]

Therapy for Alcoholics

Psychodrama is recognized as an effective group method in the psychological treatment and rehabilitation of alcoholics. It is generally used in conjunction with other forms of individual and group psychotherapy, marital therapy, drug therapy, Alcoholics Anonymous, educational health courses, and/or vocational rehabilitation.[6] Alcoholics vary tremendously; even the individual drinker changes the pattern of his drinking from time to time, so clinical treatment needs to be as comprehensive as possible. The usefulness of psychodrama lies in its flexibility and the variety of techniques that can be used to treat those who are resistant to facing emotional tension and conflicts. Typically, psychodrama ties into the other programs to clarify the content of and the expression of anxious feelings. The group uses concrete situations of misbehavior to educate the patient on the nature of his behavioral response.

The popularity of group treatment developed from the nonmedical model of Alcoholics Anonymous, as many drug abuse programs are fashioned on the nonmedical approach of Synanon, Daytop, and Odyssey House.[7] Unable to find the help necessary to function, either in a doctor's office or through hospitalization, alcoholics banded together to help each other. Experimentation with group therapy began in the mid-1930s. Since then, many types of group therapies have been tried. Psychodrama was first used in a veterans hospital as part of the overall emphasis on the treatment and management of the hospitalized patient. It has spread to the point of being included in some form of action technique in the conducting of group therapy sessions both here and abroad.[8]

It wasn't until the fifties that group therapy with drug users was reported,[9] principally in prisons and with adolescent drug users in hospital treatment centers.[10] Both AA and Synanon encourage their members to share their experiences; they accept only persons who admit to the problem of alcoholism or to drugs. The common problem draws people from all walks of life. However, unless the therapist is a recovered addict, it is felt he cannot succeed in helping the patient, for he is not able to understand the "addict mind."

At this point, there is some value in reviewing briefly the general form of AA because of its widespread acceptance and influence.

Alcoholics Anonymous

Alcoholics Anonymous does not tolerate drinking, although a member who relapses into drinking is not rejected if he declares again his desire to stop drinking. Each member is encouraged to find a sponsor (an auxiliary ego) who gives encouragement and provides emotional support in overcoming the desire to drink. He is on call at all times. Each member is kept in social communication through regular meetings, visiting, and calling among members. The group support of sobriety, reliable friends, reliance on spiritual values gives its members an opportunity to re-establish social relationships with other people. This form of group treatment, which bypasses the conflicts that cause the drinking, differs from group psychotherapy as adopted and practiced by trained therapists and so is called *social therapy* by Howard Blane.[11] There is currently a change of emphasis in the AA program as it moves toward exploring the personality factors that lead to drinking. No doubt this expresses the interest of the younger alcoholic as he reflects the attitude that alcoholism is a multifaceted problem that includes the sociological, physiological, and psychological state of the person.

It may be seen from this that the self-help movements, AA and Synanon, are based, according to Hendrik Ruitenbeck,[12] on one or another analytic principle. Jules Masserman believes that AA and Synanon methods parallel religious and psychiatric methods, especially those utilized in the dynamics of group therapy—"the delusion of the omnipotent servant" of "the group therapeutic magic."[13]

Psychodrama and Its Value

Psychodrama in a treatment program can identify and alter the social distortion of an alcoholic's world. The sessions are set up to help the alcoholic move toward his eventual rehabilitation in the community. The problem of lost skills (including losing a driver's license, a job, social roles) is variously handled in this chapter. Useful techniques for teaching social skills are described which can be used with both the alcoholic and the drug user. Some sessions bring an individual's lifestyle into focus, either for an emotional release or to motivate a change of behavior.

Psychodrama sessions develop skills for coping with problems through fostering an increased awareness of the self as it interacts with others. The alcohol that the individual uses to anesthetize himself, to block out unpleasant experiences or inadequacies of behavior, and to fog-up encounters with people is replaced by encounters with a sober group of people in therapeutically controlled acting-out sessions. The drinking crowd, with its feigned gaiety, superficial sexual encounters, and destructive relationships, is replaced by a group that examines in specific terms the life situation and the observable behavior of each member. Thus behavior reveals a person's low self-esteem and how this affects his interpersonal transactions. All this becomes sharply and vividly drawn, particularly when the action deals with work or family roles.

Psychodrama in work with alcoholics is used in several ways. It may be used as intense therapy for an individual with group empathy, in work-oriented sessions developing skills of social communication, or as an aid to foster an experience of group cohesiveness brought about by movement and nonverbal behavior. Psychodrama is especially valuable for introducing a newcomer into the group. As the patient explores old and new patterns of behavior, he is much more able to select those modes of behavior most likely to succeed in the less protective world outside the group. He has, optimally, an increased appreciation of other people as well as of himself. He develops social concern.

The sessions help the staff and the alcoholic understand his relationship to the person closest to him, in many cases, his spouse. Experience has demonstrated that this interaction is cooperative; the drinking affects the behavior of the spouse, but the family, in turn, contributes to or, at the very least, does little to alleviate the alcoholism. We see in role playing how the family encourages sobriety or reinforces alcoholism. "Nor can it be concluded that the 'cause' of drinking is the family." Role playing prepares the patient for further therapy through marital groups of alcoholics or family group counseling.[14] The groundwork for repairing the troubled relationship is laid in role playing, and progress can continue with the real people in other forms of therapy.

Understanding the Alcoholic

Dependent behavior, seeking to be with others in times of stress, is common to all people. It has been pointed out by military psychiatrists that when a soldier landed in Vietnam, he reacted to the stress of family separation and the anticipatory fears of enemy action by making friends with his combat unit. This sometimes included smoking marijuana as proof of solidarity. When the unit didn't provide the security of solidarity, the incidence of psychiatric breakdowns and other escape behavior increased.[15] Stress may be experienced under less life-endangering situations, such as entering a group of people at a party. Before moving into the group, one may first go to the bar for a drink to reduce one's anxiety. The goal of the behavior is the same, in combat and at the party—to become a part of the group. Each person expects to be able to rely on others for emotional satisfaction.

One of the major sources of interpersonal difficulty is an intense feeling of not being able to meet external demands. A manifestation of this is a demanding, blaming attitude, as well as avoiding situations that might expose the person to humiliation or failure. Anxiety and depression are frequently accompanied by punishing and self-destructive ideas. An exaggerated feeling of helplessness often occurs, especially with the female alcoholic, at a time of critical loss such as divorce, death, or disappearance of youthful attractiveness. With the male alcoholic, this response is more diffused and pervasive and seems to be easily triggered by criticism. He has a strong tendency to be sensitive about his mistakes. He may seek service and sustenance from others. The role conflict is resolved by his becoming completely dependent on others.

Three characteristic attitudes of the alcoholic personality are observed in the following cases (protagonist-centered sessions) that summarize the alcoholics' problem with felt deficiency (dependent needs). Since everyone experiences the discomfort of the feeling of weakness and helplessness, the crucial factor is the way the alcoholic solves this sense of powerlessness. The behavior is observable as becoming openly dependent on someone; another solution may be to deny the dependency and overcompensate by acting independent of "others." Yet another solution is independence that is "flexible, modulated with dependency, and not easily challenged."[16] This attitude presents a confusing and perplexing behavior pattern to the mental health worker.

Case One: Passivity and Withdrawal

The alcoholic's spontaneity is often low and rigidly constructed. Alcohol provides his stimulation as well as preserving his dependency. The private logic may be expressed thus: "I can't get what I want through my own efforts. It all depends on what others do for me."

Jim, forty-two, was the younger of two brothers from a working-class family. They did not experience extremes of poverty, since the father was a moderate man who worked regularly. The mother overprotected her younger son. She was concerned for his health because he was sickly, and she insisted that the older brother make sure that Jim didn't get picked on or hurt when they went out to play. High school was uneventful and lonely for Jim; he showed little interest in anything other than sports. He made few friends and didn't date girls. He began drinking as he spent his time after graduation "hanging around" the gym. He lived at home with his parents and drank as much as he liked, but rarely became drunk. This low-keyed, sheltered life, with "jobs not worth mentioning," continued until his parents died. His brother by this time was married.

Jim's drinking increased, and he spent the next ten years in and out of hospital programs. He made the rounds and at first interested the staff and group; his quiet reserve, sensible responses, and good looks were appealing. He remained in a program as long as no demands were made on him. He selected (and was accepted for) a day-care program for the treatment of general psychiatric disorders. He never attended the group when drunk, but occasionally skipped a few days, returning red eyed and depressed and reporting that he had been drinking too much to make it. His hermitlike existence continued in the group, since he rarely, in a six-month period of day care, brought in a personal problem.

When efforts were made to place him in a job, his tension became so great that he was totally hospitalized and even attempted suicide. He could, and often did, play an auxiliary ego to another patient; under protest he became the necessary "other" with skill and understanding. In an unusually open period, after a suicide effort, he played out this scene to show the futility of trying to be comfortable during a holiday weekend with his brother (an alternate solution to his isolation).

The scene takes place as his brother picks him up at the station to spend the weekend with the family. Jim was asked to begin the scene in the role of the brother, "the significant other" person, so the other individuals in the group could observe the way Jim cut himself off from others by portraying them as offensive, stupid, or insensitive to his needs (the way he externalized the resentment).

JIM *(as brother)*	Thank God you haven't started to drink yet. You know Mame [his wife] hates it when she smells the stuff on you. It's okay when we all are drinking—you know, it's social then, not compulsive. My psychiatrist says you should stick with the program. It's good for you. Now tell me, how do they analyze you?
PATIENT *(as Jim)*	Well, they try to establish some regularity of attendance.
JIM *(as brother)*	And you don't make it, do you? You never could, not even when you went to school. Half the time you stayed home with mom. *(Falls out of role.)* I wanted to leave then. It's like being

in a prison, a captive. Then
Mame corners me and
complains about him. Finally
I make some excuse—like
I'm not feeling well. I go
home and—the hell with it.

His unrealistic search for comfort and security was directly grati-
fied with alcohol and hospitalization. This behavioral pattern is appropriately called "passive mastery."

Case Two: Passivity and Anger

Some patients are more productive than Jim but meet the ever-
increasing roles of work and marriage with a passive acting out of anger
and frustration. They are either unwilling or unable to meet the role
requirements, and they blame others for the difficulties they encounter.
They seldom find a better solution for themselves, except in alcohol.
The private logic may be: "I've gone as far as I'm going. It's getting
too much for me." Spontaneity is dissipated by the enormity of other
people's expectations.

This patient also was the younger of two, but the older sibling, a
girl, died of a lingering illness when the patient was in his teens. Tim
was four when the family realized that his sister was seriously ill. He
couldn't remember anything associated with this period other than feeling bad when his sister died. His mother was a nervous housewife whose
life became devoted to preserving the life of her surviving child as her
husband and son slowly drank their way to extinction. Tim, at the time
of this session, was in an alcoholic rehabilitation unit.

The purpose of the following is to demonstrate a type of alcoholic
patient as well as the interrelationship of psychodrama to other aspects
of the program. Tim was chosen as (and accepted being) the protagonist at the session, since the staff felt he could be helped through psychodrama to change his relationship to his mother. He had attended three
times prior to this participation and had sat tensely out of range of the
action.

The interview between Tim and the director could best be described as prying out bits of information. Many alcoholics have families
in which one or both parents drink excessively. Feelings toward the
parental figures are crucial to the patient's feelings of self-esteem. He
can identify with a drunken bum or, as in this case, a father who slipped
off into drunken slumber and left his son to receive all the mother's con-

cern. Tim's resentment was not verbalized, for it, too, was cut off by his deeply felt and unhappy memory of his mother's mourning the death of her daughter. The relationship was lacking in warm human exchange. He began drinking in high school, and by the time he graduated from college his drinking was a problem. Four years after graduation he met a girl who agreed to marry him although she knew he was an alcoholic.

These identifications came out in the enactment of a childhood scene in which Tim played all the roles. It was a short interaction in which his sick sister told him to go out to play and he did. The mother was hovering over the sick girl and the father was asleep. Ergo: There is not much I can do for others but play or sleep.

Another interaction followed as typical of the mother-son relationship. Tim and his wife are washing the storm windows and putting them on the window frame. Tim's mother arrives unannounced.

TIM *(as mother)*	Tim, why are you doing that heavy work? You know it isn't good for your kidneys. Let me do it.	*The director asks a patient to take over the role of a stereotypical overly concerned mother as Tim becomes himself.*
TIM *(as himself)*	Damn it, I guess I know what's good for me. Just let me alone. (*He raises his voice and begins sweating.*)	
PATIENT *(as mother)*	Now, Tim, don't get upset. You sit down and I'll finish this with Agnes. I'm right, aren't I, Agnes? We'll do it. You rest, Tim.	
TIM *(as himself)*	(*Turns to his wife.*) See, I told you she won't let me be. Now you know I'm not a mamma's boy. But she won't let go no matter what I do.	

Tim's helplessness and feeling of inadequacy were revealed in the short scene. A member of the staff stood beside him and, as the double, spoke to the mother: "You scare me—you may be right. Maybe I am an invalid. I feel desperate and empty when you remind me of sickness. Cut it out!" This helped the patient separate his problem from his mother's. The pattern as shown here is that when Tim's feelings of anger are aroused, he may respond by drinking.

Another scene was played in which Tim's mother took the matter of his being fired from his job into her own hands by calling the employer to ask for leniency. She tried to arrange for his return to the job using sickness, not alcoholism, as the reason for his frequent absences. Tim was furious. The group was sympathetic to his misfortune in having so managerial a mother. But what could he do about it? In the discussion that followed, successful ways of stepping out from under this tyranny were suggested. Then the director summed up the problem: "Tim, you have cared for your mother and handled her anxiety about life and death for so long that you have trouble extricating yourself from her. You think that she should stop being the way she is. You love her, and you don't want to hurt her, but you are angry at her for hovering over you and acting toward you in a way which frightens and humiliates you. Let's try another approach. You decide what you are going to do when she interferes. Try not being angry at her. What would you do when she comes into your house to wash the windows?" The scene was replayed, and with a little coaching from the group it went like this:

PATIENT
(*as mother*)
Sit down, dear boy, and I'll wash the windows. It's too much for you.

TIM
You know, Mom, you may be right. Are you sure you won't mind doing the work? Agnes and I were wondering when we'd find the time to go shopping, but now that you're here to do this dirty work—so long—give my regards to Pop—we're going shopping.

Tim's current relationship with his mother (and incidentally his wife) was a "reality" problem. His predicament was vividly portrayed in the interview and in a short excursion back to his early childhood.

The group saw his previously learned solution of passive avoidance of anger and frustration. The goal of the session was to help him become aware of this feeling of victimization so that he could be free to feel differently about himself and to respond more adequately to anxious mothering.

Case Three: Aggressiveness

The aggressive patient shows adequate masculine behavior and hides his anxiety and feelings of weakness. His spontaneity is hot; he reacts quickly to what may be interpreted as depreciation. His concern with personal superiority may be expressed as: "I'm somebody and don't you forget it. Show a sign of weakness and you're done for—look what happened to Vietnam." The common feelings of inadequacy and anxiety are denied, and the denial is heavily defended. This person's behavior is aggressive and confident. He drinks because he likes it and denies any discomfort from drinking large amounts of alcohol.

The following case represents an effective working through for a problem drinker, Pat, using a psychodramatic presentation of a psychotic episode at the end of a drinking bout. The enactment revealed Pat's lack of control in his striving toward acceptance and the effects of this on an already well-established sense of personal worthlessness. Pat watched and evaluated psychodrama for a few sessions before he volunteered to become a protagonist. His participation in this therapy impressed the critical individuals in the group, for he was its unquestioned "star."

The technique used was a straightforward reenactment of the events leading to Pat's hospitalization. The staff played the roles of the important people in the drama, since they knew Pat's history and had had conferences with his family. Pat was asked to play the significant other—the boss—for the core problem was Pat's perception of the man who made him and who seemed to be able to destroy him.

The scene begins on the floor of a factory where Pat is working as a foreman. He has been there about four years. One day the boss of the firm stands at one end of the room and roars:

PAT   Hey—you with the brains—
(as boss)   Pat. I'm putting you in
               charge of production. Let's
               have a drink on it.

STAFF MEMBER
(as Pat)

I'll take the drink and the promotion. Thanks, boss. *(Turns to one of the workers.)* Do you think he means it or is he loaded again? See you tomorrow, just in case this is some sort of gag.

Pat and the boss went for a drink, and whether the boss was drunk or not, Pat got the promotion. It was the beginning of a relationship that was a mixture of alcohol and promotions. Pat's family saw less and less of him as he spent more and more time drinking with his "benefactor," and as the demands of his position became more pressing. In a few years he was in an executive position. Then it happened. One night, in a drunken frenzy, he tore the bar apart—hitting, throwing, and attacking. He was unable to recall anything that had happened when he woke up in restraints on a public hospital ward. The scene at the hospital was played next.

PAT
(as boss)

Pat? Pat? *(Walking from bed to bed.)* Oh, there you are. *(Stops and looks.)* You look like a piece of shit. See you later when you're dried out.

PAT
(as himself)

Is that all you can say? What are you going to do to get me out of here? *(He leaves the role)* The SOB walked out and I came here.

STAFF MEMBER

You must have a lot you'd like to tell him. Why don't you do it now? I'll be the boss. It's still unfinished business, you know.

The catharsis was a tirade, a struggle between blaming "the other" and a dim realization that he had participated in the destructive relationship—in fact, had profited from it—so that he was in a tortuous position of self-doubt. Was he chosen as a drinking partner or an efficient businessman? One minute he felt that his actual performance on the job kept him there, and the fact of a prospering firm attested to this; the next, he canceled this feeling out with a feeling that his promotion was luck, the times, the breaks. He used alcohol to subdue these doubts; the session ended with talk of the future. Will he rejoin the firm? "Not in a million years. I've had it." But, he did. A year later, when he returned with his family to a reunion of his graduating class, he was still with the firm and was managing himself without alcohol.

Some sessions centered on a single individual such as those just illustrated. Identification with the protagonist's problem is intense and is particularly helpful in the treatment of the alcoholic. This form of psychodrama is spontaneous; the development of the scene is derived from the client's behavior. The constant goals in the development of these sessions are: (1) to define the role of the protagonist; (2) to discover the antagonist; (3) to see what resolutions to the conflict are made; and (4) to help the protagonist modify his perception of the antagonist through a realistic evaluation of the situational behavior, accomplished through feedback and discussion.

Case Four: A Work-Oriented Session

Sessions may be designed to prepare the alcoholic for a job interview.[17] Role playing an employment interview frequently prepares the sober alcoholic to account for his bad work record, that is, frequent job changes, long periods of no work, and poor references. Most people are anxious while applying for a job, even if they have good references. If one has a bad work record, however, the job interview is an even more discouraging experience. The interviewee is asked to look at his quick discouragement, how he quit trying before he was accepted or rejected.

The scene starts with the arrangement of the job interview. The applicant may have found out about the job by seeing a help-wanted sign, by reading a newspaper advertisement, or through a vocational service recommendation or the recommendation of a friend. He enacts his arrival at the place of employment and the completion of his application. The application is filled out verbally, with one of the other patients speaking as the application form: "Name? Address?" A patient or staff member may be selected as the personnel interviewer. Often a member of the group has had this experience and makes a reliable personnel director. The warm-up is designed to help establish the applicant's motivation to get work or to consciously or unconsciously avoid it.

The interview is enacted with special attention to the way the applicant manages his anxiety. The interviewer and the applicant may change roles when the behavior of the applicant shows negative motivation to get the job; he is either very passive (using weakness) or arrogant (using unwarranted conceit) in his search for work. Other patients are invited to apply and to show how they have successfully or unsuccessfully handled the problem of getting a job by being truthful about the alcohol problem, by hiding it, or by denying it. The group is invited to discuss the value of each mode of behavior and of the initiative and energy shown. After this training phase is over, the job applicant is given a second chance at the interview to see if his selection of a response has improved.

A patient often profits when the group's attention is focused first on his present job and then on the job he would like to have. The compatibility of these two roles may be observed if the patient makes a realistic appraisal of training and preparation for the longed-for job, or the discrepancy between reality and future goals may be observed in an exaggerated striving for a position of affluence without considering the possibility of not being able to manage it.

One patient, the proprietor of a Laundromat, played the roles of all the people surrounding his work area—the owner who met bills on the tenth of the month, the employee who asked for a raise, and the customer who needed help in running a machine. He was then asked what his preferred work situation was. He selected and was preparing to be a "great white hunter" on a safari with gun bearer, tourists, et al. He regarded himself as being able to function in this capacity, based on his reading and seeing movies on the subject. But clearly this job was inappropriate to his urban Chicago background and his experience as a small businessman.

Many unemployed alcoholics refuse to face their actual performance level before alcohol took over. Some exaggerate the importance of the jobs they held; others minimize their job efforts.[18] It is helpful to clarify this point by examining the actual work situations that each has experienced. Break the group up into threes with the instruction to present to the others a difficulty on the job. One person plays out his problem with the other two playing auxiliary roles; when the situation can be presented by two, the third becomes the commentator.

Carl, a TV repairman, was in his early fifties. The group knew he was married and had some marital difficulties, but the area to work on was the immediate job problem. In the scene, Carl is at the shop. A distress call comes in. He goes to the house, and a woman answers the door.

CARL	I'm from the TV repair shop. I'd like to see your set.
WOMAN	It's right here in the living room. I hope it's nothing serious. We've only had it a short time. Must be a tube.
CARL	I'll check the tubes. *(After a short interval during which Carl simulates checking out the set, the woman begins.)*
WOMAN	I understand you fellows are real gyps. How can I be sure you'll be honest with me?
CARL	Madam, I do the best I can. I've been a TV repairman for ten years.
WOMAN	The Better Business Bureau says to be cautious. Can you fix it here?
CARL	No, ma'am, I can't. The tubes are all okay. It may be the condenser or something.
WOMAN	There, I knew it. You're trying to make a week's salary on me. Is it possible you made a mistake? I better wait until my husband comes home and let him decide if you're a big gyp or you know what you're doing.
CARL	That's up to you, but you'll have to pay for two service calls, you know. *(Turns to the group.)* Two or three of these and I've had it!
DIRECTOR	It seems that the woman's attitude toward TV repairmen is shared by many and is like the attitude many	*The director, as analyst, summarizes the role playing as not being a straightforward*

people have toward alcoholics. Maybe it's because of all the publicity about TV robbers. Did you have whiskey on your breath when you made the call? *(Carl shakes his head no.)* Well, I think you acted as if you were afraid she knew you were an alcoholic—no authority. After ten years of looking over those boxes, you must know something— but you didn't act it. Let's give it another try. Change roles. Carl, you be the woman of the house, and Jim, when you play Carl, do what he did, only put it on heavy so he sees it.

statement of his skill as a television repairman.

The director, as therapist, reflects the feeling of fear being expressed. This helps bring the interactions into focus: two fear-ridden strangers meeting.

This training period should last long enough for the group to observe the patient's interaction with the antagonist. Although he assumed the role of "the other," the patient continued to act out his own emotions. He expressed his own anger as he exaggerated the woman's suspicions and stupidity. This scene lasted only as long as it took to make that point. During the group discussion that followed, Carl and his actors sat in the center of the room. The three could have planned a new presentation or acted it out spontaneously, expecting that Carl would change his attitude toward the antagonist as he attempted to deal with her anxiety. Here is the replay:

CARL

Have you had any dealings with our firm before?

WOMAN

No, I haven't.

CARL

Then I can understand your being worried. All the warnings, and some of them justified. How did you get our name? Through a friend or from the directory?

WOMAN	In the phonebook.	
CARL	That figures. You have no way to know whether we are on the level or not. Well, I've been with the firm for over ten years, and the firm was in business before that. Come over to the box.	*The replay helps him answer the woman's anxiety and lessen his own.*

When a patient is unable to face hostility directly, symbolic action is used to move him from his passivity to effective action. For example, Carl is seated on a chair; the woman stands up and continues to charge him with crooked machinations. An auxiliary stands in back of the patient and speaks:

AUXILIARY EGO	This woman is on my back— the witch. If I close my eyes, she'll go away. *(The auxiliary presses harder.)* Don't talk up —stay on your butt—you can always get a drink to forget it. You're no good.
CARL	Hey, you're hurting me.
GROUP	Give it to her, Carl. Stand up and tell her what's what.

Carl stands up and takes an aggressive stance facing the provocateur. The group is satisfied and rewards him with applause and jovial kidding. He turns to the auxiliary ego and says, "I thought you were going to break my shoulders." The director answers, "Passivity is painful, too."

Each work situation summarizes the feelings of the patient as he copes with discouraging, critical, or discernible stress. Because the alcoholic has learned to manage frustration with alcohol, it seems that any situation can trigger the compulsion to drink. The significance of the scene with Carl was not that the lady questioned his integrity but that he felt helpless to counteract any question of his ability. He instantly felt inadequate. Alcoholics often strongly deny this connection and focus instead on the lost sale, the demanding supervisor, the long hours. The auxiliary ego can supply the more relevant feeling of not being quite good enough to make the grade.[19]

Case Five: The Dry Period and Return

The next example deals with an event common to a group of alcohol or drug addicts. One of the treatments for alcoholics at the Veterans Administration Hospital in Houston, Texas, is the BUD (Building Up to Drink) program, originated by Jorge Valles, director of the program.[20] It treats the period of abstinence, and its premise is that the alcoholic shows specific involuntary behavior patterns that, in effect, are warning signals that a relapse is imminent. BUD is the urgent pattern and is carefully and systematically watched for.

It is generally observed that the alcoholic is easily upset and, therefore, creates the situation that pushes him toward alcohol. The upset may be a response to physiological or psychological distress; he undergoes some experience that seems to predict a relapse into drinking. In any program, the time comes when an alcoholic or a drug user begins to get restless and feel an urgency to leave. This urgency is assumed to be a signal that the BUD is in the danger zone.

The patient may handle his stress in one of two ways—by taking a drink or by working out the anxiety symptoms, principally through psychodrama. The illustration given here is a flashback, a recall, not the moment of the stressful situation. (Valles reports successful management of the BUD symptom *during* the period of agitation.) The goal is to help the alcoholic understand how he creates his symptoms. Nervousness is a distressing emotional state. It can be helpful to the alcoholic who wants to break his drinking habit to be able to see how he plans a drinking situation, and why.

In the psychodrama one person is asked to present a series of events that led to his decision to start drinking again. The protagonist may begin by saying: "I just got tired of not drinking." This is a strong denial of the emotional state in which the drinking occurs. The director begins.

DIRECTOR Let's move to your house. Tell us where you live, who lives with you, and what was going on.

TONY
In a house, with my wife and three kids. She's a quiet chick and wants me to finish the oils I started last year. She's always saying, "Go to the basement and finish the landscape. You're a good painter. Get with it."

DIRECTOR
Select someone to play your wife. Does anyone here know her? Have you seen the two together on visiting days?

Someone volunteers, and the scene proceeds from general to specific pressure as Tony changes roles with the auxiliary ego to supply the characteristic interpersonal behavior of himself and his wife.

WIFE
I know you don't like being down there painting alone, so I'll iron while you paint. You can sell it if you finish it.

TONY
Christ, I've been at the board at the office all day. I'm sick of it. Lay off. I'd rather have some love. Let's go to bed.

WIFE
The children are still around. I'm going to iron.

TONY
And I split! I can't paint after working all day. I need to get charged up.

DIRECTOR
What we are going to do now didn't happen. I want you to continue the action. You be your sponsor who runs into you and tries to stop you from buying a bottle.

PATIENT *(as Tony)*	She's going to iron while I paint. That's a hell of an inducement. So we're both working. I can't paint anymore. I've lost it.
TONY *(as sponsor)*	Calm down. She's not a bad sort. Just boring.
PATIENT *(as Tony)*	I can't get her off my painting. Always pushing. I'll give her something to yap about!
TONY *(as sponsor)*	Talk, man. What are you afraid of? Not being another Picasso? Let's go over the nervous feeling you have. Or maybe you're a lousy lover as well. Talk, talk, talk!

The impulse to drink is experienced as a destructive response to an emotionally charged situation.

Case Six: Impatience

The response of impatience (the omnipotent dependent wish of an infant), an insistence on getting what is wanted on demand, is common and becomes clearly evident as roles and counterroles are investigated. Drink by drink, the alcoholic extinguishes his occupational, familial, and community roles. Time, past and future, seems to disappear as immediate satisfaction becomes urgent. Manipulatory handling of people, money, and sex goes hand in hand with alcohol, becoming the principle concern of the alcoholic. This is a characteristic that alcoholics have in common with drug users. Sexual acts by men with their daughters, and other culturally disapproved partners, satisfy sexual urges; sex is consummated with the nearest and most easily available outlet. Sexual jealousy may be strongly felt, a projection of the view that since one is entitled to get what one wants when one wants it, a spouse or other sex partner must hold this view too.

At first, the director should focus on the less threatening aspects of this impatient behavior, for example, a patient's walking away when an appointment isn't easily arranged or his keeping other people waiting. One patient, a salesman for a national organization, showed how he had made a long-distance call to set up an appointment with a big account of his firm. When he arrived at the appointed time in the far-away city, he was told that the executive would be delayed. This is not an unusual situation for a salesman to encounter. This salesman filled the time drinking.

The session dealt with building up to a drink by having a double join the patient as he went to the bar. The double began a restless pacing, mopping his brow. Then he said, in sharp, irritable tones, "I gotta get out of here. Look at my hands. They're trembling. I don't want to be seen with shaky hands. This'll cost me my job, after twenty years with this firm. Those bastards." The patient acknowledged that the double was correct and added some details of his own. "I'll go for a walk. That'll calm me down. What the hell is that buyer's name? God, what's happening to me? I know it as well as my own. (*To the secretary.*) Tell the big boss I'll be back at the appointed time. I don't think she caught on that I couldn't remember his name. Maybe she did." He was creating, out of the physical distress that is undoubtedly present, a reason to drink. As he fought the symptom, the desire to drink increased.

For the next scene two chairs were placed facing each other. The patient sat in one chair as the alcoholic salesman and talked to the empty chair as though he were sitting there *before he began drinking*— the pre-alcoholic self. The patient was instructed: "Tell your pre-drinking self how you feel as an alcoholic. Then switch chairs and tell your drinking self how it felt when you weren't drinking." Out of this came a re-call of a similar situation when, as a pre-alcoholic, he had been similarly delayed and had spent the time visiting with the president of the firm, whom he had known for years. The director moved to the chair of the pre-alcoholic patient and asked, "How can we restore the role that alcohol killed off?"

These sessions not only highlight the pre- and post-alcoholic roles, but seek to repair the damage to the patient's shrinking role relationships.

Role Playing the Significant Others

In order to afford each patient in the group an opportunity to role-play a significant relationship, the director selects the role area and invites the group to select any relationship within that area. When the selected area is the family, the roles open to enactment are: son to father; daughter to mother; brother to brother; sister to sister; husband to wife; and so on. In the directed warm-up, not only the role area but the directives may guide and stimulate the patient to recall past experiences. For example, the directive question may be "What relationship in your family is the one you'd like most to change?" A situation is then enacted to show the interpersonal disturbance. Each person in the group who is ready with a situation becomes a protagonist and presents his dilemma. After the last situation is played out, the group discusses the similarities and differences in their interpersonal problems. Hopefully, such discussion can help them to improve their relationships.

For many groups, role playing of family relationships is the warm-up to a discussion of family values or of a family atmosphere. For others, it may lead into a protagonist-centered psychodrama, with one person presenting all the relationships within his family.

In one session, when a patient was asked "What relationship would you like to improve?" the patient showed a husband-and-wife relationship with an alcoholic member playing the role of the bottle. The bottle stood between the two and kept the action centered on himself. The husband and wife did not talk to each other; they talked about the bottle. The bottle excused and prevented sex. The whole group, one at a time, joined the bottle, making the distance between the couple greater and greater, until finally only the bottle was holding forth.

These sessions are reminiscent of morality plays, in which Temptation stands on one side of man while Temperance stands on the other side and fights for his soul. One member of the group becomes Alcohol, the solution to the problem. The protagonist waits for his girl friend, or asks for sex from his wife or girl friend and makes jealous accusations at any sign of indifference. Then Alcohol exaggerates the situation, expresses distrust in and indignation toward women, and urges the patient to get relief from the problem through drinking. On the other side of the protagonist are figures pulling him away from Alcohol —wife, mother, and so on. A tug-of-war develops, first verbally then nonverbally, with the patient a passive agent in the struggle.

Case Seven: The Exit Situation

A patient can benefit a great deal from acting out going home— his expectations of being met by his family, employer, and drinking pals. If he has to look for work, the job-hunting task is enacted. Through a series of these enactments, the sober alcoholic can be helped to anticipate the frustrations and disappointments he is bound to encounter and be prepared to withstand them.

Al was a middle-aged man who had been sent to the alcoholic unit by his firm, which was located in a small town. He was a longtime employee of the firm and had been married a long time. Both the firm and his wife had made either/or statements, and he was frightened to leave the unit for fear of earning the "loser" title most alcoholics recognize as their trophy. He expected to be met by his wife and daughter at the bus depot, to be driven home to a welcoming dinner and a visit with the neighbors, and to reestablish a sexual union with his wife. He left the unit and, about six weeks later, sent a long letter to the unit explaining what had happened. He compared it to the experience of the psychodrama, which at the time he thought had little meaning for him.

"I got off the bus and the little wife wasn't there, so I walked across the street to a bar and filled up on B&B [beer and bourbon]. This lasted a couple of days, then I suddenly was tired of it. Just because she didn't meet me wasn't reason enough to blow the whole situation." The letter was read to the group, who were surprised at his strength and amazed at his insight, for during his hospitalization, he had seemed to be negativistic and rejecting of the program.

Resistance to Psychodrama

Resistance to change is frequently discussed in all forms of therapy. It is demonstrated by acting against the therapist with verbal hostility or baiting, by staying away from the group, or by silence that says that this is a waste of time. Often the defiance is openly expressed; at other times, it is cleverly and slyly repressed. These behavioral responses, in action therapy, also include resistance to acting. For a group of patients who are studiously avoiding examining themselves, the usual curtains of secrecy are lifted as a drama begins.

Stagefright takes many forms; the first signs are the anxious feelings of not being able to perform—"I'm not an actor." Walter E. O'Connell further identifies avoiding statements by alcoholics.[21] Patients say psychodrama is "kid stuff," that they are too nervous to perform, that they can't act, that they need time to think out their problems, that they have already solved their problems, that the director should give someone else a chance, that they don't want to be embarrassed or made a fool of, that they can't think of a problem. The director, of course, recognizes the patient's effort to irritate the therapist and to direct attention away from self-examination through action therapy, or for that matter through any form of therapy.

Some measures can be taken to deal with an alcoholic individual's resistance: a friendly, reassuring recognition of the anxiety or a request to use this feeling as the theme of the meeting. The reluctant actor is asked to discuss any problem he may have, perhaps his present attitude toward therapy. The talking may be extended through the entire session or until the patients realize that acting is another dimension of learning. The next step is to ask some member in the group to act out a concrete problem. It may be a sleepless night, full of pacing and smoking one cigarette after another in anticipation of the psychodrama session. The therapist addresses himself to the reluctant one: "Is that the way it was? Did you pace that way or was it a slow, meandering walk around the unit? We are interested in seeing your walk—make it a personal statement about you. Will you try it? I will walk up and down with you." This usually works; when it doesn't, the next person discusses a problem and the group acts it out. The pain of exposure is necessary to therapeutic gain.

When a group is composed of peers—all adolescents, all adult offenders, all alcoholics, all drug users, and so on—the group may be able to band together in resistance to the session. In many cases, such cohesive resistance is an expression of their frustrations about and their sensitivity to the depreciated role of "patient." The members of this group act out their hostilities and aggressions on others. They put the blame for what is happening to them not on themselves but on something or someone outside themselves—psychodrama, the staff, society, and so on.

It is a mistake to ignore hostility. It is a warning signal that communications between patients and staff need to be improved. Talking to the staff after one of these angry outbursts can encourage them to think of what provocation the group is responding to and to find a better solution to the problem. Also, explore the staff's attitude toward psychodrama, for often it is negative for some of them.

At the time of the hostilities, it is necessary to endure the group's antagonistic behavior without defensive reactions. Perhaps most important is to remember that each one in the group is an individual of value.

Conclusion

These techniques are a sample of the procedures found to be useful in practice. When an alcoholic is sober, we can see the "real" person and treat his constricted view of life. The here and now, as well as the there and then, become a part of the social contact and help in the identification of some of the problems that lead to drinking. Family therapy helps relatives understand this transaction. The acting out of relationships (work, love, and friendship) helps the alcoholic recognize alternate patterns of behavior and reverse the retreat into alcoholic oblivion.

The effects of alcohol may be likened to the growth of a child. When he is small, all his tricks and tyrannies are smiled at and talked about. But as the child grows, the same moods and demands become a source of aggravation and finally of despair. Being a good drinker is considered a masculine attribute and is greatly admired until the alcohol controls the man. The alcoholic then meets with annoyance, avoidance, and, finally, separation from significant others. In treatment the therapist must believe in a person's capacity to change (to stop drinking) even though the therapist cannot know that the alcoholic will change.

> Bacchus that first from out the purple grapes
> Crushed the sweet poison of misused wine,
> After the Tuscan mariners transformed,
> Coasting the Tyrrhene shore as the winds listed
> On Circe's island fell; (Who knows not Circe,
> The daughter of the sun? Whose charmed cup
> Whoever tasted lost his upright shape,
> And downward fell into a grovelling swine).
> —JOHN MILTON, Comus at line 46.

15

Drug Abuse
and Psychodrama

This account of psychodrama on a residential treatment unit with heroin-addicted males is included for its timeliness and to describe some of the communication conflicts that arise when a psychodramatic consultant is introduced into a drug treatment program.

Therapy began shortly after the formation of the twenty-bed unit, which offered carefully screened applicants long-range goals of occupational and social rehabilitation. The hospital had other programs to treat the addict: detoxification, methadone maintenance, a wide variety of other forms of therapy, and out-care clinics.

The therapeutic community as a mode of treatment for the narcotic addict was originated by Synanon in 1958. While not geared to returning the addict to the community, self-help management by ex-addicts and encounter therapy are accepted techniques for reaching the addictive personality. In many communities, the ex-addict directs groups and, in this role, is concerned with encouraging honest transactions in the here and now.[1] While the hospital unit was staffed with professionally trained therapists, psychiatrist, social worker, nurses, and others, the counselors were the chief facilitators of therapy and the connecting link between staff and community. The professional staff assisted in explaining the addict to himself.

Psychodrama was held once a week for two hours, ideally with all the staff present. The hospital was situated in the center of a predominantly black neighborhood that provided a flow of patients for treatment. The age range was from twenty to forty-three; over 70 percent were blacks. All were specifically addicted to heroin. They presented problems of general concern such as marriage, jobs, and sexual maladjustment, complicated by drug addiction. The majority, including the counselors, had had one or more offenses that led to prison; most of the patients had a history of delinquent behavior prior to drug use.

Social Roles and Normality

A characteristic of mental health, whether it is viewed as cooperation or as intimacy, is an attitude toward life that enables a person to develop a socially useful, satisfying existence; thus the person is able to seek alternate choices for his social problems.[2] His success is estimated by the number and kind of roles he has fulfilled and by the amount of flexibility he has used adjusting to his life situation. A person cannot take a role for which he lacks the necessary response patterns. When he attempts to take a role for which he lacks prior experience, the individual manifests an inadequate performance, even psychopathic behavior. This is characteristic of the addict personality. Reliance on a chemical starter hinders role development and eventually disrupts an individual's ability to fill the roles necessary for his participation in the life of the community. The spontaneity of the individual is insufficient to meet the complexities of the social situation. Psychological problems may be viewed, in this framework, as a decreased social sense and a lack of courage to undertake the responsibilities of social living, compounded by an increased feeling of inadequacy and discouragement in regard to making friends and achieving a satisfactory adjustment to work and marriage.

The Group

Grouping a number of individuals who have the common characteristic of drug abuse results in a session quite different from a meeting with an individual drug user or a treatment that integrates the addict into other psychiatric programs. Sociometric status on a drug treatment program is principally achieved by the hard-core addicts through being highly skilled in street survival techniques. The street addicts, by choosing each other and ignoring the staff, stimulate power struggles and defeat authority. A resourceful group leader will avoid reinforcement of the struggle with a variety of approaches that confront without stimulating rancor or revenge. Humor is often useful to offset the tension.

The addicts behave like an adolescent group, which of course they are not; they have physical and intellectual development, wide life experiences, and the expertise to survive in a subculture of crime and hostility. But, just as adolescents are uneasy and irritable in the presence of adults, so are drug users among nonusers. They prefer the company and advice of the addict group. The language of drug users, a special argot, reflects the distance and breakdown of communication between the drug world and the establishment. The special language and mumbling responses convey antisocial behavior and opposition to social conventions. The argot links one to another and removes the sense of isolation drug users feel that they interpret as pressure from the outside world.[3]

Another characteristic of drug-abuse groups is periodic disturbances of an antisocial nature. The role creativity of the addict is limited to the creation of drug-related (criminal) acts. This symptom is as effective in isolating the addict as the assaultive and abusive behavior of the schizophrenic. It accounts for the large turnover of staff as well as patients who can't tolerate this behavior and so leave the program. Support for this type of program persists because of the proven value of treatment *in situ*. The addict lives in this type of group, so the group is treated.[4]

Motivation for Treatment

Some addicts enter treatment because they are tired of their way of life, which is a continual struggle to get enough money for drugs. They are happy to wake up in the morning and not need a fix. But they find it difficult, even after physiological withdrawal, to stay away from the drug scene. Many patients recognize this but don't know how to change. Treatment must prepare the patient for the world outside and give him a new view of life, a new role. Some come to the program to recuperate physically and to have a place to stay. One spoke earnestly: "I went to the first program because my wife urged it; the second time, the court; but this time, I want it." This sounded sincere, but many in the group were suspicious and believed that the cost of the habit had become hard for him to handle and that he was using the hospital program to reduce his drug needs. Another spoke of the great attraction he felt for the drugs and especially for the beautiful people in the drug culture. But he feared the getting-no-place-fast aspect of this attraction.

Others come because they have been ordered by a court to undergo treatment. They personally may see no reason for it, since in many cases they feel (sometimes quite correctly) that if the world were less unfair, they would have no difficulties.

Paul, a white patient from a small western city, told of his attempt to stay away from drugs after his release from a rehabilitation center where he had been for eight months. "I moved away, far away from everyone I knew, to a small town so I wouldn't be tempted. I got a job at a factory, no sweat. The first day, I looked around. There he was. I knew he was on the stuff. I knew it the minute I saw him. Before the day was over, I was back on the scene."

Drug users vary in the intensity with which they warm up to the stimulus of drugs. This young man, like many others, repeated his old pattern. He became intensely aware of the availability of drugs and was completely unconscious of the other people around him. He forgot his eight months of hospitalization. He was not ready to drop the old role and produce a new one.

If a person has not developed person-to-person relationships, he is unlikely to be competent in role taking. Flexibility, a capacity to re-evaluate goals and shift viewpoints, is needed in order to deal success-fully with people and problems. Paul's estimate of the world after he left the hospital was polarized. He viewed all people as either users or nonusers. The known is always more attractive than the unknown, and this rigidity of thinking created the very problem he was unable to solve. He clung stubbornly to his old behavior and resisted change.

When interaction by some drug users with the environment in-volves a frustrating obstacle or challenge, they may attempt to amelio-rate the situation with drugs. The obstacle may be simply the usual problems of life. The drug user may also see an empty world, and he may feel too handicapped to tolerate it except as a deviant. His unique-ness and individuality are reinforced in the drug culture. Others exag-gerate their individuality and seek in the drug culture an unrealistic haven. Their idealism usually leads to disappointment. Idealism, then, justifies destruction of oneself and others. Drug taking becomes the accomplishment, a status symbol on the drug scene, and the horror of the rest of the community.[5]

David Laskowitz[6] points out that heroin provides oblivion and is usually associated with the ghetto addict. The violence of the environ-ment is internalized, and the opiate dulls the threatening feelings of rage. A patient describes it: "I'm a violent man, but when I'm high, I get along better with people." As with the alcoholic who feels successful when "high," the reality of failure is ever present.

The type of drug used depends on what the addict wants from the drug and is a clue to his personal striving. The effect of a drug involves more than the drug itself, for one's state of mind and other circumstances affect one's response to the drug. For example, many people who smoke marijuana expect a pleasant intoxication, with an intensification of visual images, sharpened emotionalism, and a stimulated sexual desire. These last for an hour or two and then the sedative effects lead to relaxation and sleep. One veteran reported reaching for a joint each time he had to do something tedious or demeaning—making deliveries; watching TV, which he hated; and going home to his wife, which he also found boring. He obliterated that task and the relationship by smoking marijuana.

Another patient reported a different effect of marijuana: "When I landed on Nam, the unit I reported to was a bunch of bastards. They tried to make up to me by giving me some joints and alcohol. It just intensified the terror. Everything I saw was dangerous—the leaves, trees. Enemies, that's all I saw." He found heroin as the answer to his persistent feelings of being in enemy country, both in Vietnam and in the ghetto.

At a therapy session, each participant was given an opportunity to show his first experience of taking drugs—alcohol, marijuana, LSD, or whatever. The following reasons were given as the original motivation: (1) to join in the fun; (2) to gain peer approval; (3) to impress others that he was a tough guy; (4) to substitute something else for alcohol which his girl friend hated; (5) to calm his nervousness; (6) to get with it, feel spaced out; (7) to find some excitement; (8) to satisfy curiosity.

Patients were reluctant to link the causative factors of experimentation to any early family experiences, that is, they did not say that they found in the peer group the security that seemed more attractive than that which the family provided. Lifestyle was an acceptable referent, but to them, lifestyle meant present behavior, without its relevance to early recollections or family transactions.

The first steps in working with the group were to establish a good working relationship with the staff and the consultant and to discuss the treatment method. This was begun before meeting with the patients. Salient events of the patients' behavior were discussed, and a general strategy to meet the situation and the techniques available were established. It was hoped that this core group would give more than lip service to the principles of equality and cooperation in running the session, for each contribution is potentially therapeutic. A loosely structured type of group psychodrama might free the patients from the usual resentment and anger about established authority—the group leader and the director.

Sometimes consultants spend time with the staff and work out the role conflicts away from the patients. In this case, however, the consultant decided to start immediately with the entire group, aided by the staff. This decision was based on what was felt to be the needs of the patients and the experience of the nursing staff, who had worked on a psychiatric unit and were comfortable as auxiliary egos. The four counselors (ex-addicts) were unfamiliar with psychodrama. Although superficially interested, they had other job priorities. They took turns attending the sessions until one finally elected to attend regularly. (While a high degree of staff participation is desirable, this goal is not always reached.) After each crisis in the group it became apparent that nonattendance was due less to a heavy schedule than to the counselors' failure to remain drug free. Nonattendance preceded leaving the program.

Acting Out

During the early sessions, with the support of the staff, some meaningful situations were developed, such as emotional attitudes toward bosses, girl friends, and difficulties encountered on a pass. There were one or two protagonist-centered sessions that explored the relationships surrounding the person. Then, members of the group began requesting sessions of job interviews, while others ridiculed the effort as not guaranteeing results, as being no magic method of job placement. Their interest was away from personality growth and toward jobs and whether or not they could hold them. The intense professional competition of the staff was reflected in the behavior of the patients. This situation climaxed with a staff meeting that revealed that the counselors were under pressure because they had promised jobs to the residents (patients) and the job placements were not being handled. This failure was being played up by three older addicts to make the program look ridiculous.

Any commitment a therapist makes can be used to defeat him. It may inspire an addict's declaration of war with society, expressed as: "Why are you in *this* shooting gallery when there's lots of bread on the street?" The conflict ended when the three patients were given administrative discharges. The staff decided not to offer more than the program could give, which was the potential for growth.

A New Group Structure

During the period after the discharges it became easier for patients to bring up situations depicting feelings of weakness and the accompanying anxiety. A group of five patients had been selected as counselors-in-training, which pleased the chosen ones and angered the unchosen. The group developed a new pattern of relationships. It had always excluded patients who were not heroin addicts, and without group support those patients would soon leave the community. The reshuffling disturbed one of the older members in the group, who said, "I don't belong anywhere in the group. I'm left out." An action sociogram verified his statement. The following sessions demonstrated the rivalry and how the anger was expressed.

Case One: An Undirected Warm-Up

Rick was a drug counselor-in-training. He was married and had children for whom he expressed love and concern. His wife kept him in constant turmoil with a battery of complaints that ended with a threat to leave him. In spite of this, he stayed away from heroin but turned to alcohol on the weekends he spent with his family. Unknown to the director at the time of the session, he was passed over for a job placement, perhaps to give him time to resolve his marital conflict. He sat down as the session began and started without reference to his disappointment:

RICK   I move we dismiss the group.

ART   Second it. I'm bored.

RICK   So am I.   *This is a symptom of withdrawal: a task that requires some future planning is potentially unsafe.*

AL   Let's stay. I like the meetings. If you're bored already, how are you going to make it on the street?

DIRECTOR   Rick, what are you running away from? A fight with one of us? Or a decision you have to make?

RICK	Do you get paid for coming here?	*He answers a question with a question, which distances him from the problem.*
DIRECTOR	Yes, I do. Why do you ask?	
RICK	Do you make a lot of money? I've been here for six months and I don't get anything out of it. Would you come here without pay?	
DIRECTOR	I don't think I would. But I also paid to learn. I still do. Am I the issue?	

Rick got up and left the group. His indirect anger, although self-defeating, blocked the movement of the session. He retained control by limiting the freedom of the group and the therapist. The community supported Rick's hostile withdrawal.

Case Two: The Counselor in a Catalyst Role

This session began in the presence of two new residents who had recently been admitted to the community. The director offered the time to the older members to continue working on the unfinished problems of the week before; they refused. Someone suggested that the new members be introduced to the community. Two counselors were present.

NEW PATIENT	I have a problem. But before I present it, can a decision be made here?
OLD PATIENT	No. This isn't a community meeting.
NEW PATIENT	Then I won't discuss it.
DIRECTOR	A good way for us to get to know you is through the problem—and perhaps we can shed some light on the problem.

NEW PATIENT	*(Glances at the counselor.)* Okay, let's go. I've been trying to get a pass to go to my church, to worship.	
DIRECTOR	What did you do to get the pass?	*The director wonders how he utilizes the therapeutic milieu.*
NEW PATIENT	Pressed everyone I could. Wrote letters, met with the counselor. You *(To the counselor)* are interfering with my constitutional right to worship at the place of my choice.	
COUNSELOR	You didn't mention wanting to go to church during the screening interview. Why not?	
OLD PATIENT	Does it have anything to do with your shoes? You were talking to me about some expensive shoes.	
NEW PATIENT	No, my rights are being violated. *(To the counselor.)* How do you handle this with others? I am a Buddhist and I must go to worship.	
COUNSELOR	We have no precedent for it. No one has raised this question before. But you made a contract during screening to stay two weeks without privileges. Now that you are on an open unit, you insist on going to church. What's your point?	

The patient quickly interpreted the refusal of privileges as a hostile attack directed at him, but the counselor's admission of its being a first request of its kind restored his feeling of self-esteem. He still wanted a special privilege, however, as a guarantee of his place in the group. If he gave in, he would be a nobody, a loser.

New Patient	It's a good thing you said that.	
Counselor	I know better than to hassle you.	
Director	How do you feel now?	*Director considers moving him into an enactment on the issue of anger.*
New Patient	How should I feel? Fine.	*It is difficult for him to become involved in a meaningful relationship.*
Director	I wondered if you felt angry.	
New Patient	I'm a nonviolent man. The last time I was angry was three months ago, when I was being pistol-whipped by this dude. I really got mad then. I managed to run away, but when I found him later, my partner and I broke his legs. I control myself. In my religion I make the choices. If a building gets bombed I make the decision to enter the building. That's what I'm taught and what I believe.	
Old Patient	I went to some of those meetings and had two weeks of bad luck.	*Without hostility the counselor is refusing to allow the addict to "make a deal," demonstrating that the rules are for his welfare as well as that of the community.*

NEW PATIENT	*(Turning to the director.)* Anything else?	
DIRECTOR	Yes, now you can deal with us. You told us something of the events in your life and your beliefs. What effect did you have on the group? Say how you think each one feels about you. Start with John—he'll tell you honestly how he was feeling—if you're right or wrong.	
NEW PATIENT	That can't be done! I don't know anyone well enough to know how he reacts to me.	*"I can't maintain my position on unfamiliar grounds."*
DIRECTOR	Yet we live each day on less information and feedback than you've gotten. Try guessing.	
SOCIAL WORKER	Start with the counselor. Does he like you?	
NEW PATIENT	All right. He likes me, thinks I'm intelligent and someone who stands up for his rights. How is that?	
COUNSELOR	I do like you—I like everyone in the community. I believe you but you bullshit. I'm a violent man and I know it. You talk a lot about control and use airtight situations to lay on violence. Sure, I like you. You're intelligent, too, but you bullshit.	
NEW PATIENT	You like everyone, so that's nothing special.	*He shows sensitivity to depreciation.*

DIRECTOR	Let's try John now.
SOCIAL WORKER	Before we go on, does bullshit mean lying? I think he was telling the truth.
COUNSELOR	Bullshit means to manipulate. He was trying to get something from us with a story calculated to get him what he wanted, a pass.

The new patient went along with the self-perception test and then stopped abruptly. The project had served its usefulness. He was the center of attention but became restless as he realized that the group recognized the behavior in him that they knew and disliked in themselves. He was a mirror of the manipulator and rule-maker residing in them.

The drug counselor is the authentic double of the addict, since he's walked more than a mile in his shoes. Walter O'Connell points out that a therapeutic community is constructed in this way or by walking hand-in-hand two miles with the addict.[7]

Case Three: Preference for Drugs over Therapy

The next session began with an empty chair placed in the center of the circle. The director invited anyone to take the "hot seat." Several members of the group began urging John to "run it." He slowly moved from his seat to the center. John was a young white addict from a well-to-do family and had avoided participation in any of the psychodramas. He never risked disclosures of a personal nature or feedback, except to ask, "What's the point?"

JOHN	Well, I don't want you to take it personally, but I don't like psychodrama. You're okay, but there's no sense to psychodrama. *(He trails off.)*	*John is unwilling to confront the director and wants to withdraw into his usual silent critical attitude, but the group wants to see if he can make the director angry.*

PAT	Run it like you did last night. Come on. You weren't so polite. Start running.
NURSE	She can take it. Let it out.
JOHN	I don't think you know anything. You come once a week and get our names wrong; you called Bob, Tom.
DIRECTOR	If anyone can play John by being his double (not alter ego) and get him to say what he isn't saying, go ahead. Is that okay with you, John?
JOHN	I'll say it. *(He will not risk the exposure of all he has said.)* You rush into the nurse's station, get a rundown on what's going on, drink three or four cups of coffee, smoke like a fiend, drop some words, and get paid. That's what I said. I get something out of the drug education classes, not from this.

DIRECTOR	Drugs are helpful. Therapy is not.	*Director sidesteps the personal attack but should have asked for a role reversal.*
JOHN	That's what I mean. You never say anything we didn't know already.	
DIRECTOR	I couldn't tell that from you; you never said anything before. You must be going through some changes.	

JOHN   You really don't make any
                sense. *(He leaves the chair.)*

DIRECTOR   What else do I do that you
                don't like?

The empty chair was then offered to anyone willing to take it. No one would, so John kept the role of the hero as some continued to blame and accuse the director of being highly paid for inefficiency. Before the session ended, the director was willing to accept part of the blame for mixing up the names, but not all of it. There was give and take between the group and the director, but not enough give from some of the group. It was agreed that they would decide in advance of the sessions what problem and person to work with. The psychodrama experience might then prove more effective.

Resistance to Switching Roles

The following session began with a replay of a fight between two white patients, John, the silent man from suburbia, and Frank, a new admission. Frank had been in other drug units, so he began to express his feelings aggressively as John slouched in his chair, not moving into the situation. Most sessions did not focus on encounters between the members of the community, but on their value systems.

FRANK   *(In the center and pointing to
                John.)* Man, I don't dig you.
                In fact, if I found you on the
                street, I'd avoid you. You're
                a snake, not to be trusted.

SOCIAL WORKER   What did he do that made
                you decide he's a snake?

FRANK   He doesn't have to do
                anything. I know. I have to
                know a snake when I see one;
                otherwise I'm dead.

JOHN   *(Remains quiet and averts
                his eyes.)*

FRANK	Where I come from, a white ghetto, I'm tough. I've been on the street all my life and you're a . . .
DIRECTOR	Is it because he comes from the suburbs? Will you switch roles with him? Walk around as John; put yourself . . .
FRANK	*(Breaks in.)* Oh, God, you don't know anything. I got a feeling and it's never wrong. It doesn't matter where he comes from. No, I don't have to switch. I know him.
SOCIAL WORKER	It might help John and clear up the fight issue.
FRANK	Shit on John. Listen, I was married a few days and I break into this store. A dude cops on me and I'm suspicious. He's a snake and when I find him, I tramp him. He got his, man! He's in prison!

The group was then asked for feedback, both to check Frank's rising hostility and to find out how he was influencing the group. (An antagonistic member who openly defies the goals of the community has an easy access to group cohesion which then is directed against the leader.) With quiet recognition of his savagery, the group agreed one by one that Frank knew how to live on the street. The counselor volunteered his reaction: "I see him as a hostile man. He's entitled to do as he pleases and he knocks out anyone who interferes. It sounds like he wants to stay that way. Drugs and violence, that's it. What a lifestyle!"

Discharges

The following weeks were spent in preparation for some members of the community to leave. John lost his case in court and was transferred to prison, Frank left, Rick was placed in a job, and other members also left with job assignments. The tension caused by members leaving the community was relieved with alcohol and the group's willingness to discuss the reasons for substituting one poison for another. One session began with the problem of drinking among the members and ended with a new member's admission of heroin injection on his first pass. His explanation of his misbehavior in "shooting up" was an interesting example of the way in which drugs suspend self-criticism and destroy close relationships. The group was able to separate the new man's drug dependence from his perception of his wife's misbehavior, the neurotic transaction of "It's your fault I shot up."

J. W. had been married for three years to a hard-working woman who, according to J. W., the patient, didn't drink, take dope, or cheat on him. She arrived at the hospital to pick him up for a weekend pass after his three weeks without privileges. His speech and logic were disorganized as he attempted to role play the scene.

J. W. (as wife)	You don't look so good. Do you want something?
J. W. (as self)	No, I'm all right. (Aside.) I lied—I did want something, but I didn't want to take it. You see, she's a square and doesn't understand.
J. W. (as wife)	Well, you don't look right. I thought maybe you wanted something.

Later on in the evening J. W. and his wife went to a bar. He bought a half pint, and she said, "I don't want you to be without money— here's thirty dollars." J. W. left the bar and got a fix.

Pat	You need a new wife. She wants a passive man.
J. W.	You don't understand. It was three weeks since we were together, and I can't make love when I don't have drugs. She wanted me to feel good so I'd be able to stand up for her. She wanted me to be nice to her. That's the way I am.

PAT   We need your wife here.
She's dumb. My wife would
never give me money to get
into bed or anything. Did
she tell you that?

J. W.   No, but I knew it. She
wouldn't fool with another
man.

This brought the discussion to the effects of heroin on each of them. All agreed that lovemaking is the last thing you think of when "you've got the Jones on your back" (a craving for heroin), but each had a different reaction to heroin; some used it as a stimulant to sexual activity and others in place of it. Then, following the director's example, several patients played J. W. waiting for his wife, telling in soliloquy how uncomfortable he began to feel when he thought of his sexual responsibility, how he needed a fortifier to meet it. It was his fear of sexual failure rather than her need for him that mobilized his drug hunger. The session may not have provided J. W. an insight into his behavior, but the group arrived at a dynamic understanding of behavior expressed as "You must have put on a good show for her to ask, 'Do you need something?' " Even in role playing, J. W. demonstrated that the technique he used to cope with the interpersonal aspects of a situation was manipulating others by increased sadness, pain, and suffering; even more insidious was his cognitive style, with its self-centeredness, rigidity, and stereotypic responses, which proved inadequate to meet life situations.

Summary of Adult Drug Program

It is too soon to evaluate the overall effect of psychodrama in the drug program, but it has produced many positive results. The interaction of the professional staff with the ex-addict counselors was perhaps the experience of greatest value. If these two groups understand each other, the controversial question of who shall treat the addictive personality may not be raised; it will be understood that each supports the other, that the alliance is as necessary to the ex-addict (who often is thrown into a program before he has had a chance to separate himself from drugs) as to the staff, who have a difficult time in establishing a relationship to the drug community.

Communication is a social exchange based on cooperative action.

Psychodrama is a challenge to cooperation, and is viewed at times with distrust and disdain when it fails to move in the direction of clarification. But its value lies in its ability to awaken the addict to the practical issues of his life. This may be done in a minidrama (a short interaction of day-to-day living), by self-perception exercises, or by breaking the group into small triangles so that the warm-up is carried out by the patients.

A therapeutic community is made, not born, and the outside consultant is able to measure the changes taking place in the encounter of the director, the counselor, and the group. He may be met with reticence, defiance, suspicion, or trust, as the group moves slowly toward social integration. The psychodrama helps the patient see how the drama is his; he can rewrite the script when he sees the possibility of living something other than a tragedy.

Adolescent Drug Experimentation

A group on a private hospital ward included three boys and a girl in their late adolescence, all of whom had been experimenting with an assortment of drugs—hallucinogens, marijuana, amphetamines, barbiturates. One session was organized around the girl, Debbie. The other patients forming the group were of the usual type to be found on a closed psychiatric unit and ranged in age from late adolescence to middle age. In the prepsychodrama period with the staff, the four teenagers were discussed, in particular their lack of motivation to participate in the therapeutic programs on the unit. This adolescent drug group defined their hospital stay as a happy holiday and made few responses during the warm-up interview. It seemed that the young boys were inadequate to discuss (or were afraid of) the aspects of the patient role that hospitalization signified. Their resistance to taking the therapeutic setting seriously was a manifestation of the behavioral difficulty that brought them to therapy. Distrust covered with superficiality was a defense against disappointment. Continued distrust prevented them from using the therapeutic resources of the unit.

This kind of negative attitude sometimes can be reversed through an intercessor, one patient who warms up to the session positively by willingly cooperating with the director (even though this attitude may be a part of a mistaken attitude toward life—to cooperate in order to show life's futility).

When Debbie entered the unit, she didn't walk, she ran, and she jumped over chairs rather than go around them. This behavior, along with the fact that she had taken an overdose, was checked against the nurses' observation that her behavior showed more adolescent spirit than uncontrollable excitement. This was, indeed, the case. She quickly organized herself as a responding ego to the director's question, "Do you have a problem you'd like to work on?" She sat cross-legged on the floor in the middle of the group and said, "I've never done this psychodrama before. Where do I begin?"

Choosing the people to enact the roles necessary to portray the problem was left to Debbie. She selected one of the boys to help act out a telephone conversation that she had just received. He turned his back to show the lack of eye contact during this type of communication.

DEBBIE	I'm glad you called back. I thought maybe you wouldn't.
BOY	I always do what I say. How about it? Have you thought about moving in with me?
DEBBIE	You don't know me, never even saw me. Why do you want me to live with you?
BOY	I'd like to get into you. Your voice sounds good.
DEBBIE	He didn't say that. (*They reverse roles.*) I want to help you. What are you in the hospital for?
BOY (*as Debbie*)	Drugs, an overdose.
DEBBIE (*as the boy*)	That's a hard one to get over, but I did. Maybe I can help you. Oh, well, we can try it.
DEBBIE (*as self*)	Call me later. Someone wants the phone. (*To the group.*) I don't know if I should move in with him. I don't want to get hurt again, but I have no place to go except to my old boyfriend. (*This is an appeal to the group as she considers his offer.*)

A double joined Debbie, and the truth came out that she couldn't go back to her parents; they didn't want her. She'd go to her old boyfriend if he'd ask her. The next scene between the old boyfriend and Debbie grew out of this clue and was the presentation of the problem. The scene as she began to describe it was so familiar to the young boys that they formed themselves into a tight circle on the floor. But she corrected them: "The friends don't come in until the evening."

Debbie selected someone to play her boyfriend, a twenty-year-old who sits around the apartment (it's his) as she cooks and cleans and stays out of his way. There is little interaction between them except on the subject of money and how to get some. She is anxious to be helpful about money, too, and steals whenever she feels she must. At night a group of friends drop in and encircle her boyfriend, and she is left out. He talks only to them, not to her; she sits on the outside of the group, but serves beer as the group smokes marijuana and talks about drugs and music. She curls up on the outside of the circle, covers her face with her hands, and quietly begins to cry. She notices that one of the girls is on her boyfriend's lap. She brings him a beer, and the girl slips off. Debbie rushes into the bedroom and cries uncontrollably. The young boy patient who is playing the boyfriend—with insight that came from his own experience—goes to her (after the friends leave) and consoles her with a couple of pills, the way a parent gives a bottle to a crying baby. The police arrive, and she is charged with stealing. She swallows more pills and ends up in the hospital.

A situation from Debbie's family life followed. The similarity of Debbie's enactment to the theme of Cinderella—doing all the dirty work for others, but without a fairy godmother to save her from her misery—aroused the staff and patient group to help her face, not the invitation of a new rescue agent or the old boyfriend, but a long-term treatment center as an alternative to a prison term. What did Debbie get out of being with her boyfriend? "Sexual responsiveness," she said. "I had a sexual hang-up before we had the nights together."

The period ended with a discussion. The boys pronounced Debbie "stupid," a term commonly used by drug users and meaning that the person has put forth effort to have a good time and has failed to do so. The decision to find excitement in the flow of images of LSD and an enjoyable experience of marijuana is not stupid, but the tactics that lead to disaster are. Each feels that the fun of the drug experience can be had without untoward consequences. For some this is true, if they are smart enough to manage it. So the term "stupid" refers in this case to Debbie's role relationship, not to drugs but to her boyfriend. The message is: Don't blame drugs if you are messed up.

A psychotic woman looked sympathetically toward Debbie and, holding her hands against her face, mumbled, "You're so young to be grappling with the problems of adults. You are only a child, but you seemed to enjoy playing house—cleaning, washing, and cooking—a real little housewife." This was an accurate observation, since housework to Debbie was fulfilling. At the end of the session, one of the teenage boys requested that he be placed on the carpet at the following meeting.

Interest in therapy picked up when the interest level of the young patients was met.[8] Inattentiveness is a form of opposition. One good reason for working with many patients in a group is that it helps overcome this resistance. Debbie is now in a drug treatment center.

Role Confusion

Children nearing adolescence can be expected to experience role confusion as they enter a new phase of the life cycle. They feel powers that until now have been dormant. Children who are brought up to believe that doing what they want is more important than the consequences of their acts become models of misbehavior. Their lack of social feeling comes clearly into focus.

When an adolescent suffers a great amount of role confusion, he may participate in the drug scene, in criminal activity, and/or in other destructive acts. Such behavior indicates serious distortions of attitudes toward the community and may include reckless driving, drug overdoses, sexual promiscuity, and homosexuality.[9] Girls at this stage are seriously vulnerable if they have felt themselves to be slighted at home. They become susceptible to the attentions and flattery of others and can only believe that they are of value when they are receiving this attention, especially from men. Adler points out that many are completely hypnotized by this craving for appreciation.[10]

Debbie is a case in point. Her slavish subordination to her boyfriend in order to feel her worth made it difficult, if not impossible, to find a satisfactory relationship. The sex role was separated from the other roles in the way in which human values were expressed.

Disintegrative Influence

An approach that is similar to the action sociogram of the family, and that shows the role relationships in a drug group, maps in action the roles that this drug community expects of its members. The challenge of role development is not felt by this group because of their low social concern. The group values of the normal, psychiatric, and criminal groups are expressed or implied in a series of rules that achieve the purpose of the group—whether it is toward societal aims or antisocietal goals. *The rules are developed as roles* and give the group direction. The patient's role is constricted by the expectation of the membership rules in the group and his private goal of success or failure.

In another session, Ken, a seventeen-year-old dropout, became the center of the group's attention. He had been sent to the unit following an arrest for reckless driving while high on drugs. He arranged a group of four auxiliary egos who were stand-ins for his circle of friends —three boys and a girl. The girl was his lover. He wasn't certain of what to call her, for he felt that she was more than a sexual mate, a love mate. The boys were a twenty-year-old pusher and his flunky, and an unemployed musician. As Ken reversed roles with members of this group, he had to prove to them that he was a man, a quiet, smart man. Suspicious evaluation of "the other" became his modus operandi except in the case of the girl, for whom he seemed to have a genuine regard. This became even more apparent as he reversed roles with the members of his family group. The same contempt was readily seen as he acted the family members: an older brother who was a drug addict, and a father who was distressed about his sons. This arrogance is often seen in children who have been excessively pampered. They regard others as inferiors, as servants.

There was, in one session, a quick realization by the director that the distrust and movement to outsmart others included the therapist. This would make Ken's getting his head together long and difficult. The diagnosis, in this case, was simple; the treatment would be harder.

A Final Word on Adolescent Drug Users

The adolescent drug culture is part and parcel of the social scene both in America and abroad. It is a frightening development not only for the parents but for all concerned adults. Many adolescents who are into drugs are using them as a plea for help. Masserman says, "Try to understand the nature of the patient's desires and tribulations, the deviant way he tries to deal with them; and the relative accessibility of these patterns to therapeutic influences."[11] Successful work with adolescent drug users depends on helping the patient to build a good relationship with at least one member in his family or with a substitute.

Dr. Jordan Scher, executive director of the National Council on Drug Abuse, writes: "My own experience has been that, for the most part, American youngsters have escaped serious involvement with drug abuse. And of the 25 to 40 million who have tried marijuana only 20 percent went on to psychedelics, 20 percent of these went on to amphetamines and barbiturates, and 20 percent of these went on to heroin and other narcotics. Thus the actual number involved at the bottom of the spiral is small by comparison with those at the top. Furthermore, it has been my experience that most of those who experimented with drugs, and did not advance to the more serious stages, tended to have a two to five year period of mild to intensive involvement, prior to a return to the more usual virtues, vices, and bad habits of the rest of us. With this in mind, for most youngsters the picture, at best, is not necessarily so depressing and disturbing as one might be led to believe."[12]

16

Training for Psychodrama on the Psychiatric Ward

Psychodrama is one of the few forms of group therapy that can accommodate a large number of people and still be of therapeutic value. This chapter will show the procedures used in introducing psychodrama and sociometry to the patients and staff of a large state hospital. The members of the psychiatric staff were not interested in becoming psychodramatic directors, but once the initial hurdles of exposure and of acquiring trust in each other were over, they were able to profit from a fuller knowledge of the group method. The director believed that those who were qualified and who showed interest in directing a group could be given additional training, perhaps using their talent and skills on other wards of the hospital.[1]

A Group of Strangers

The psychiatric ward is a community of individuals facing everyday problems of working, living, and playing together. The patients know one another, at least marginally, and continue to be together for a period of time, in some cases for years. This population requires a special alertness to its problems and understanding of such symptoms as auditory hallucinations and delusions. It is important to know not only the role each individual plays as a patient to another patient, or as a patient to the staff, but the purpose of a particular interaction. The purpose behind the behavior is a clue to the basic overall pattern of motivation.

The hospitalized patient frequently has cut the lines of communication by inventing a language. Unless the staff that works with this patient learns to translate the language—both the words and the expressive behavior—they cannot succeed in therapy. Techniques of an action therapy like psychodrama help the patient portray his problem and show the patient a way to establish contact with another human being, a way into the group.

While the general format of working with hospitalized patients is the same as one would use with people outside the hospital, a warm-up to a personal enactment, with interaction and audience reaction, the means (techniques) used are to form a relationship to the patient, to confront a patient with his aberrant behavior, and to encourage socially acceptable activity. Hospitalized patients seem to have given up on problem solving and to feel more alienated from people than those outside the hospital. Patients with psychoses have little tolerance for closeness and emotional interaction; therefore, the director's technique has to be directive and supporting. Goals are specific: to discuss realistic problems, to help the patient become friendly with the group members, and to discourage exaggerated patterns of behavior.

The Unique Climate

To establish a social climate conducive to rehabilitation, a wide variety of people must meet and work cooperatively with each other. Rudolf Dreikurs described the social climate of a therapy group in this way: "The most outstanding aspect seems to be the fact that in this group each member has his place regardless of his personal qualities, his deficiencies and assets. Nowhere else is this true in our society. In any other field of action, the individual is constantly judged according to his abilities and deficiencies, his accomplishments and his mistakes. Not so here. One may say that the values which make him a person higher or lower anywhere else in society are discarded here. But no group can exist without definite values."[2]

The values of a therapeutic milieu may be summarized as: (1) attending group meetings regularly (showing interest and concern); (2) revealing oneself as one really is, without pretense; and (3) discovering value in others. These values give the patient an opportunity to be directly affected as soon as he feels recognized as a fellow human being. Most likely, many of his previous contacts made him feel something less than others because he did not measure up to the value system.

Psychodrama provides each ward with a physical setting and a way to understand and treat the patients as people of equal worth, to offer them either individual or group treatment. The patients need the staff as auxiliary agents to help them develop skills in living. The staff usually must undergo a change in attitude to discharge their functions in a democratic rather than an authoritarian manner. "As the patients become persons instead of objects, the staff members become persons instead of functionaries."[3]

Staff members often do not appreciate the value of psychodrama as a treatment method, so a demonstration may be necessary. Merely verbalizing the value of group participation is not enough. Also, the staff needs to practice handling typical and unusual conflicts or ward problems in order to develop new attitudes toward the patients and to feel comfortable in the management of a group.

Introducing a Psychodrama Program

Successful psychodramatic programs in many hospitals begin with the full support of at least one influential member of the hospital staff.[4] A psychodramatist may be invited to direct a series of daylong workshops, usually six consecutive meetings, to which representatives of all the psychiatric services of the hospital are invited. The first meetings may take this general form: The morning session deals with some of the theoretical and practical problems of forming groups. Mutual introductions are made, and acquaintance testing is done, all for the purpose of enabling the staff members to get to know one another. It is expected that a few persons will form a core of individuals who will be responsible for the psychodrama program. The afternoon is devoted to demonstrating with patients in front of the staff audience.

In subsequent meetings, team leaders are chosen, and the sessions are moved to the ward. Later, the psychodramatist may spend a full day on each visit working with each group as director, and the trainees become the auxiliary therapists. The program can be maintained with a monthly visit or meeting when the psychodrama consultant lives out of town; however, a weekly visit is more effective.

The First Meeting

At the first meeting with the staff, the psychodrama consultant introduces role playing and sociometric techniques and tries to provide a significant group experience for the ward personnel and patients. The purpose, of course, is to persuade the staff to accept psychodrama as a treatment method and to show that this action technique can improve the communication network of the hospital. Attendance at this meeting may be high.

The major problem facing the psychodrama consultant is to get from the group a free, spontaneous, feeling reaction to the program. This can be done sociometrically. In one such session I invited each person to get up, look around, and move toward someone in the group he thought shared his attitude toward participation in the psychodrama. Using this procedure, the consultant found it possible to show that there were networks of information and a pattern of inter-action that exerted an influence on the development of this group. The acquaintance-action diagram broke the group into small and large clusters of people, making it a simple matter to get each subject in the mood to role play the way he was invited to the meeting and to say aloud in a soliloquy the thoughts that he had about psychodrama. Here is an example:

SUPERINTENDENT   Did you find a consultant in psychodrama who would be available to come here?

PSYCHOLOGIST   Yes, I did. We are negotiating, setting up time and deciding on payment.

DIRECTOR   Now, turn your heads away from each other and say what you are thinking but not saying to each other.

SUPERINTENDENT   He'd better get with it while I still can fit it into the budget. I wonder if he's stalling, dragging his feet, because he's not too interested in this type of program.

PSYCHOLOGIST   I'm not sure whether to rush in and produce this program or wait until another brainstorm hits him. He gets flashes and crushes on all sorts of approaches. I'm interested, but is he?

The audience laughed and enjoyed the good-natured ribbing. The next group to role play were six staff members from the adolescent unit. This group followed the role-playing instructions more closely. The head of the unit, a social worker, announced at the end of a staff meeting, "You won't believe it, but we are going to have a psychodrama seminar." The reaction was positive. During the soliloquy the members expressed concern, first about how difficult it would be to learn, second about the best size group to work with, and finally about the competitive aspects: "I wonder if I will be selected as a leader."

The nursing supervisor had attracted a large group who had moved toward him as a person who was against the program, even though they knew he had tried to get a group therapy program going and had failed. The reactions in this group varied from slight reluctance to getting involved to a definite stand against it. They believed psychodrama was too much work, that it would fuzz up the climate and make management of the patients difficult. The director resisted the temptation to stop with this group and go more intensively into the negative attitudes being expressed toward therapeutic engagement with patients. Up to this point, the members of the staff had been getting acquainted with each other and the director in an important aspect of the work situation. It was not the time to abort the process. It was important to continue role playing with the other groups.

The director made a positive comment on the frankness of the group and encouraged the rest of the members to speak up with equal openness: "This illustrates an individual's behavior in a group setting, and we are seeing in a psychodramatic method the way private thoughts and feelings are brought out in a soliloquy."

When the last group had finished role playing and expressing themselves in soliloquy, they were asked to illustrate another pattern of interaction in the group through a self-perception test. "Now, let's use this group and begin with you. How do you think this person [pointing to a member of the group] feels about you since you have declared yourself 'neutral' about this project?"

FRANK	She thinks I'm lazy—too lazy to take a stand.
DIRECTOR	And what does Harold think?
FRANK	He thinks I've latched on to a good attitude. Don't stick your head above the crowd and nothing terrible can happen. Is that enough?

DIRECTC   Yes, thank you. Is it evident
to everyone that a person
has some definite ideas of
how other people react to his
attitudes and that this
becomes part of everyone's
behavior in a group?

The director summarized the results of the sociometric rating of the psychodrama program by pointing out the attraction-repulsion pattern, but, by a happy circumstance, the core of the negative feeling was diluted by the prior interest of the nursing supervisor (an influential figure) in group therapy. The director pointed out the value of this kind of information and suggested that simple diagnostic tests, like the ones the group had just experienced, could be helpful in eliciting patients' problems and their relationships to hospital personnel.

The Afternoon Session

During the afternoon session, which was devoted to demonstrations, a group of adolescents sat in a semicircle as a front row of the audience. The director faced the group and began: "The objective of a demonstration with a patient group is to present the staff with the experience of observing patient interaction in a psychodrama; this means to study the enactment of a patient's relationship to important people who may be absent from the group—a brother, a sister, a mother— and become acquainted with these people in an intimate way through the eyes of the patient. The patient group gains from having the audience here, for the information they get from the audience helps them understand themselves and others and make plans for a return to the community. Now, even in a demonstration, the audience can join in spontaneously. There should be no separation between us. The relationship of a patient group and a staff audience is shown in the performance that warms each up to the other and to the issues. The audience not only shares but contributes to it by its presence. The audience will be expected to participate in the discussion that will close the psychodrama."

The director turned to the patient group and asked, "Will you help me give this demonstration?" He pointed to one of the young boys and continued, "Come up and let's begin by visiting together." After some giggling from the adolescent group, the boy came up.

JIM	What do you want to know?
DIRECTOR	I want to get to know you, but let's wait with the questions. Will you look out over the audience and choose someone you'd like to talk to? After all, I chose you.
JIM	Anybody? You really mean anybody? Okay, her. (*He points to a staff member.*)
DIRECTOR	Will you come up and visit with Jim? Then you can choose someone you'd like to visit with. Jim, while she's on her way up here, why did you select her?
JIM	I've never seen her roaming around here and I wondered.

The choosing and the visiting led to a personal problem that was enacted with the auxiliary egos selected from the whole group. In the final discussion that closed the psychodramatic session the group was asked to answer these questions: (1) What happened here to help you understand yourself better? (2) What situation had special meaning for you? (3) What person helped you the most to reach a satisfactory understanding of the problem?

In subsequent sessions the staff members were given the opportunity to have a wide variety of interaction experiences with other staff members.

Didactic Psychodrama with Staff

The staff audience may be invited to draw on their own experiences and role play experiences with patients. Typical of situations enacted by the staff are:
1. Getting a psychotic patient off the floor.
2. Coping with the restless agitation of a new patient.

3. Dealing with a patient's profanity and sexual overtures.

At the first meetings, the ward personnel deal primarily with staff-patient relationships. It is helpful to the staff, who are cautious both in tackling a new method and in showing "clumsy" tactics with patients, for the patients not to be present at these first sessions. As a further face-saving device, it is best to put the nurse-with-a-problem into the role of the difficult patient, with another staff member improvising the response (as one has to in the real situation). Reversing roles, then, becomes a safe way to show what actually happened or to try a different approach.

After the interaction between the two, the staff audience is encouraged to describe the behavior of the patient as played by the nurse and the auxiliary ego. What feelings does the patient (as played by the nurse) show? What response did they produce? Some possible feelings may be itemized as:

antagonism	friendliness
panic	self-possession
disorganization	control
puzzlement	certainty
playfulness	seriousness
sexual teasing	politeness
suspicion	trust
embarrassment	boldness
stubbornness	compliance
fearfulness	courage

The group evaluates the action *not as good or bad* but as recognizable, realistic, or unusual. A good question to ask is, "Did anything happen in the interaction that surprised anyone in the audience?"

Restraining Phase

It is helpful to draw the observers into an action situation. The director may say, "We would like to show the difference between the 'common' sense we share with people outside the hospital and our not being able to be sure what a psychiatric patient means when he refuses to comply with a request to eat, bathe, talk, or take medication. It is easy to understand and be either angry or not angry when a family member or a friend acts in this way." Then the director can ask the group to enact a circumstance that might occur both at home and at a general hospital with a patient and compare behavioristic responses.

"Immediate purposes in interpersonal situations," writes Bernard Shulman, "are usually movements in regard to the therapist. The patient may be trying to move away from the therapist, to move toward him, to depreciate him, to discourage him, to outmaneuver him, to enlist his help, to obscure the issue, to win him as an ally, to prove the therapist cannot help him, to stop communication, to get approval, to poke fun, to impress, to assess his power or wisdom, etc."[5] Role playing and psychodrama are excellent means to recognizing the private significance of the patient's behavior.

Specific Cases

The nursing staff needs to develop skills to respond to immediate problems in a constructive way. Many of the staff personnel feel at a loss when a patient displays bizarre behavior, thinking disturbances, or erotic and aggressive expression. The psychosis has meaning for the patient, and it is a major training task to help the staff understand the indirect messages of the behavior. Frequently the staff have a tendency to overlook the disturbance because they do not know what to do.

Quite often, on a ward, a patient's behavior is withdrawn, with little or barely visible response to outside activities; spontaneity is low: and the role pathology may be that of a corpse.

Bertha was a heavy woman who had stretched out on the floor one day and announced her death. It was not inconsistent with her role of a corpse to get up off the floor for meals or to roll over to ask for cigarettes; at other times she lay face down, arms drawn around her head, deaf to the social demands of the ward routine. Her decision to move against the order of living took an extreme form; the patients and staff walked around her, for they were met with violent resistance each time they tried to move her. The more the staff and patients pointed out the inconsistencies of Bertha's behavior, the tighter became the arms circling her head, and the angrier the staff became with her. "She's feigning; she's putting us on. She knows she's not dead; she comes to life when she wants."

What message was the patient's behavior sending to the staff? It was not easy to fit it into a single category. If she wanted to be left alone, why did she stretch out in the middle of the dayroom? Also, the amount of anger the staff felt approximated the amount of defiance the patient felt.

It is a waste of time to tell a corpse what to do or to argue the point of being dead since a corpse is accountable only to God. To persuade the staff to this attitude it seemed timely to tell them the story of another patient who thought he was a corpse. The psychologist (so Harold Mosak tells the story) who had this patient in treatment asked, in an effort to have him admit being alive, "Does a dead man bleed?" No, said the patient, a corpse does not bleed. Forthwith the psychologist pricked him with a needle and drew some blood. The patient remarked, "It proves that this corpse bleeds."[6] The staff relaxed and laughed; they felt that the director understood the type of patient they were supposed to help.

A nurse was invited to begin with the expression "I wish I were dead," and throw herself on the floor and feel "dead." It was hoped that by having the nurse assume the patient's posture, she could empathically communicate with the patient. The rest of the staff was asked to show the many attempts they had made to interact with Bertha. Some of their remarks were hostile; others were timid, as if directness would crush the weak ego of the patient. (Often a statement showing understanding of the motivation for behavior is an encouragement to the patient and is useful for drawing him into a relationship.)

As the nurse was stretched out on the floor, she was directed to review, as if she were Bertha, what was known of Bertha prior to hospitalization. She spoke as in a dream reverie: "I worked hard at that factory for years with a lot of raises. Why did they hire that bitch and put her ahead of me? I'm gaining weight—ten, twenty, thirty pounds. I don't understand what's happening. I'm fat, ugly, and mean. I knocked the bitch around the floor. She deserved it, but I'm a goner. I'm not me. They jumped me and sat on me, pinned me to the floor. Then they fired me. I'm a goner."

The nurse began to capture the rage and hopelessness of the patient. A nurse approached the prone Bertha, saying, "I'm sorry you feel dead. You must think the world doesn't need you anymore. Well, we do, to help with Agnes [an elderly cripple who needed to be helped at meals]. Can you help her get to the table?"

Within a week, the real Bertha responded to this approach. She jumped up at mealtime, clutched at Agnes, and began to be her helping ego. A few months later, Bertha was able to talk about her "death" in a matter-of-fact way: "I really thought I was dead." She never referred to what brought her back to life; she said only that a sudden weight gain was a signal that she was getting sick and that she would diet to avert her psychosis.

Another type of patient that often puzzles a nursing staff is the new patient who is disorganized and in a panic as he enters the unit. An aide who expressed discomfort with this kind of patient was asked to form a mental image of a specific person, to be a particular patient. She began warming up: "I'm fortyish, well dressed." She paused. Then she said, "Oh, God [wringing her hands and rushing about], they were all killed. My husband is dead. My sons, one by one, are dead. I'm alone." She repeated this with tears and wailing. "The tragedy is too much. Oh, God, let me join them."

Then the aide dropped the role and said, "I don't know what to do; she just keeps repeating it over and over."

One of the nurses in the group went to the aide-playing-the-patient. "Mrs. F., I can see you are feeling deserted. But your husband and son brought you to the unit last night and, as they left, I explained that we don't allow phone or visiting privileges. That's why you aren't hearing from them. You'll hear from them as soon as your doctor thinks you are ready for visitors. Let me show you what happened last night." With the help of several patients, Mrs. F.'s arrival on the ward and her family's departure were reenacted. The aide-playing-the-patient felt comforted. As a staff member, she needed sufficient information and a way to use the information to respond adequately to the patient.

The staff is shown through psychodrama how to encourage patients, how to reduce the misery of being locked up, how to stand as helping egos. A staff member sometimes finds a clue when he tries out the body position of the patient; this conveys messages that otherwise may not be understood. When a difficult patient is known to the staff, it is helpful to enact all the encounters the staff has had with him. This may lead to the discovery of the conditions or terms under which he will relate.[7]

The sessions end with suggestions for new approaches to a patient. The nurse who is embarrassed by a male patient who asks "Will you marry me?" and then walks away muttering obscenities is helped to look at the movement as an awkward gesture of reaching out, which he quickly withdraws. When the nurse's anxiety is lessened, she is able to manage the situation comfortably and to respond to the private meaning of his behavior ("I have time to talk to you now, if you'd like to stay."), and to discourage the obscenities by examining with the patient the purpose they serve ("Your cussing makes it hard to talk to you, but go ahead if it makes you feel better. Sometimes a person expresses unpleasant feelings in this way. What's bothering you?").

Subsequent sessions usually begin with an informal discussion in which the director summarizes the techniques introduced at the previous meeting. The staff is encouraged to relate how they felt doing psychodrama. How effectively had the patients been managed who had been the subject of the past week's work? It is important to verify the results, to note what activities helped in understanding the patient, and which ones fell short of the mark. As a rule, groups feel it to be a stimulating and helpful experience to review the level of responsiveness of both the patients and the staff. As the discussion develops, the staff is encouraged to show what has happened to make them feel impatient or angry with a patient. Auxiliary egos are selected from the group, and the scene is enacted, almost as in a typical psychodrama session. More interruptions and discussion periods may occur as a bit of behavior strikes a familiar chord in someone in the group. Impressions of patients are exchanged in order to increase understanding of their behavior and the behavior of the staff.

The patient discussed in one session was a young man of twenty, named Harold, who was recovering from an episode of being mute. He was willing to talk to the staff and other patients in a limited fashion, answering questions and responding nonverbally to requests for help in putting things in the dayroom in order. Both he and the staff felt he had become considerably better.

The nurse was asked to place an empty chair in the center of the room and introduce Harold to the group. The nurse, pointing to the empty chair, began talking: "This is Harold, who has had three years of college, a mathematics major. He came to this ward after two months of being hospitalized in an acute catatonic state. His behavior is showing considerable improvement." The nurse took a seat in the empty chair and became the patient, Harold. She held her body in an upright position. She focused her eyes away from the group and did not allow them to follow the movements of others. The rest of the staff were asked to acknowledge "Harold" (played by the nurse) by walking up to him and commenting on how his behavior made them feel. One member accused him of being negative; another commented on his being cooperative; still another found him sensitive to the isolative needs of other patients. "Remember," she said, "when Thea didn't want to participate, you responded in the go-around by saying that you thought we should respect her privacy." The feedback ended with the conclusion, as pointed out earlier, that "all actions and events have communicative aspects as soon as they are perceived by a human being."[8] The nurse reported that she felt she understood Harold better for having followed this procedure and could appreciate momentarily the significance of his withdrawal.

The problem of Harold is then presented in psychodrama. The scene opens as he is being approached by the nurse.

NURSE	Harold, we need you for a game of Monopoly. How about it?
HAROLD	Sure.
NURSE	Let's set the game up here. (*He complies.*)
HAROLD	(*After the game gets started.*) I'm not going to my sister's for Thanksgiving.
NURSE	Why?
HAROLD	My mother will be there.
NURSE	Are you angry at your mother?
HAROLD	I'll kill my mother if I see her!

The nurse must make a judgment about the patient's readiness to face her anxiety. She seemed not to know what to do with the patient's hostility. It came as a bolt out of the blue. The director requested an aside, to check the hidden thoughts and feelings of the nurse. Often she is expected to cover up her feelings as she talks to a patient, but now she can safely react to the remark.

NURSE	(*In an aside.*) Still water runs deep. I wonder what to do with this? I thought you were getting better, and now you come up with this crazy talk. Or maybe it's not crazy. Maybe his mother did something horrible to him. I'll check it out. (*To Harold.*) Why are you so angry with your mother? Does she give you a hard time?
HAROLD	She killed my father.

NURSE	That's a horrible thought. How did your father die?	
HAROLD	Of emphysema and heart trouble.	
NURSE	Well, Harold, you know that heart disease is America's number one killer.	*She is thinking, "I'm back to my original thought—it's a crazy idea."*
HAROLD	But she could have stopped him from smoking, and she didn't. She made him smoke more!	
NURSE	I guess it's a good idea for you to stay away from your mother until you can forgive her for not being able to stop your father from smoking. (*To the group of nurses.*) Did I handle it all right? I'm worried about him.	

The importance of the psychiatric staff was pointed out in this management of the patient. Because the staff and patients spend so much time together, relationships naturally develop, even with those patients who are not easily reached. It was explained that the nurse was experiencing the other side of the coin. Harold's mute period no doubt concealed his hostile feelings, but as he began to talk, his anger was there to be understood, either as something he wanted to be rid of or as something to have and to hold. Everyone agreed that the nurse had kept the door of communication open; she did not argue with Harold's conclusion about his mother's culpability, but she did not agree with it. Instead, she supported his decision about staying away from his mother because of his angry feelings. She was able to find an area of agreement and work with it.

Another approach is to have staff members interact with patients. In role reversal they may find a new perception of each other. The staff experiences the role of a patient, and the patients learn the social role of the staff.

The results of psychodrama training programs indicate that hospital personnel can be drawn into a therapeutic service and profit from it. Success, however, depends on a sustained program in training and the use of patient groups as instruction for the staff.[9] The expectation of becoming group leaders adds importance and worth to working with patients. The subtlety of playing the roles of helper, student and teacher, group leader and member can enlarge the role range of the participating hospital population and lead to meaningful interaction.

17

Psychodrama
and Psychosis

The difficulty of reaching the psychotic patient is well known to hospital staffs. Doctors and others, past and present, have attempted to understand and help the psychotic patient achieve a less painful pattern of living and a more rewarding relationship to his environment or, desperately faced with their own limitations, have feared and destroyed him. There are many psychotherapies, and each approach depends on the concept the therapist has of the psychotic state.

The Approach

Treatment of the psychotic patient may begin by encouraging him to act out within the controlled situation of an audience. He is urged to "stage" the symptoms of his psychotic behavior. The psychosis is produced and staged by the patient with the members of the audience acting as auxiliary egos. Or the patient may sit in the audience as an auxiliary ego mirrors the psychotic behavior as experienced or observed by the staff and other patients. The production of the patient's problems becomes a cooperative act, an explicit move toward consensuality. The problems are no longer something fantasied by the patient, but are made real to all and shared with the members of the audience. This brings the patient into contact with real people and is the period of realization.[1]

The therapeutic principle is disarmingly simple. The disorganized

265

world created by the patient is present, and the audience is able to see him not as an isolated person but as he sees himself. This self-presentation fosters a reorganization of the patient's imagined world "by creating them [the symptoms] *at will*, by exaggerating or multiplying them *beyond* the dynamic needs of the mental syndrome proper."[2] The patient reexperiences with others what he has previously kept private, and this fantasied material is extended and enlarged to make it appear as real.

In certain forms of psychosis, the hallucination is an accusation aimed not at a single person but at a number of people—the opposite sex, the whole of humanity, or the entire world order.[3] This becomes slowly evident in paranoia and may be intended as a belligerent turning away from life. In psychodrama, the life difficulties that enveloped the patient are uncovered, and it becomes possible to understand the patient through his production. Therapeutic measures can then be directed toward helping the patient deal with some of the life tasks from which he withdrew, and offering a number of alternate ways of meeting his problem situation.

At a demonstration of psychodrama in Copenhagen (1962) for the psychiatric staff of the Frederiksberg Hospital, and for visitors from all over the world, Dr. Geert Jørgensen, chief of staff, introduced five patients and an interpreter, Ruth Holger Nielsen, to the group. The interpreter, a psychologist, was highly experienced and translated my English into Danish rapidly, sending my messages along to the patients as if I were speaking Danish. I was the director, and she was the amplifier. As a patient talked, she repeated quite naturally what was said.

The three male and two female patients in treatment were known to some of the members of the audience. One male professed to know a little English, so we began with him. The interview with the patient revealed the following: He was unmarried, lived at home with his parents, worked in a civil service job, and was preparing to take a test that was crucial to his future. If he didn't pass the examination, he was doomed to stay at his present level for years, perhaps for the rest of his life. He was invited to select someone to portray the person who helped him prepare for his trip to take the examination. He selected a staff member to play his mother. The scene between the mother and son revealed that he had a good record and should have no difficulty.

He reenacted leaving home and getting on the train. As he approached the test situation, sitting alone on the train, he said aloud, "I'm afraid. What will happen to me if they ask a question I can't answer? I'm not sure that I know all that is expected of me. I jump off the train and start running. The next thing I know, I'm in the hospital. I never took the test."

The situation was defined: a massive retreat before the difficulties of the test or imagined inadequacies and failure to avoid humiliation. His fantasy was primary and had little to do with his actual capabilities. He had created his own dilemma, so the movement of the drama was toward the future. He was asked to get back on the train, finish his journey, and show how he would like the outcome to be. The emotional block was still there: he couldn't imagine taking the test. As the interaction was being prepared, Dr. Jørgensen interrupted by pointing to a female patient in the group who was trembling, crying, and barely able to stay in her chair, and asked me, "How do you handle this when it happens during the session? What do you do? She is very upset." I replied that I'd work with her, and we began.

This situation demonstrated one of the positive benefits of having an audience.[4] Each member is not only a spectator but a possible protagonist. Viewing the drama of another arouses patients, making it easier to bring their problems before the group.

DIRECTOR	When did you begin shaking like this?	
PATIENT	(*Trembling and crying.*) I don't remember.	
DIRECTOR	Let's try to think about it. Were you trembling when you came into this room?	
PATIENT	I don't know.	
AUDIENCE	Yes, she was!	*This gives support and courage to the most disturbed patients— they are noticed.*
DIRECTOR	Tell me, were you shaking before you came to the hospital?	
PATIENT	Yes, I was. At home.	

DIRECTOR   Can you remember where
            you were when you first
            began shaking? In the yard?
            In the kitchen?

PATIENT   In the living room.

DIRECTOR   Show us what you were doing
            in the living room. Walking
            around? Sitting in a chair?
            Where?

PATIENT   I was sitting on a couch
            listening to the radio.

DIRECTOR   Now, let's be in the living
            room. You are there now.
            What is happening?

PATIENT   I am sitting, listening to the
            radio.

DIRECTOR   What is on the radio?

PATIENT   My favorite singer is there,
            and he is singing to me. (*As
            she calls his name and the
            song he is singing, the
            audience murmurs
            recognition of both the singer
            and the song.*) He tells me
            that he loves me and wants to
            visit me.

DIRECTOR   Here he is, the renowned   *The audience supports*
            singer who wants to visit you.   *the delusion through*
            (*A male patient stands in   *participation.*
            front of her as if on a radio,
            faces her, smiles, and begins
            to sing the love song. On a
            cue from the director, the
            audience joins in.*)

PATIENT	That's how it was. Then I sent him a letter and told him that I returned his love, and he should visit me when my husband isn't at home. (*She writes the letter.*)
DIRECTOR	Oh, you have a husband! We must choose some one to play his part. (*A staff doctor volunteers.*)

The lover (male patient) arrives, puts his arms around the female patient, and begins to make love to her. He caresses her, discovers her slashed wrists, and says, "My dearest love, I will kill the man who makes you so unhappy." He kisses her wounds as a father consoles a hurt child.

The male patient's tenderness reaches this thin, worn, prematurely aging woman, and her shaking stops. As the kissing continues up her arm, he becomes a lover. Her body stance changes as she returns the passion with shyness. He continues kissing her with real ardor. She exchanges her fantasy lover for a real man.[5] The husband (auxiliary ego) walks in on this scene. As he shows surprise and consternation at his wife's love scene with this famous singer, he takes his pipe out of his mouth. The male patient, who has problems of his own, mistakes it for a gun and begins to wrestle for it.

The male patient warmed up as quickly to feeling attacked as he did to love. When the wrestling takes on a meaning of real danger to the auxiliary ego husband, the female patient separates them, sits down, and calmly announces, "I don't want my husband dead. I know that I had no lover who came to see me. I just want my husband to stop drinking." Her social feeling interrupts the psychotic process.

The session ended on this note of self-clarification.[6] The patient had reorganized her world. It was no longer peopled with a fantasy lover and vast intrigue, but with a dissolute husband. She showed us how she returned from work and found her husband stretched out on a sofa, drunk, after he had made a solemn promise never to drink again. We saw what followed.

The patient and I sat together, holding hands, she speaking Danish and I, English, with the interpreter nearby. We talked about the session. "We all saw how alone and frightened you felt with your problem, but you were able to see and feel the support of all the people in the group.

This is a big move in the right direction. These people will help you learn to live with your husband and his drinking problem and perhaps also to help your husband."

A Theory of Psychosis

The alcoholic husband was not the cause of the psychotic break but the precipitating circumstance. A psychosis is created when the person's attention is directed toward the inner experience of fantasy selected from the ever-present fantasy-reality track. According to the spontaneity theory of child development, the origin of psychosis is to be found, in all probability, in the "development of infantile spontaneity, the early breech between fantasy and reality experience in the child, the sociometric evolution of grouping."[7] A psychotic episode may stem from faulty role development in early childhood training; role confusion may find expression in a weak attraction to real people and a strong attraction to imaginary people or objects or symbols and lead to the person's forsaking the development of positive interpersonal relationships. This theory does not necessarily assume that there is a constitutional or genetic explanation of the condition; however, telic strength is considered a genetic factor. It does assume that the response is one of choice. The person selects this special role with the conviction that psychosis frees him to construct an environment, to produce a drama, more suitable to his goal of absolute fulfillment. It is an attempt by the person to exchange his discomfort, as perceived by him, for a special state or position that gratifies his desire for the extraordinary, again as perceived by him. He lives detached from real people and things and creates a strong attachment to imaginary ones. He develops a technique for nonliving by refusing to accept the logic and feelings that lead to social organization. He denies the influence of others since he is his own playwright, actor, and producer. The roles are all self-assigned and played out unassisted by others. The isolation is so great, at times, that there is no conflict. "In catatonics, we have been able to observe that they play the role of a doll, a corpse, a hero, and similar roles."[8] There is in all these manifestations an intelligent but unreasonable chain of thought that supports the subjective, private world of the patient.

In the foregoing illustration, we saw how an auxiliary ego picked from the patient group was an agent of change for a delusional patient. The patient was able with his help to turn away from her fantasy existence and face her troubled world. This is the chief purpose of the auxiliary ego, "to free the patient from this extreme form of isolation-hallucination."[9] The auxiliary ego began as a fantasy character but quickly was accepted as a real person. The auxiliary ego (male patient) was first a spectator, warmed up and attracted to the distress signaled by the female patient. Then he was able to come out of the audience to soothe and free her from her fantasy.

Another way in which the audience serves a therapeutic function is by providing motivation for the psychotic patient to perform. The "stage" and audience are a symbol of unreality and fit well into the playwright's (patient's) dream of fulfillment. Of what use is it to create a drama unless there is an audience to see it to completion? The most effective audience is the staff—doctors, psychologists, social workers, and nurses. In this demonstration we had the added incentive of dignitaries from all over the world.

An audience is a source of satisfaction to the psychotic patient. Few people listen to him. He is seldom respected to the extent of being taken seriously, for most people have difficulty making sense out of the garbled figures of speech or poetic symbolism that typifies the speech of the psychotic. If anyone is ready to listen to him, the patient shies away from a direct confrontation, for that would mean giving up his social isolation and becoming a fellow human being, which is not part of his plan for living. As the director and cast make sense out of what seems nonsensical, the audience sees the patient differently and is better able to deal with him since they understand him. The audience, then, becomes a group of involved participants.

The patient usually sits in the audience as a spectator of someone else's drama, sometimes for many sessions, before he is invited to place himself on the stage. This is important, for it reassures the patient that he is, after all, still in control of the situation.

Finally, an audience answers a basic concern of man, namely, to feel that others care for him. The audience serves at times just as an audience for the patient; at other times it serves a supportive role to help the patient bring his life's predicament—his reality, fancifully created though it may be—into line with the common goals of society.

Psychodrama on a State Hospital Ward

Psychodrama on a ward of a large state psychiatric hospital usually takes place in the recreation room. Chairs are arranged in a semicircle, allowing an area for the action to take place. Some patients may be seated, waiting for the session to begin; others may be standing along the wall, sitting with their backs to the group, or lying on the floor;

others may be pacing back and forth. In the room are patients who are depressed, confused, overactive, hallucinatory, delusional. Every category of behavior that exemplifies the lonely, isolated, hospitalized patient is usually represented.[10]

On a closed ward, the number of people attending a session may find more patients sitting away from the circle than in it. On an open ward (this varies from ward to ward) the number attending is usually smaller and depends on the weather, the attitude of the staff toward attendance, feelings of the patients toward the group and therapy sessions, the composition of the group, and the timing of the sessions. If psychodrama is programmed after a long ward meeting, the active patients leave and only the quiet ones remain. After a time, some may wander back to take part and then leave again.

The size of the group rarely is under twenty patients. Under favorable conditions, there may be thirty-five patients who attend the session. The staff (ward psychiatrist, social worker, psychologist, nurses, psychology trainees, aides, training aides, student nurses—all those who meet and interact in this setting) are invited to participate as audience, auxiliary egos, discussion leaders, or resource people. The acting area requires nothing more than a table and two chairs. The total ward is the group. Seeing and hearing one another are most important and may be difficult to arrange.[11]

Introducing Psychodrama to the Group

The psychodramatist is usually introduced by a staff member. The psychodramatist explains when the meetings will be held, usually once a week for an hour and a half. He may say, "This is a learning method —learning by doing, by feeling, and then through discussion with the group. We want to know how we see each other. This time can be of value if you bring to the group things that are bothering you, whether it is something on the ward or something that has happened on a pass, on your days away from the ward, or in your family. You can, when you feel ready, invite any member of your family to join us during the psychodrama session."

A director who is too wordy will depress the spontaneity of the group; the patients will let him talk on and on and seldom interrupt, perhaps even falling asleep. It is important, however, to clarify for them the types of problems common to the group and the possibility of discussing them. The comments can be specific, for example, "I went home on a pass and nobody was there when I got there." The director considers the organization of the group and pitches his comments and questions to the level of their spontaneity (ego development). He might notice that the group is made up of people who are quiet and fearful of each other and say, "Who would like to work on how to show friendliness?"

The Warm-Up

The director looks around the room and comments on the composition of the group and the seating arrangement: "Are there any new people in the group besides me? How does it feel to be here? I'm new here, too. Oh, there are student nurses on this ward. How long have the student nurses been here?" The director notices that a patient, Warren, is trying to kiss a student nurse. The student nurse wrestles in a playful manner with the patient. We have a situation.

If the director is sensitive, the subtleties of the interactions that are taking place at the moment are useful clues to beginning the session —an uneasy movement in a chair, an unusual facial expression, or, as here, an inappropriate interaction between patient and student nurse. If the group is willing, the director can move quickly into action; otherwise, he should continue questioning the group.

The Interview

As Warren and the nurse sit in the group, the director calls out to the patient, "Warren, you're treating the nurse as if she were a girl friend." They stop wrestling.

WARREN	(*Angrily, to the director.*) It's none of your business.
NURSE	Oh yes it is! He tries to kiss all the student nurses, not only me. We spend most of our time running around being chased by him.

The nurse's response helps the director define the interaction as a specific area of difficulty.

DIRECTOR	Will you come and sit beside me, Warren?

WARREN   No, I won't. (*Still sitting
                beside the nurse, but smiling
                broadly.*) But I have a juicy
                problem for the group.
                There's a lot of masturbation
                and fornication on the ward,
                and I want to learn how to
                sublimate our sex drives. I
                don't approve of
                masturbation, fornication,
                adultery, but I would like to
                know what we should do. I
                won't mention names, but
                they know what they are
                doing is disturbing to the rest
                of us.

PATIENT   What does fornication mean?

WARREN   It's illicit lovemaking of
                unmarried people. Adultery
                is illicit lovemaking of
                married people, and I
                disapprove of both, as well
                as masturbation.

STAFF   Are you married?

NURSE   Yes, he is, to a nice girl.
                I know her.

STAFF   Are you telling the nurses
                that you are only playing
                games with them and have no
                illicit intentions?

WARREN   Tell them, Miss Student
                Nurse, what you said to me.

DIRECTOR   Will both of you come up,
                please?

Significant issues surrounding Warren's malfunction are observable in his negative reaction to the interruption of his disruptive behavior. At times, the director may feel more comfortable ignoring such behavior. But when he chooses to act on the behavior, his choice should be based on a considered judgment of whether he will help clear the air or if he'll only stir up more than can be managed. In Warren's case, while he expressed hostility, he quickly covered it up with a request for help by saying, "Why do you pick on me for such a small thing when there's real misbehavior going on?" A member of the staff properly spoke up, establishing a therapeutic role in the group; the group was beginning to understand Warren's attitude. The patient rejected the director's strategy, but warmed up to the group's interest in him.

Scene One

Mr. V. is a forty-two-year-old patient who has stalked into the acting area.

MR. V.	You shouldn't use words like *fuck,* or *SOB,* or *motherfucker* in front of the ladies; I don't think it's right for Jim to masturbate unless he has permission from the "high authorities."
PATIENT 1	Shut up, Mr. V. Do you think it is right for that patient to talk like this, or act like that, without the doctor's permission? You're more vulgar than anybody.
PATIENT 2	It's the first time I have ever heard Mr. V. talk in the group; he's usually out there talking to the trees and the grass. Maybe we should listen to him.
PATIENT 1	Do you really think this is a problem we should discuss with the ladies present?
DOCTOR	Sex is certainly a problem of relationship, a problem of social cooperation. It should be discussed here.

MR. V.	(*Wags his forefinger at the group, flexes his right arm muscle, and shouts.*) I am a fourteen-year-old boy, too young for sex, but strong and old enough to work. Look, Doc, at the floor; do you like the way I cleaned it? I'm a good worker.
DOCTOR	You're changing the subject from sex to work. Have you given up on being a ladies' man, a sexual, virile man, and settled on being a hard worker?
PATIENT 1	He doesn't work; he didn't clean the floor. He only talks to himself or to the trees.
MR. V.	Isn't the floor clean? Do you like it?
DOCTOR	What happened to you at fourteen that was such a challenge that you gave up the idea of being a full person?
MR. V.	Oh, shit! (*Leaves the ward and goes to find the kind of answers he wants to hear in the whispering trees and murmuring grass.*)
DOCTOR	He may try us again, but from this encounter we are better prepared to approach him and break through his social isolation.

PATIENT 4	(*An old-timer on the ward.*) I've known Mr. V. a long time. He got into trouble on his last visit home. It must be at least a year ago. He worked as a plumber's assistant with his brother and tried to make love to his brother's wife. They haven't invited him to come back. He hasn't any other place to go. (*A deep silence falls over the group.*)
DOCTOR	(*To the director.*) It may be uncomfortable for you to come here expecting to do psychodrama and find us going off on a tangent.
DIRECTOR	This *is* psychodrama, a real encounter.

This spontaneous act evolved out of the interaction between Warren and the student nurse. It brought responses from many of the patients and staff, but it particularly aroused Mr. V. He was sensitive to the love-making as it was unfolding on the unit. For a moment, the group members became the trees Mr. V. usually talked to, but unlike the trees, the group responded to him out of their involvement. Mr. V. emerged from his fantasy and briefly played a social role, that of a proper man reprimanding the patients and staff for "dirty talk" in front of ladies. The counterspontaneity of the group confused him, so he returned to an environment without counterspontaneity—the trees. He wasn't able to ask us for a home visit, just for work.

The director responded to the interruption of the warm-up as Mr. V. began to describe in detail the "juicy problem" on the ward. As a general rule, if a patient interrupts, the director hears him out and gives him an opportunity to respond to the situation. Although this patient was psychotic, he was speaking on the subject the ward was discussing. Rejection by the group at this point certainly would not have been profitable to the group or to the patient.

We have here a sample of psychodramatic process; the most remote patient can be pulled into the group on some issue. Mr. V. was able to come to the group and hint, "Love is a dangerous thing. I know that now, but I'm ready to go back. I'm strong enough to be a plumber's helper, and I won't make love."

The social worker made a note to contact the brother to see if he would give him another chance.

Scene Two

The director, recognizing that the student nurses' presence on the ward had stimulated the patients to thinking of themselves as sexual males, turned the group's attention to the incident of the kissing patient and the wrestling nurse.

DIRECTOR	Who else in the group did Warren try to kiss? Raise your hands. (*All student nurses raise their hands.*) Each nurse choose a patient and break up in pairs. I'd like each incident to be enacted as it really happened to the nurse. We'll take five minutes for the nurse to tell her partner how he must behave.	*The mirror technique aids the patient in observing his behavior from a distance.*
WARREN	This is the greatest. (*He laughs as each actor shows how he teased the nurse and chased her around and around.*) That's exactly the way it was. (*He tried but never succeeded in getting a kiss.*) I like this.	
DIRECTOR	Warren, will you show us now how you act with a nurse?	
WARREN	Sure. (*As Warren and the nurse come forward, Warren begins chasing her.*) I want a kiss. I want a kiss.	*The beneficial effect of the production is being expressed as Warren takes his own role in the interaction.*

NURSE	(*Stops, faces him.*) Sure, if that's what you want. Let's.
WARREN	Oh! (*He bolts, and everyone laughs.*)
DIRECTOR	Let's break up into groups of ten and discuss this. How do you see Warren now? What was the purpose of his behavior?

The various group reports were: (1) he didn't want to get a kiss; (2) he was running after slaps; (3) Warren needs love; maybe his mother did not love him enough (a frequent catch-all).

DIRECTOR	Someone in the group thinks your mother did not love you enough. How do you feel about that?	
WARREN	My grandmother raised me.	
DIRECTOR	Warren, since you're the only one who knows how your grandmother treated you, you be your grandmother and the doctor will be you.	
WARREN (*as grandmother*)	You're the finest one of the lot, Warren, baby, the only one I can rely on. You're smart, make good high grades in school, work after school, and bring me your money. You're a good boy. You'll amount to something some day—I just know it.	*He is the favorite child who gets privileges and burdens.*
DOCTOR (*as Warren*)	But I'm tired of being good; you keep on expecting so much of me. The only peace I get in this family is by knocking my brains out being good. Lay off.	*He can't be as good as she expects him to be, but he'd like to.*

WARREN   (*Falls out of role.*) I never talked like that to my grandma.

DIRECTOR   Did you ever feel like it?

DOCTOR
(*as Warren*)   You bet. But it never lasted, at least as long as I lived with my grandmother.

WARREN
(*as grandmother*)   (*Falls back into role playing.*) Now, son, don't go and ruin everything and your chances in life by marrying. You got to finish school or you'll end up on a construction job. And don't you forget it— you'll just be nothing. (*He lapses into being Warren.*) You know she was right. I couldn't make it after I married. It was hard to study, so I quit. I'll never make it now, especially since my wife is pregnant.

He is discouraged by his grandmother's warning, but he's accustomed to getting what he wants—so he marries.

DOCTOR
(*as Warren*)   But I can make girls squeal. It may not be much, but I do that well and easily. I like that. It's almost as easy as impressing Grandma. I wish others were as available as Grandma.

He creates excitement in one way or another.

WARREN
(*as himself*)   (*Walks off and sits down.*) That's not right.

He recognizes the useless goal of his behavior.

DIRECTOR   (*Trying to elicit feelings.*) What's not right? What the doctor said? Why don't you talk out loud what you're thinking about and feeling?

WARREN   It's someone else's turn.

DIRECTOR   (*To the group.*) Now, what
                  do you see?

NURSE   He's telling the truth. He was   *He knows how to win*
                  the most popular guy in high   *recognition.*
                  school, an athlete and on the
                  honor roll.

DIRECTOR   Does anyone have an idea
                  why Warren stopped
                  so abruptly?

PATIENT   You embarrassed him.

DIRECTOR   We may have. (*To Warren.*)
                  Were you embarrassed?

WARREN   No.

DIRECTOR   In a way, this is a little bit   *The director explains*
                  like your life. You were   *the patient's behavior as*
                  going along just great, and   *resulting from his*
                  then you stopped. We're   *self-concept.*
                  trying to figure out, with
                  your help, what made you
                  stop being productive. It may
                  be that you're sensitive to
                  the same provocation outside
                  as you showed us here.

WARREN   You may have something.

PATIENT   My mother was a lot like his
                  grandmother, always
                  warning me that I wouldn't
                  amount to anything without
                  an education. That really
                  gets you.

RESIDENT   Parents are anxious, too,
            about meeting the harsh
            competition of business life,
            and instead of encouraging,
            they scare the wits out of
            their kids. That's what I saw.

DIRECTOR   This is our first session in   *In this summary, the*
            psychodrama. What did you   *metaphor of sports*
            think of it? There are many   *meets the interest level*
            situations in Warren's life   *of the patient.*
            that need to be acted out—
            his relationship to his wife, to
            his boss, and to the baby
            about to be born—before we
            can see the conflicts that
            brought Warren to a grinding
            halt. He knows intellectually
            that one can toss a ball and
            make the basket from many
            positions. There's no one
            position in life that must be
            assumed, except that one has
            to throw the ball in order
            to make it.

One of the features that contributed to the movement of the session was having the nurses act out the kissing episodes with the rest of the patient group. This gave the patients an opportunity to experiment with a new role, since most of them were passive and wouldn't dare approach a female in this way. Warren's behavior might be described as a delightful backward movement into early adolescence, when he was the chosen son of the mother surrogate, and whatever he did pleased her. The auxiliary ego projected a portion of Warren's behavior in an attempt to identify the meaning of the present situation. The patient seemed to feel a growing confidence in the group and a growth of self-esteem. Mirroring the behavior of the patient through selecting a variety of situations that have actually occurred allows a patient to see his behavior and the effect it has on others and provides him with the continuing opportunity to correct the situation as it is occurring before him. Patients are sensitive to ridicule; so it is the staff's responsibility to keep reassuring the patient that *the goal is understanding, not making fun of him.*

After the session, the kissing stopped. Warren's pattern of behavior changed when the student nurses responded more positively to Warren. He was encouraged to talk "sensibly, like an adult," and was able to give up the need to succeed in a sham battle, chasing the girls around the ward.

Second Session of an Open Male Ward

A week later on the same ward, it is as though one were facing a new group. So many things happen in a week. Old patients are gone, and new ones have arrived. The director may refer to the previous week's session, asking the group if there are any loose ends, any questions, or any changes resulting from the session of the week before. The director, in a sense, is warming himself up. The immediate behavior of the patients is a guide to the session: some are sitting together and some are alone. A pattern of interest and disinterest begins to form.

The Warm-Up and Interview

The director takes his place at the center of the room and looks carefully at the group.

DIRECTOR	You're a community of experts. Does that surprise you? You're experts in the art of defeating and being defeated.
PATIENT 1	I don't get it.
DOCTOR	How do you think you made Mrs. Starr feel with that comment?
PATIENT 1	How should I know? That's her business. She's supposed to know everything.
DOCTOR	Who do you think won in this little exchange in this conversation between Mrs. Starr, the staff, and the patient?

NURSE   It seems to me the patient
               won. Mrs. Starr was trying to
               get him to understand
               something, and he wouldn't,
               so he won.

PATIENT 1   I don't get it.

DOCTOR   You can't win from him.
               Maybe we ought to find out
               if there are any problems on
               the ward today.

PATIENT 2   Yes, somebody stole my
               things last night.

DIRECTOR   Did this happen to anyone
               else last night? (*Several
               people raise their hands.*)
               Each of you who had
               something stolen last night
               should choose people from
               the group and dramatize the
               moment of loss. Break up into
               little acting groups; when
               you're ready, let us know.

The director sensed the passivity of the group members and diffused their resistance by asking them to organize into small subgroups. The opening statement was for the staff; they, too, faced the resistance of the patients. An important source of satisfaction for the staff is being successful in what they are doing. The remark was intended to help them modify their behavior and to "help each other work through the feelings aroused by their more personalized contacts with the patients."[12] A staff member demonstrated the expertise of a patient in always winning an argument, but then he was able to disengage himself and move the group toward dealing with a problem—stealing.

Scene One

The first patient places two chairs together, pretends they are a bed, assumes a sleeping position, and makes snoring sounds. Patient 2 lifts the trousers from the foot of the bed and slips money out of a pocket.

PATIENT 1	(*Wakes up with a start.*) Oh, what are you doing? (*Patient 2 doesn't answer and runs away. Patient 1 turns over and goes back to sleep.*)
GROUP MEMBER	Didn't you even tell the attendant what happened? Who stole your money?
PATIENT 1	No to all your questions.
DIRECTOR	Let's have a series of these experiences before we discuss each event of theft. Who's next?
PATIENT 3	(*Gets into bed and assumes a position of sleep.*)
PATIENT 4	(*Takes patient 3's cigarettes and tiptoes softly away.*)
PATIENT 3	What the hell are you doing with my cigarettes? Give them back to me.
DIRECTOR	We have a different response here. Did he give you back your cigarettes?
PATIENT 3	No.

Patient 5 sets the scene in the dayroom; he takes off his shoes and sets them beside him. Patient 6, playing the role of a confused, disoriented person, picks up the shoes and slips them under his shirt.

PATIENT 5	Those are my shoes. Give them back to me.

PATIENT 6	No, they're not. They're mine. (*A fight ensues.*)
DIRECTOR	We've seen three different incidents of theft. Are there any more? This is not a court of law. We are not trying to punish the offender, but we want to make this a more harmonious environment. That is possible when people learn to protect their possessions and to respect the feelings of loss in others.

Whenever there is fighting, stealing, smoking in bed, or other ward problems, the psychodramatist examines the issue and makes the problem explicit through role playing the situation. Close attention is paid to the patients' responses to the provocation.

When patients bring up ward problems, they expect the staff to take some action. In effect they are saying, "You have power—we are helpless; so do something about it. Punish the offenders and reward the good guys." These enactments are forms of helping patients become aware of what they are doing when faced with problems and of what they could do. It is important for them to learn to express their feelings and ideas, to be assertive.

Scene Two

PATIENT 1	We all know who was roaming around last night. Why doesn't he admit it?
PATIENT 2	If you know, why don't you say; I don't know.
PATIENT 1	It's not up to me to say; he should say.
DIRECTOR	Is the person willing to come forward and say "I roamed around last night and rifled through people's pockets"?

PATIENT 3	Don't everybody look at me. I didn't do it.
DIRECTOR	That's one of the difficulties. Everyone feels accused whether he's guilty or not, so that when the thief discloses himself as being the thief, he gives back part of what he's taken—your trust in each other. What he stands to lose is your trust in him and the items he has taken.
PATIENT 4	(*With a great deal of bravado.*) I took some junk last night.
DIRECTOR	Let's see what made you decide to take things. When did you make this decision? Did you talk it over with anyone?
PATIENT 4	I called my mom.
DIRECTOR	(*Interrupting.*) Has anyone seen Arthur's mother? Does anyone know her? Who will be Arthur's mother, talking to him on the telephone?
AIDE	I will. I know her.
DIRECTOR	(*Warming up the group and the aide to the role of Arthur's mother.*) How old a woman are you? What do you call your son? Arthur? Artie? Do you work? All right, someone be the telephone and ring.

When the auxiliary ego shows a lack of information, the director may request a role change, using the patient as a resource person. The simple act of making a ringing sound is an attractive role for a very withdrawn member in the group. He may be unable to enter into the situation at a higher level or in a more sophisticated role, but he can make a sound of a telephone ringing. It may be a first movement toward communication with other people.

ARTHUR

(*Turns to a patient.*) Lend me a dime; I want to call my mom. I don't have any money, and I need some. (*The patient starts to give him a real dime.*)

DIRECTOR

This is pretend; pretend to give him a dime.

ARTHUR

Oh, hell. I almost got away with that. Hello, Mom. Are you coming out on Sunday?

AIDE

No, I can't, Honey. We're going to a wedding.

ARTHUR

(*Looks up, laughing.*) That's exactly what she said. Were you listening in?

DIRECTOR

Were you listening in?

AIDE

No, I was guessing.

ARTHUR

Well, I need some money. Will you send me some?

AIDE
(*as mother*)

I just sent you five dollars. What happened to it? What do you think we're made of? Money? I bet you were gambling again. No, I'm not going to send you any; that will have to last you.

ARTHUR	I really don't have any. When are you coming out?
MOTHER	We'll see. Call me next week, and I'll let you know.
DIRECTOR	Was anything left out? Is this essentially what went on between you and your mother?
ARTHUR	Yes, it is.
DIRECTOR	All right, Arthur, talk out loud. What are your feelings? What do you think?
ARTHUR	She's mean. I think she doesn't understand what it means to be without money here. I have to get some. I owe a lot. I think I'll try the lockers. I know how to spring them open.
PATIENT	(*From the group.*) He does. I saw him. I saw him tampering with the lockers.
ARTHUR	(*Unashamed, runs over to the lockers and shows how easily they spring open.*)

The group got excited and turned to the staff. "You see, there's no safety here. Why don't we have lockers that are safe? Why don't you do something about this? Locking something up doesn't protect our possessions. Anyone can spring lockers open." The staff admitted that this was true, that the lockers were inadequate. A request had been put in for new lockers. Until then, though, what should be done about Arthur?

The director pointed out that the group had placed the whole responsibility on the lockers, not on the people who had participated in the looting—Arthur and those who had not interfered with Arthur's actions. The victims of loss often participate by being indifferent to the incident. Stolen property should be returned or a reparation made, otherwise the culprit enjoys the advantages of putting something over on "society."

The original three victims of theft were asked how else they could have reacted at the moment of stealing. Then the scenes were acted by three other patients, but this time alternate modes of reacting to the theft and alternate modes of reacting to Arthur's tampering with the lockers were demonstrated.

The director concluded by saying, "We have seen that some people on the ward encourage the misbehavior of others through indifference or carelessness. Some forget that many here are so confused they are unable, at this time, to recognize the difference between 'mine and thine.' Others only sense their own predicament, as Arthur did, and have no feelings except a sense of accomplishment in being able to get what they want. We hope this session has helped them to alter these attitudes."

This session demonstrated the exhibitionistic quality of Arthur. His relationship to the audience had a childlike trust, indicating a simplicity of affect: "Look, Ma, no hands." The effort toward concealment of misbehavior, as found in the criminal, was lacking here. Arthur had a much more infantile response to problem solving. His childlike openness was also shown in the ease with which he showed his feelings, his misbehavior, and his skill in opening the lockers. This patient showed a shrewd manipulative attitude that charmed both the staff and the patients. He was able to engage people with his apparent openness and willingness to participate as long as he felt he was getting out of the situation what he wanted—sanction to rifle, a hospital discharge, or whatever. Usually, Arthur wanted a discharge, and when he didn't get it, he ran away. Diagnostically, he was listed as a paranoid schizophrenic.

Other patients may learn from a session like this; patients like Arthur do not. He performed for the joy of the action, the personal benefit, and only went through the motions of therapy. He learned little, if anything. Role reversal with patients with this type of disorganization is of little use, for their perception of others is minimal. Soliloquy in Arthur's case was helpful in establishing the impulse to act. The psychodrama session was not used to punish by making a decision about Arthur's theft, like requesting that he return the money or that his privileges be taken away, but to help the group feel the strength of their position and encourage them to handle it.

Stealing never stops on a state hospital ward (as it is always with us in the community), so it can always be used to provide the group with a shared experience of loss and a chance to examine their reactions to it. For this reason, whenever a stealing episode happens, the director should allow the drama to emerge spontaneously; it offers the possibility of insight into the mental state of the patients.

Family attitudes toward possessions and stealing may be acted out. The director may wish to use a stealing incident on the ward as a referrant to childhood experiences of stealing, not only of the culprit, but of as many of the group members as possible. Stealing is a symptom of rebellion, and the parents' attitude toward stealing may be a reinforcement of the symptom.

The director introduces the role-playing procedure by pointing to stealing as a common experience, something each of us has tried and given up or tried and continued to do. The scene may start with a warm-up to the actual "snitching," as described in the case of Arthur. The most frequent incident that patients recall is slipping into the parents' bedroom and grabbing loose change from either mother's purse or father's trousers. When this is accomplished without detection, the director sparks the scene by asking the patient to be, first, the mother discovering the child in the act of thievery; then, the father. This shows the family value system and rules of child rearing. Some parents are so indignant that they overreact and become thief catchers; rather, they should play down the incident and not let the child have the money he got by stealing. Some parents are themselves thieves and train the children to steal. The patient's position in the scheme of family living becomes apparent: he is inclined either to follow parental rules or to act against them.

"This Is Your Life"

The following session took place on an open ward with the usual percentage of chronic patients who wouldn't attend ward or therapy sessions. The staff decided to clear the dormitories, get all patients out of bed, and lock the door during the meetings. There was nowhere else for the patients to go, so they were forced to attend the psychodrama session.

It is certainly true that you can lead a horse to water, but you can't make him drink. The active patients get bored with the slow warm-up and dull conversation of the long-term chronic patients; they lose interest and show it. On the other hand, sessions with the active patients are too fast for the chronic ones. As a result, the chronic patient gets what he seems to want—to be left out of it, to be left alone. Here is what we tried. We assigned a student nurse to each chronic patient on the ward and asked her to be prepared at a psychodramatic session to tell the general facts in the life history of her patient.

The director opened the session by saying, "Today, in psychodrama, we are going to do 'This Is Your Life.' Whose life would you like to hear?" The group showed great interest and offered many suggestions. They finally decided on Dorothy. The student nurse who had been assigned to Dorothy walked over and stood with her about twenty feet away from the psychodrama circle. Dorothy's back was turned to the group, and she was staring out the window. She was frail and untidy, with straight gray hair hanging over her face. She didn't move a muscle when the student nurse stood beside her.

STUDENT (*as Dorothy*)	I am Dorothy, forty-five years old, from Oklahoma.	
DIRECTOR	(*To the group.*) Is there anyone here from Oklahoma? No? Dorothy, where do you come from? Tulsa? Sapulpa?	*The director asked questions that could be answered with a yes, a no, or a nod. Dorothy gave no answer, no recognition of the question.*
STUDENT (*as Dorothy*)	I have three sisters.	
DIRECTOR	Are you the oldest sister, Dorothy? (*Dorothy gives no response.*) Are you the youngest?	
GROUP	She won't talk except to say "Match." That's all she has said in a year that I know of.	
DIRECTOR	(*To the group.*) Does anyone here have older sisters?	
PATIENT	I do. I'm the youngest.	
DIRECTOR	Show us what it was like to have older sisters. Does anyone in the group remind you of your sisters? Choose them and act out any experience you remember— a short one.	

The short scene was as follows. The actors were chosen from the more active patients.

YOUNGEST SISTER Let me borrow your dress, your blouse.

FIRST SISTER No, I won't. You can't have it.

SECOND SISTER I won't let you have mine either, so don't ask.

YOUNGEST (*Giggling and laughing.*) Then Mom will make them lend me the blouse.

DIRECTOR (*To Dorothy.*) Is that the way it was in your house? Is this your life? (*Dorothy gives no response.*)

STUDENT
(*as Dorothy*) I graduated from high school and became a beautician.

The director again asked the group for similar experiences, which were enacted and followed with "Is this your life, Dorothy?"

STUDENT
(*as Dorothy*) I was married three times, and I still have a husband.

PATIENT Who would have thought it? I never even had one.

The group's attitude toward Dorothy changed from one of little respect to open admiration. She began to take shape in the eyes of the patients even though the details were meager. The last scene to be played mirrored her present behavior with patients on the ward: her isolation, her paucity of words, her disarray. Although Dorothy's back was turned to the group through the whole session, she burst into tears and tried to escape the situation. It was the first time she had shown any feelings since she entered the hospital three years before. The change in Dorothy was dramatic, and after some months, she left the ward and returned to her husband. This shows that a patient can be dislodged from silence by a drama that prods the group members to change their image of the patient. For some patients "This Is Your Life" en-actments are not so effective. This type of session helps identify a silent patient and permits understanding and support to develop among other patients.

"This Is Your Life" is a technique of acting out relationships that a patient may have experienced, all the while asking him, "Is This Your Life?" The other patients, meanwhile, are enacting roles that are known to them. Since the patient often perceives and interprets reality in ways that differ widely from those accepted by most of us, the difficulty is to learn to see reality as the patient sees it. "This Is Your Life" helps others see the world as the patient does.

It is important in "a play within a play" not to let the internal scene run too long; it may alienate the "silent one." Its purpose is to warm up the mute patient as well as to keep the interest of the rest of the group. When a point is made during the scene, the director or stu-dent nurse turns to the silent patient and asks, "Was it like this at your house?"

One of the essentials is that the session stimulate the staff to inves-tigate and build on areas that were strong before the walling-off began. When it was learned that Dorothy had been a beautician, the volunteer worker encouraged her first to begin arranging her own hair and, later on, to fix the hair of the others. The patient's fears seemed lessened as the direction of her life changed. "This Is Your Life" seems to be one answer in working with the silent patient. It provides the patient audi-ence with a new look at the unknown member of the group; it warms the group up to an awareness of the former social roles of the silent one; it involves the audience by letting the other patients act out the imagined issues of the unfolding life history; it reaches the chronically withdrawn patient by including him in a very direct way. One condition for using this technique should be mentioned: it is better to wait until the group has met for three or four psychodrama sessions so that the withdrawn patient, who seems to be nonparticipating, has had some exposure to the method. It must be remembered that the warm-up time of patients varies and the silent ones are the slowest of all.

Dream Therapy

A male patient was referred into the psychodrama session from a different ward. The referring doctor believed psychodrama might be a quick way to alleviate the symptoms of his agitation and prepare him for further treatment. Tony arrived shivering, shaking, moaning "I killed my daughter," wringing his hands, and leaning on the psychologist from his ward.

In this V.A. hospital, there was a separate room with stage and lights for psychodrama. The psychologist and Tony took their places in the audience and the director explained that the group had an opportunity to help a patient from another ward. From his distress, said the director, perhaps everyone could learn a bit more about their own ways of managing life situations.

DIRECTOR	Tell us, Tony, why do you accuse yourself of killing your daughter? This is a serious charge you make against yourself. What happened?
TONY	My daughter came home sick —she was only eleven years old, and she was coughing and saying she wasn't feeling well.
DIRECTOR	In this situation, Tony, we don't tell about what happened; we act things out. How many people will you need to show us what happened to you and your little girl?
TONY	(*Turns to the psychologist, moaning and whimpering.*) I don't know, maybe a doctor.

The scene was enacted. Tony put his daughter to bed. She continued to cough, and finally he called the doctor. The doctor said, "This is not a cold. She has pneumonia," and the little girl died.

TONY	Ever since then I've had a dream of going to Hell and being punished.

DIRECTOR   We would like to see that
              dream. Sometimes acting out
              a dream helps you see and
              understand your private
              intent. Take two chairs, close
              your eyes, and see yourself
              in the dream. Where are you,
              Tony? Where do you see
              yourself in the dream?

TONY   I'm in Hell. It's hot, and the
              devil sits there and stares
              at me. I wake up trembling
              and moaning; it's a nightmare.
              (*The lights are dimmed and
              the psychologist is asked to sit
              on the stage facing Tony,
              in the role of the devil.*)

DIRECTOR   Did you say anything to
              the devil?

TONY   No. Neither of us said a
              word. I wake up, and I can't
              stand it.

DIRECTOR   What would you say to the
              devil if you could?

TONY   (*With a lot of feeling.*) What
              are you going to do to me
              for killing my daughter?

PSYCHOLOGIST Not so fast. Let's get the
(*as devil*) facts first. Why are you here
              in Hell? You say you killed
              your daughter?

A searching interview ensued between Tony and the devil. The devil decided that Tony had shown bad judgment in not calling the doctor earlier, but that this was not murder. The act was not sinful enough for him to be consigned to Hell.

PSYCHOLOGIST *(as devil)*	*(In an exhorting manner.)* Get out of Hell and go back to earth. You are not a murderer. You committed a sin of bad judgment—that is all.

Tony stopped trembling and stopped his self-accusatory moaning. His acceptance of the "verdict" was immediate and dramatic, and he said, "I guess I made a mistake that almost anyone might have made." The audience responded with reassuring words and examples that showed that even doctors weren't infallible. Tony left the psychodrama room and was subsequently discharged.

The dreamer is the author of his dream, and in it he describes his predicament symbolically. The psychodramatic approach is to put the dream out in the open, peopling it with the imaginary figures of the dream. These imaginary figures are stand-ins for the dream figures. In the presentation of the dream, these stand-ins say no more and do no more than directed by the dreamer, reflecting the dreamer's perception of the conflict. In Tony's dream, paralysis of action characterized his confrontation with the devil; both were immobilized.

In order that there may be a catharsis of action, the dreamer may be asked to redream the dream and end it in a more satisfying way. In Tony's case, there was not a clear separation between the dream and reality, so it wasn't necessary to ask him to dream again. It was only necessary to release him from being constantly confronted by the devil. The effectiveness of the exhortation by the "devil" was possible because of the positive relationship between Tony and the psychologist. Just as Tony was able to throw himself on the mercy of an avenging devil, he was able, because of his respect and trust, to accept the psychologist's reasoning. A session of this kind emphasizes the suggestibility of many patients.

Sociometric Self-Perception Test

Studies on group therapy and psychodrama report the difficulty of having a "monopolizer," whatever his diagnostic category, as a member of the group. In this instance, the monopolizer is a paranoid patient on a ward. Because he was there, he had to be dealt with. One technique that deserves consideration is the sociometric self-perception test.[13]

The scene is a male ward. One patient is standing in the center of the room reading aloud from the Bible. A group of patients are scattered around, some sitting, some sleeping, some half-listening, but all are a captive audience. As the psychodrama team enters the room, the monopolizer continues reading and explaining the Bible's text. "How long has this been going on?" asks the director.

PATIENT

About forty-five minutes, but it seems longer. He always does this.

MONOPOLIZER

And my tongue shall speak of Thy righteousness, and of Thy praise all the day.

PATIENT

He sits there with his Bible and he finds an answer to everything.

MONOPOLIZER

Let me read you this passage from Psalms. The answer to our sickness lies here. Let the good book lead you.

PATIENT

He acts like he's the therapist, but he's a patient just like we are.

MONOPOLIZER

But I don't just sit here and not open my mouth. I talk, I read, so listen to me.

DIRECTOR

(*To monopolizer.*) Much of what you say makes sense. You and I are faced with the same problem of trying to get people to listen to us.

MONOPOLIZER

(*Reading again from the Bible.*) Because He hath inclined His ear toward me, therefore will I call upon Him all my days.

DIRECTOR	(*Interrupting.*) You seem to incline your ear primarily away from the group; do they want to listen to you, or don't you care?	
MONOPOLIZER	I know what you're doing. You're trying to change places with me. You want to be in charge of this group.	*The competitive aspect of the monopolizer becomes evident.*
DIRECTOR	You're right. I do. Let's find out from the group. Would you be willing to do that?	
MONOPOLIZER	Not until I finish Psalm 116.	
DIRECTOR	Why not use that as a basis for discussion? Let's break into groups of five, and the group can discuss briefly how they feel on this subject— who they want to be the leader of the psychodrama session. We two (*the monopolizer and the director*) will leave the room and return in a few minutes.	

To assess quickly readiness for therapy, the director tests the patient's cooperative resources, that is, when he shows a movement toward a meaningful agreement. It is for this reason that the director and monopolizer leave the scene together. The contest then is not between the monopolizer and the director, for both of them are faced with the same problem of winning the group.

The director and the monopolizer reenter the psychodrama room.

MONOPOLIZER	(*Holding his Bible under his arm.*) Shall I begin reading?
DIRECTOR	Let's make a few predictions on how they voted. How about Jim? Do you think he voted for you or against you?

MONOPOLIZER   Against me. He's one of the
               men I'm trying to reach. He
               depends too much on
               medicine. I want him to come
               alive, throw away the
               medicine, be like me.

DIRECTOR   Let's give him a chance to
               answer and see if your
               prediction was right.

JIM   He was right. He's smart all
               right, but he is constantly
               yakking away, and if you
               don't listen, he threatens you
               with his cane.

The polling of the group continues, revealing that the monopolizer was aware of their indifference, dislike, or antagonism, but ignored this since he felt justified in subjecting them to his superior wisdom. The polling also showed the monopolizer that the patients respected many of his ideas and attitudes and liked him, but they didn't want him as a preacher-therapist. It further showed that he held the group through intimidation. If they tried to stop him, his excitement increased. Long before the poll was concluded, he got the point and left the room in a huff.

When a patient is face to face with another member of the group and is asked, "How does this person feel about you?" the answer reflects his perception of the other person and indicates his method of approaching the other. Had the monopolizer been less perceptive of his group and believed that they enjoyed his taking over, the movement of the session would have been different. Sometimes, as with adolescents, patients are looking for ways to win people's attention, and it is possible to show alternate modes of behavior. In this case, however, the monopolizer perceived others as inadequate and in need of him in his glorified role of therapist, so repressive measures were indicated. Each session with this particular monopolizer began by getting him to agree on what should be done when he tried to take over. The perception test was used strategically.

It was not necessary or possible to help this monopolizer gain insight; he didn't need to hear what he already knew. But it was necessary and possible to give the group a chance to deal with the basic issue of his needing the group and their needing him but being afraid to contradict, interrupt, or interfere with him because of his violence. The sociometric self-perception test helped clarify the facts and made group therapeutic action possible.

18

Working with Depression

Depression is a common symptom that takes many forms. A person's feeling of despair is expressed in body language and characterized by a loss of spontaneity. His verbal communication abilities may be impaired. Movement may be hesitant and slow; the depressed person may have difficulty walking from one spot to another. Or he may display excited agitation, with tears, wringing of hands, violent raging, and pacing.

Alfred Adler believed that "the categorical imperative of melancholia becomes: 'Act, think, and feel as if the horrible fate you paint on the wall had already befallen you or were inevitable.' . . . The symptom or attack of the patient signifies that he is removed from the present through anticipation, and from reality through empathy into a role (of a person who is already perishing)."[1] This results in the disturbance and interruption of habitual patterns of work, interpersonal relationships, and social and leisuretime activities.

Moreno focuses attention on the sociometric pattern within the social atom, the affectional relationships among members who have an emotional interplay. Moreno found in the interplay between the depressed patient and his interpersonal environment "a gross imbalance" between incoming and outgoing feelings. The depressed patient "whose motor behavior is retarded tends to produce a like reaction towards all of the individuals towards whom he is emotionally selective, whereas they assume towards him various and differing reactions." At times, the members of this interpersonal environment may express love, at other times, anger or fear; the depressed patient responds to all with a stereotyped attitude of, say, anger. This response is quite different from what is expected of him. This impaired performance may be helped by changing the organization of the social atom, that is, by finding a person or a group toward whom the depressed individual has not a fixed stereotyped attitude. This therapeutic maneuver can contribute to an improvement in an appropriate interaction with others.[2]

The causes of depression are complex. A person may be depressed by a stressful life situation such as separation or loss (the loss may be physical or interpersonal), or an important person (or persons) not providing him with what he feels he needs. "Depression in any single patient probably results from a convergence of causes. They include stressful life events, genetic predisposition, vulnerability to certain stresses based on personality and other factors, and probably biologic and neuropharmacologic abnormalities."[3]

The predominance of depression in women over men, a two to one ratio, has led some investigators to postulate a sex-linked genetic factor and to seek hormonal causes. Others feel that this ratio is due to culturally determined factors rather than genetic linkage, that the male is less prone to seek medical treatment for a feeling disorder than the female. A man may be using alcohol to stave off depressive feelings and psychiatric treatment (the known rate of alcoholism is higher among males than females). The difference in occurrence of depression in the sexes may be less than it appears.

Hostility in depression is a major theme, but the depressed person is aware only of a feeling of hopelessness, of worthlessness, or of self-reproach. Anger and resentment may not be expressed toward the helping professionals, but will be directed in the form of irritation, nagging, and vicious behavior at close family members, especially children.[4] A careful investigation of the "at home" difficulties and the violence which is taking place away from the treatment center may expose the degree of hostility felt by the patient.

Psychodramatic treatment should be planned to help the patient acknowledge and come to terms with his anger and its origin and consequences, and to construct plans for rebuilding relationships. My experience indicates that the depressed patient's ability to express anger is not impaired, but he has great difficulty communicating his needs, wishes, and feelings. In psychodrama, the covert demand for help becomes evident as the auxiliary ego and the patient identify the "opponent" and gratify some of the patient's profound needs.

Often there are many cases of depression on a hospital ward, and each psychodramatic episode is likely to have meaning for patients in the audience as well as for the participants in the drama. Psychodrama provides several techniques that can work with depressed patients.

Use of Auxiliary Egos

The group in which the following case appeared was small, twelve patients with a staff of four. Psychodrama was programmed once a week, and each session began with a brief review and discussion of the last session. In this session, the director used a direct question to get the session moving: "Who do you want to know more about?"

PATIENT 1	I'd like to ask Cece about the house. (*To Cece*) You always mention it.	
CECE	It's empty.	
PATIENT 2	Is that why you talk about it?	
CECE	I'm afraid of it.	
DIRECTOR	What will it do to you? Does it hold sad memories?	
CECE	No, no. It's an awful house.	
DIRECTOR	When did you last see the house?	*Director helps the patient portray the crucial fear she is experiencing.*
CECE	I went there yesterday, because Dottie said I shouldn't let it get me, but it did. It was as bad as ever.	
DIRECTOR	Let's see that visit. Mary, you be the house. Stand here in the center of the room. Cece, describe it in as much detail as possible. (*Mary, the nurse, stands in the center of the room, arms outstretched to give a corridor, or opening, effect.*)	

CECE | That's exactly what the house does. It opens its arms like that and calls to me. (*She recoils.*)

NURSE
(*as house*) | Come in, Cece. There's no one here. Come in.

CECE | I don't want to. You will hurt me, smother me. Your walls are like velvet, and you'll suffocate me. | *The house is a symbolic expression of her anxiety.*

HOUSE | Come in; come in. I want to smother you. | *The auxiliary ego echoes her fear and resentment.*

CECE | I push the furniture against the door and put the bottles on the window sill so that I can throw them. (*She runs "into the house" and starts to wrestle with it, breaks loose, and starts to pile up the furniture and prepare for an attack.*)

HOUSE | That won't help you. I'm going to get you. What can you do? Who is here to help you? | *The auxiliary ego suggests avenues of help.*

CECE | You feel like velvet, and you're choking me. I've got to get out of here. I'm afraid of you. You keep telling me to kill my children. Stop it! Stop it! (*Cringes in the corner.*) | *The house, not the patient, has the evil thoughts.*

DIRECTOR | You are a brave woman to test your courage by visiting that house. When did you move there? | *After the enactment of her hallucinatory fears, the patient is not left alone. The director tries to discover the series of events that led to this disorganization.*

CECE	A few months ago, when I decided to move.	
DIRECTOR	What happened that made you want to move?	*The director explores the frustration that is being resolved by moving.*
CECE	Larger space for my five children.	
DIRECTOR	Who lives with you, your husband?	
CECE	No.	
DIRECTOR	Where is your husband?	
CECE	He lives a few doors down. Every night or so he throws rocks through the window.	
DIRECTOR	Is that why you moved?	
CECE	No, I didn't mind that. It was kind of funny. He's usually drunk. He wants me to take him back.	
PATIENT 1	What about your boyfriend?	
CECE	What about him! I decided to move. (*Shows excitement.*)	*This may be the major involvement, but the director felt that Cece was warmed up to her fantasy world—the house—not to her boyfriend.*
DIRECTOR	Now, don't tell us anymore. Let's act it out. Who do we need for the scene?	*The director doesn't let the patient talk about the experience, lest it reduce the intensity of action.*

The scene is set in the office of a housing project. Cece comes in asking for larger quarters for herself and her five children. She is twenty-six, on ADC, and separated from her husband. He is an alcoholic.

AIDE (as project manager)	I have one apartment for immediate occupancy. That's it. It's nice. It's a lovely place, way out in the country.	
CECE	Oh, the Compound. I didn't want to go that far out.	*Here is a clue to her conflict.*
AIDE (as project manager)	It has a swimming pool, and a bus takes the kids to school.	*Another complication: it may be good for the children, but not for me.*
CECE	I don't know anyone. How will I get to work? I'll take it.	*She resolves the conflict by giving up everything for her children.*
AIDE (as project manager)	Now be sure it's what you want. Once you sign on the dotted line, I can't give you another apartment. It's yours, and that's it.	*This is the challenge that she must meet; to move away from her old attachments and make new ones.*
CECE	I took it, and then I went home and told the children what I had done.	

The director and staff then sat with the patient and encouraged a discussion of the role playing. Did the aide play the housing project manager accurately? Did Cece really take the apartment without looking at it? Wasn't she worried about getting to work? After the issues were integrated, the action continued. Cece was encouraged to select five people from the group to play her children.

CECE	We're moving.
CHILD 1	Where?
CECE	To the Compound.

CHILD 2	I don't want to go.	
CHILD 3	I know it's got a swimming pool. I'd like that.	
CHILD 1	What about all my friends?	
CECE	Cut out the talk. I took it. Let's go see it. There's nothing to do about it. Talk won't change anything.	*Her fears are mounting. The resentment begins to express itself toward the children.*
NURSE (as house)	Come in, come in, and welcome!	
CECE	The house began to talk to me as soon as I saw it. My skin crawls; I hate it.	*Her symptoms are directed to the house, not to her children or her boyfriend.*
NURSE (as house)	I'm a nice house. A little far out, but nice. Come in.	*Auxiliary ego attempts to modify the imagined danger.*
CECE	Kill your children. Why do you say that to me?	
NURSE (as house)	Kill your children!	*Auxiliary ego echoes in order to establish the point of danger.*
CECE	Kill your children. They don't have a chance. They are already in trouble.	
NURSE (as house)	The children don't have a chance. Kill them.	*Auxiliary ego again echoes.*
CECE	Living way out here, what chance do they have? If they manage to make it out here, the war will get them.	

NURSE *(as house)*	There's no chance to make it way out here. If they manage to make it out here, the war will get them	*Auxiliary ego keeps echoing to show her essential pessimism.*
CECE	Don't let them suffer. Kill them.	
NURSE *(as house)*	Don't let them suffer. Kill them.	*Cece is playing both roles, the house and herself. The auxiliary ego is separating out the role of the house.*
CECE	*(To the children.)* You look so afraid of me. You look frightened.	
NURSE *(as house)*	Now is the time to kill them. Do it now.	
CECE	I have a gun in my purse. I take it out and the house starts counting.	
NURSE *(as house)*	One, two—at the count of three, I want you to shoot.	
CECE	*(To the group.)* Johnny, my littlest one, turns his head at that moment, looks at me, and I can't shoot the gun. Come on, kids, I'm sick. We'll go to Grandma's and stay there. I can't stand this house. Let's go!	*She resolves the conflict by retreating into a safe environment.*

The director and participating staff sit beside the patient and talk about the scene with sympathetic understanding. Their attitude is, "You are an intelligent person who likes to think of herself as independent."

PATIENT   It seems like that to me.
                 When you decided to move
                 away from all of them—your
                 husband, your boyfriend—
                 you acted pretty independent;
                 you didn't even ask the
                 children if they wanted to
                 move. I do that sometimes
                 when I'm angry, I say the hell
                 with you all.

STAFF   When did your skin begin to
                 crawl and the house begin to
                 talk?

CECE   When I saw the house. As
                 soon as I saw it.

PATIENT   Sure you did, when you
                 realized that you'd bitten off
                 more than you could chew. I
                 hear voices when things
                 aren't going the way I like.
                 All those children, it's too
                 much. I have just one, and I
                 can't manage him.

STAFF   Does anyone here think that
                 Cece could kill her children?

GROUP   No. She's over the worst of it.

PATIENT 1   I'm not so sure. She still has
                 the same dangerous thoughts.
                 She still has the house telling
                 her to separate herself from
                 taking care of her children
                 and be free of them.

GROUP   But she's here working it out.
                 She doesn't need to feel so
                 trapped; there's lots of things
                 she could do.

CECE   Name one. On second
                        thought, maybe I could go
                        back to the project manager
                        and be released from this
                        contract.

The session ended on a high note with the project manager promising to let Cece move into a more desirable area. Cece acknowledged that this might or might not happen, but that she needn't feel so desperate about her predicament. Her icy restraint was gone; she felt better, not so tight inside. The rest of the session was devoted to others in the group who had experienced hearing voices and having dangerous thoughts.

When a patient reveals an intimate detail or a shameful act, the director must recognize the face-saving needs of anyone who has gone to such lengths to cover up his feelings of dependency. One way of showing this recognition is to assure the patient that such symptoms are a human phenomenon, that when a problem seems insurmountable, people experience unpleasant emotions and thoughts that seem dangerous.

The only techniques used with Cece were the auxiliary ego as a symbol of the imagined house and the imagined voices, and the important absent members of her drama. Cece had been in the group for about three weeks. She had been silent, worried, depressed, and negative during the psychodrama. Psychodramatic techniques can sometimes reach such a depressed patient: watching a session may help the patient break through the social isolation, and auxiliary egos externalize the conflict. The auxiliary ego reduces his own spontaneity and permits the patient's responses to be dominant. The stand-in doesn't interfere with the productivity of the patient, but merely echoes the patient's fantasies. The theme of "I am afraid of the house" in the case of Cece became "I am afraid I can't raise my children." Cece denied being annoyed with her rock-throwing husband, her unreliable boyfriend, or the children. She could acknowledge only her anger toward the rental agent. This was a clue for setting up the action situation. She was ready to show certain aspects of her predicament. The house, with its accusatory attitude, was a symbol of her murderous hostility. She had to distort the world around her to maintain her fantasy of "independence."

The following week during the psychodrama session, Cece was less inhibited but still unwilling to enact relationships that were important to her. She was given a general role to play in which she showed how ably she solved the problems of others: I call it "Dear Abby," and it is a structured situation. A patient playing Abby sits in the center of the room and is surrounded by patients who act as her consultants. One at a time, patients from the audience pretend to write about a problem, read their letters aloud, and mail them to Abby. Each letter is received and discussed by Abby and her staff before an answer is given. Cece managed the role of Abby comfortably: she showed warmth and understanding toward the behavior of others. She did not use her staff as a resource, however, showing her bossy attitude.

The following week, the original symptoms of quiet disorganization reappeared. All she would say was, "I haven't been able to sleep for three nights." The goal of the next session was to help her see what she was up to and gain some mastery over her predicament.

DIRECTOR	You didn't sleep last night. Any dreams?	*The director makes an effort to establish the precipitating event that resulted in this despair.*
CECE	No dreams.	
DIRECTOR	Just before you went to bed, what were you doing?	*The director is prodding the patient from a different angle.*
CECE	I was sitting at a table, writing.	
DIRECTOR	Say out loud what you were writing last night.	
CECE	Thank you so much for your expression of sympathy at the death of (*She stops and looks up.*) . . . my mother-in-law.	*The physical activity of letter writing released her pent-up emotions.*
PATIENT 1	(*With feeling and concern.*) You were close to your mother-in-law.	
PATIENT 2	Sure she was. She used to care for the children when Cece worked.	

CECE	(*Nods.*) I loved her. She was sick for a long time and suddenly she died a few days ago.	
DIRECTOR	Since it was sudden, there may be many things you would have said had you known she was going to die. It sometimes helps to say them here. Will you be the mother-in-law, Catherine?	*The director selects an auxiliary ego, a person the patient relates to positively.*
CATHERINE (as mother-in-law)	You were a good daughter to me. I'm sorry that my son failed you.	*The auxiliary ego moves in quickly since she brings into the situation enough information to give the necessary support.*
CECE	I'll miss you. (*She begins to sob. The "mother-in-law" holds the patient close to her as she cries on her shoulder.*)	
CATHERINE (as mother-in-law)	Cry—it's good for you to show how sad you feel that I'm gone. Don't worry so much that you can't sleep; you'll find others willing and able to help you. Others will help you if you let them.	*The nurse, out of her own experiences as a daughter who has suffered loss and her knowledge of the patient's relationship to the mother-in-law, is able to respond to the patient.*

In this session Cece cried for the first time since she was a little girl. The patient was absorbed in the role of mourner and was unable to distinguish the feeling of mourning from melancholia or depression. She was frightened of the depressive feelings and was unable to express sadness for fear that it would arouse some of her homicidal impulses. The auxiliary ego, as the spirit of the mother-in-law, was in a key position to encourage and sanction feelings of sadness, grief, and unhappiness over the loss of a loved one. The auxiliary ego reinforced the role of the good daughter-in-law and tried to stop Cece's self-recriminations.

This experience brought about a catharsis of action in a crucial situation in the life of the patient. Instead of employing verbal analysis, the group replaced the loved one, and the feeling of separation was reconstructed in the here and now. Some patients are inclined to think only of loss and not replacement, and if they can experience their loss and be held or reassured at that moment, they may find a replacement. Under proper guidance this can be an excellent therapeutic tool.

In Cece's case, the immediate result of the session was her increased ability to handle her moody boyfriend. When he threatened to leave her, she wasn't thrown for a loss, and he didn't leave. She seemed to come to grips with issues. She continued to attend the day center, and the staff and patients, having shared some of the crises in Cece's life, were better able to confront her with her repressed aggression.

Use of Sociometric Arrangement

A patient's presentation is affected by his feelings toward the audience and individual members, and toward the director. In a first psychodrama presentation with acutely disturbed patients, and particularly adolescents, the director may be the least "liked" person in the room. The patients' feelings toward the director or other patients may be expressed in outright anger or in refusal to participate.

To overcome such initial resistance, the director may utilize the principles of sociometry by inviting the members of the group to seat themselves next to someone they find it easy to talk to. The arrangement may be staff and patient, or patient and patient. The tele or positive feelings for one another, should be utilized.[5] The director then asks the pairs to visit with each other and prepare a simple situation to be shown to the group—something that is significant to the patient and that relates to people either on the unit or away from the unit.

In the following session, the first pair invited to perform were George, a male hippie, with long hair, beads, and jeans, and Harry, a middle-aged businessman. The scene begins as George walks into the older man's room.

GEORGE   Good morning. What's new today?

HARRY   You ask me that every morning. It's still nothing. I can't do anything. You can't either, can you?

GEORGE	(*Smiling.*) No. No energy. We're just alike.	
HARRY	I can't do anything. You can't do anything.	*The symptoms are alike, but the causes must be different.*
DIRECTOR	Each of you choose from the group all the people you need to show this lack of energy when you can't do something, wherever it is—at home, at work, or somewhere else. Leave the room briefly with the actors and come back and show the scene to us.	

In this arrangement, the interviewing of the patient is done by an auxiliary ego. They are a mutual pair, since they have chosen each other. There is no insistence that each pair act out a situation; but there is the opportunity to talk, and this may be important for some patients. When a pair has found a situation that can be presented to the group, the director helps them portray it.

Since both George and Harry were patients, each was worked with separately. This is not always indicated, but there was such a disparity between the roles of the hippie and the middle-aged businessman that their only observable similarity was their recognition of depressive feelings.

GEORGE	This is my girl friend, Maggie. I've known her for two months. This is my friend Jerry, who owns the land, and this is a guy who lives with us. I need at least three hundred more people for the commune.
DIRECTOR	The group can pretend to be those people. Where are they?
GEORGE	Scattered about, out in the fields or someplace. But Jerry and I were in the living room and Maggie, my girl friend, was in the bedroom.

DIRECTOR	Were you sitting, standing, walking? What were you doing?	*The director is focusing on the dialogue between the two of them.*
GEORGE	We are tripping—sitting and talking. I don't feel so good. You gotta get rid of Joe. I feel terrible. How you doing, Jerry? My biology is off.	
PATIENT 1 (*as Jerry*)	I think things are all right. We have some things we have to figure out. You don't feel good, huh?	
GEORGE	There's too much, there's too much to plan. We don't know enough to run all this land.	*He expresses a feeling of inadequacy.*
PATIENT 1 (*as Jerry*)	We have enough to eat. You sure don't feel good. I don't want to sell it. We'll be able to work it out.	
GEORGE	Sell it, man. Get rid of it. It's too much, especially Joe.	*George resists the reassurances of Jerry.*
PATIENT 2 (*as Joe*)	(*Entering.*) I want some grass—a few joints.	
PATIENT 1 (*as Jerry*)	There's lots of it in the other room. I'll take one, too.	
GEORGE	How are we going to make it through the winter with all these people who don't know what to do? I don't know either; I'm sick. Bad trip.	*He begins to recognize the inadequacy of the commune.*
PATIENT 2 (*as Joe*)	(*To Jerry.*) Give me a quarter, man. I want to get an ice cream cone.	

GEORGE	That's when I began to puke. I went to the bedroom.	*The body expresses rejection of the situation.*
DIRECTOR	Keep it in the present tense. Go to the bedroom; who is in the bedroom?	
PATIENT 3 (as Maggie)	(*To Jerry.*) You really have to do something about Joe; we can't stand him.	
PATIENT 1 (as Jerry)	What's going on?	
PATIENT 3 (as Maggie)	George asked me to wake him up this morning so that he could go to look for work. He woke up, turned over, and went back to sleep. He's getting limper and limper. It's too much.	
GEORGE	(*Falls out of role.*) And then I came to the hospital. I couldn't do anything; I still can't.	*A loss of spontaneity reflects rejection of the role of member of the commune.*
DIRECTOR	Let's choose people to represent all the issues that brought you to this impasse.	
GEORGE	I can't think of any.	
PATIENT 1	The draft.	
DIRECTOR	You come and represent the draft issue.	*Multiple doubles express the various dimensions of the problem.*
PATIENT 2	Your dislike of Joe.	

DIRECTOR	You come and represent that issue.	
GEORGE	The commune. Should I go back to school or work for the commune? Die, that's one of the things, die.	*George begins to be productive.*
PATIENT 3	I'll take that issue. I know it.	
PATIENT 4	Jerry's wealth. (*The patients crowd around George and try to arouse him, taking turns talking to him.*)	
GEORGE	That's it, man. I can't do anything about it.	
MULTIPLE DOUBLES	Go back to school. Sell the land. Take a trip. Die. (*The arguments become louder and louder, with no decisive act from George. A double stands beside him and helps him face the issues, one by one. George is slow to initiate any move, but finally he is able to push an issue away from him. One by one they are pushed back—symbolically—as George ends the scene.*)	*The doubles are warned against the patient's strategy of covering up as they do all the talking.*
GEORGE	This is a hell of a time for the commune.	

The function of the multiple doubles is to expand the issues surrounding the problem, open up communication with the patient, and help the patient expose the feelings around those issues. They are not to be used by the patient for further concealment.

The patient (George) seemed to show more affect, particularly when the audience burst into applause. The contrast between the search for a simple life as defined by the idealism of "let's keep life uncomplicated" and the use of drugs to support passivity became apparent when George's dependency was externalized in the role of Joe. He grabbed his stomach the moment Joe asked for a quarter to buy an ice cream cone. (This seemed to be more than he could stomach; his body spoke his thoughts.[6]) It was as if he were exchanging places with Joe; the utter despair of his search for a simple life, his inability to discuss it, complicated no doubt by drugs, brought him to the hospital.

The director summarized the behavioral changes that had taken place during the enactment—how the patient became more involved—and reminded the group of the original problem: To compare George's lack of energy with that of Harry, the businessman. So, the next drama involved Harry and his problem.

HARRY	I'm in my office; I have papers, plans, decisions. I tell my secretary.	
DIRECTOR	Not so fast! Act it out.	
HARRY	(*To a patient.*) I'll be gone for about a half an hour.	
PATIENT (*as secretary*)	Where can I reach you?	*Roles such as this warm up the patient to the act of being at the office and provide an interference in the reverie of the patient.*
HARRY	(*Riding along in a car, talking in soliloquy.*) I'd like a drink. I can't do anything. I can't even keep an appointment; I run out on them. I was better off when I was drinking. Oh, no, I wasn't, but I could go to the tavern and sit. Now I don't know where to go, unless I go home. It's too early. I'll just ride around.	
DIRECTOR	In psychodrama, we can push time backward and forward. Let's push it ahead and go to your home. Who is there when you arrive?	

HARRY   My wife and ten kids—no,
nine. One is away.

DIRECTOR   Look around the group and
choose your family—
according to character, not
looks.

Harry carefully selected patients to play the members of his family, accurately matching personalities. He chose a volatile, explosive patient to play his bad-tempered fourteen-year-old son and a managerial woman to be his wife.

In the scene, he demonstrated his sensitivity to what people do to him by construing each remark, especially those made by his wife, as being for him or against him. He somehow overlooked that he had given his wife reason enough to take over. The scene showed the lack of respect that many children of alcoholics feel. An argument over the use of the family car became an issue that resulted in Harry's violent outburst, "Who the hell wears the pants around here?" He began knocking a few of the kids around (to feel a sense of power), and one by one the others left him alone, each child going to his room and the wife going to visit a girlfriend. He got into his car and began driving around, this time with a double ego. "I'm a failure. It's like being at a shooting gallery. I fire and I miss; I never hit the target. I only feel offended."

DIRECTOR   When we have a feeling of
hopelessness, it sometimes
helps to dump it in a
psychodramatic shop, the magic
shop. It is a place where you
can leave what you no longer
need and take away what you
want and value. Let's set up
such a shop. (*The director
selects a staff member to be
the shopkeeper.*) Your shop
is filled with dreams,
anything a person wants, but
he must bargain for it. He has
to be willing to give up
something in order to get it.
(*To Harry.*) Think for a
moment. What is it that you
really want?

HARRY   Health.   *This is an undefined,*
                                          vague statement for
                                          this envious, hostile
                                          man.

The bargaining began between the shopkeeper and Harry but fizzled out because of Harry's inability to achieve good human relationships even at the symbolic level.

It is interesting to note that the hippie and the businessman were alike in their aloofness and inability to compete with others. The businessman used alcohol to cushion his encounters with people, and the hippie used drugs. The magic workshop was meant to help the businessman identify the areas of his life that were in need of change—the social roles of father, husband, and so on—but his chief concern was in the development of the physical role of a healthy man. The magic shop could have helped clarify Harry's distorted goals and suggested a way to change them. But Harry failed to "bargain" or to concentrate on modifying his acute sensitivity to what others did to him, and this interfered with his ability to cope with others. His mounting hostility erupted and destroyed the interpersonal relationships around him.

The director closed the session by encouraging the group to break up into small units and compare the situations of the two men, reminding them that the session had begun with George's saying, "We're just alike." Were they?

Use of Fantasy

Fantasy is often a helpful means of externalizing an interpersonal dilemma. Frequently, withdrawn patients are absorbed in their feelings of inadequacy to the exclusion of the issue or of the group in which the problem occurs. The magic shop technique can be helpful in placing such a patient in circumstances in which he can participate and be helped to explore the issue.[7] The following session took place in a day center with the psychodrama team and approximately twenty-five patients. The audience was accustomed to psychodrama, since the center held sessions weekly; the director, however, viewed the group as if this were their first session. Much had happened during the week, and if a new member had joined, his presence would have changed the group interaction.

A patient who had been discharged was back. She was sitting with her coat on in a relatively warm room, head bowed, and hugging herself tightly. The patients greeted the director with "Let's do something funny today." The magic shop was what they agreed on. The director perceived that the presence of the returned patient was discouraging to the others. What they were saying was "Let's think of other things."

For the scene, three group members assumed the roles of the shop-keeper and his assistants. The "sale" began with one of the assistants going around the group, looking for customers. Some came up spontaneously; others needed to be invited. When it became evident that the returned patient, Jane, was excluding herself from participation, she was taken into the shop (into the stage area).

SHOPKEEPER	We have a shop full of goodies: fame, fortune, husbands. What are you in the market for?
JANE	Happiness.
SHOPKEEPER	We've got a lot of that. What will you give for happiness?
JANE	Unhappiness.
SHOPKEEPER	You're not giving up anything. You've got to think of something else.
JANE	Depression.
PATIENT	Give us your anger.
JANE	I'm not angry.
SHOPKEEPER	If you're going to give us your depression, then show us what you're giving us. Why are you depressed?
JANE	Monsignor died.
DIRECTOR	You loved him very much, didn't you? Would you like to talk to him? Often there is so much left unsaid that it helps to say it out loud and stop going over it inside oneself. (*A member of the staff stands up as Monsignor, and the dialogue begins.*)

JANE   I wish you hadn't died. I
                need you.

MONSIGNOR   Yes, I know you need me,
                but death comes to each of
                us. Death is a part of living.
                Tell me, Jane, who will you
                turn to now that I'm gone?

JANE   I don't know; I don't know.

MONSIGNOR   There are many who love you
                besides me. I became not
                only your father-confessor,
                but your father after he died.
                As your father, I was able to
                love you, and as I was able to
                love you, so others will love
                you.

JANE   That's true. I'll talk to people,
                and go back to the day center
                and get my part-time job
                back, and do the best I can.
                (*She looks up and smiles.*)
                You know, I really feel better.

SHOPKEEPER   We can't give you happiness
                right now. You're mourning
                the loss of a loved one. All
                we can give you is relief, but
                don't mourn too long. Come
                back later for happiness.

The original intent of the group was to have fun in order to deny the possibility of marginal recovery from mental illness, as evidenced by Jane's return. The spontaneous development in the dramatic situation of Jane's loss became the particular concern of the group. The magic shop momentarily gave Jane the physical arrangement possible for her to show her distress. The simplicity of the situation made it easy for Jane to throw herself into a state of happiness, unhappiness, depression.

As with other sessions, the point at which the director began depended on where the patient was. The skills of the director and staff were needed to integrate the performance into a meaningful life situation. The auxiliary ego playing the role of the Monsignor spoke in commonsense terms, focusing on the central issue of love and asserting in an encouraging way that all is not lost. The issue was clearly stated so that it would not be misunderstood. A confused patient has trouble when conversation is vague or complicated; he may muddle over a remark that is open to interpretation. Jane's verbal productions were a clue to the thread of her thinking and furnished the auxiliary ego with the literal statements necessary to communicate with her.

It is well to remember that one should not always insist that the patient express anger when he says, "I am depressed." An attempt to do this, only a week after the Monsignor's death, would have closed Jane up. While anger toward loss or death may have been basic to the dynamics of the problem, mourning was the primary feeling. The idea of anger (tentatively suggested) would have made Jane feel criticized, and instead of helping, might have pushed her into a deeper isolation. It was necessary for a therapeutic gain in this situation to show love, to give love, to be a substitute "loved being" for the patient.[8] "Another helpful approach for mastering the grief is to encourage the patient to reexperience it in regard to each action, place, or event that reminds him of the loved one."[9]

The role of the audience is important here. First, the group was reassured to learn that Jane's return was understandable, since many people, not just the mentally ill, suffer setbacks when death comes to a loved one. Second, the confused, withdrawn patient needs exposure to the group, since a depressed patient seldom avails himself of the positive values of contact with real people. The withdrawn patient becomes a mystery to others, and as the mystery thickens, the distance between himself and others becomes greater. The magic shop solved this mystery in the case of Jane, and a line of communication was established to a wide range of people, offering replacements in Jane's social atom.

Use of a Double

Often patients have private thoughts that they are unable to share, thoughts that may be unformulated and so cannot be verbalized. This is evident in depression. An auxiliary ego as a double attempts to identify with the patient in the moment of a feeling response and to express it. The double joins the patient's mood, unearths the underlying circumstance, and creates a change in the patient's attitude toward the problem. This requires a frame of reference, acquired either through clinical experience or by simply living and gaining insights into what goes on in one's own and in another person's mind. The value of the double is that he makes the patient feel that he is understood.

The following session centered on Jane. The group observed that she was quieter than usual and suggested acting out a home situation. She selected from the audience a mother and three sisters. They took their places in the stage area. The mother began:

MOTHER	Agnes, did your fittings with the bridesmaids work out all right?	
JANE	(*Looks up.*) That's the way she talks.	
AGNES	Well, we'll have to have another fitting.	*Jane's body posture indicates a glum mood.*
SECOND SISTER	I think the shower last night was cute. I'd like to have one when I get engaged.	*Jane's expression is definitely sad, and she seems to be reacting to the oncoming wedding.*
AGNES	Jane, don't you want to invite someone to the wedding? (*Jane doesn't answer. Her head gets lower and lower on her chest. A double stands besides Jane and assumes the same body position.*)	
DOUBLE	Life is passing me by. I'll never get married. (*Jane shows no recognition.*)	
SECOND SISTER	What about the wedding cake?	*They continue general conversation relating to the wedding.*
DOUBLE	Why don't they quit talking about such trivia when they see I'm suffering?	*The double is feeling her way into the mood of the silent patient and tries anger.*

JANE	No, no, I'm not angry at them. I don't mind them talking about the wedding.	*Jane denies anger. Double accepts the denial and continues exploring.*
DOUBLE	I accept the wedding, but I wonder what will happen to me.	*The double senses the utter despair of Jane's plight.*
JANE	That's it! What will happen to me? (*She bursts out crying.*)	
DOUBLE	My favorite sister is leaving, the only one in the family I felt close to. What's going to become of me?	*The double echoes, and sobs silently with Jane, "What's going to become of me?"*
AGNES	(*Stands beside Jane, puts her arms around her.*) I'm really not leaving. John and I both will continue to be close to you.	
JANE	I hope that's true. (*Still crying.*)	
DOUBLE	I feel better now that I cried. I get discouraged too easily and think all is lost when it really isn't. I'll tell Agnes how I feel and let her help me.	*Double corrects the mistaken idea of instant loss.*

Jane's attempt to hide by closing up and suffering quietly was interrupted by the double. While Jane was driving people away through silence and hiding from help and understanding, the double searched for the common sense, or the social sense, in the stuporous behavior. The double made several attempts to understand how the wedding was a crisis situation. When Jane denied her unexpressed anger at the wedding of her favorite sister, the double realized the despair of the patient. Jane felt utterly lost and therefore recognized the double's verbalization of her feelings. By expressing the exaggerated feelings of inadequacy ("What will become of me?"), the double allowed Jane the catharsis of tears. Meanwhile, the auxiliary egos playing the roles of mother and sisters searched for the precipitating cause of the patient's despair by talking about different aspects of the upcoming wedding. The double and the patient were aroused to spontaneous reactions. The auxiliary egos helped the patient recognize and repair her desolate feelings. Jane was included in the solution of the problem, as the double told her what she could do about her depression: "I'll *tell* Agnes how I feel and let her help me."

Reaching depressed patients and arousing them to an expression of appropriate feeling are therapeutic gains that can be seen in this sample of interaction. Jane reinstated her self-esteem by being a good girl, wishing her sister well, and meeting the expectations of the group by responding effectively to the double's eagerness to be helpful. Her "basic mistake" may have been overambition to be so good that she felt lost because she was not good enough. This is a learned attitude derived from early experiences.

The Death Scene

With depressed patients, the theme of "I want to die" may also be handled with the "death scene" described in Chapter 9. The director begins by asking the patient who expresses this wish to visualize his death. In the warm-up interview the director asks the patient how he died, how it feels to be dead, and who would mourn his death. The mourners may be named: mother, father, husband, and so on. Persons from the group are selected to stand as mourners. Through role reversal with these significant persons (the persons against whom the anger is aimed), the patient's emotional problems which led to this despair are clarified. There is light at the end of the tunnel as the issues are worked out.

19

Outpatient Groups

The term *patient* has traditionally meant a person who is under a doctor's care. But the increase in trained nonmedical therapists has given new meaning to this term. Now it may be used also to refer to a person who is being seen by a worker (or a team of workers) in the mental health field, such as a social worker, a psychologist, a nurse, a hospital aide, and an occupational or activity therapist. The term *outpatient*, then, refers to a person who is not hospitalized but who is receiving help at a clinic attached to a hospital or at one of the many community health clinics. In a clinic, therapy groups are often formed to help the aged, children, families, adolescents, young adults, and others. Staff members also receive training and supervision here in group therapy and psychodrama.

A group consisting of ten to fifteen participants who are strangers is different from a family or a couples' group in that the significant figures in the controversial relationship are not present. The group members spend a lot of time talking about the difficulties they experience with these figures, who are vague and shadowy to group members that do not know them. The psychodrama situation in which scenes are enacted allows direct expression of the interpersonal emotional disturbance by focusing on a specific situation and a particular moment. Acting out life situations helps group members recognize how they influence and contribute to the situations in which they find themselves and not project blame onto others.

The psychodrama experience facilitates the development of new role behavior. It is somewhat easier to try out a new role with a group of strangers than with the family group. The tendency to fall into established patterns of behavior is greater within a family or a couples' group. In a gathering of strangers, each person has the opportunity to take responsibility for his own behavior and attitudes and to modify them. It should be noted, however, that the longer a group of strangers stays together as a group, the more the group resembles a family.

The cases selected to demonstrate psychodrama in this chapter come from an outpatient clinic for psychiatric patients. The clinic serves mostly low income urban female adults who have at least a high school education. Before coming to the group psychodrama sessions, each patient has been evaluated in an interview with a social worker or referred from the individual treatment program offered by the clinic. Patients are referred when the therapist and patient decide that a group experience might be beneficial before they terminate treatment. In general, the patients are not likely to be acutely ill, although some are in the ambulatory psychotic range. These groups have the usual number of patients with behavior disorders that need treatment.

Because all the patients are employed (a requirement), the group from which these examples are taken met during the early evening hours. They met once a week with the same female therapist-director, who teamed up with a male codirector since the group was all female. After referral to group psychodrama, the patient had an individual interview with one of the directors, not for reevaluation but for orientation to the group. The interview generally proved helpful in alleviating some of the anticipatory fears of walking into a room full of strangers; it also lowered the dropout rate of patients who came to the clinic expecting individual therapy.

Jerome Frank, psychiatrist and author, has observed that group therapy is more stressful than individual therapy for some patients, especially those susceptible to the "disease" of other patients and those who need strong support from the therapist.[1] This stress becomes observable when a patient becomes upset and rushes screaming from the room followed by the staff. This stimulates some of the others to "catch" the same feeling of discomfort and manifest it. In an outpatient group, this type of patient may not return, unless he can be dealt with therapeutically.

Patients who were unwilling to stay in the group may have felt deprived of the undivided attention of a therapist or confused by multiple interactions; or they may have been frightened by the openness of other patients. Patients who stayed with the group usually accepted role-playing methods as a help in exploring attitudes and discovering new ways of relating to others. With little more than a question or two from the director, they dealt directly with personal problems.

Like most people seeking psychiatric help, the patients treated in this program had problems in getting along with people. However, they presented the problems specifically as wanting confirmation that they could find someone who would love them and that they would be able to maintain good relationships with their work associates. Many of the young women complained of nervousness and a variety of physical symptoms, which, for the most part, they did not connect to disturbed relationships. A confrontation with the meaning of this behavior (the physical symptoms) led them to understand the purpose of the symptoms.[2] We may assume that they felt a lack of productive contact with others and used a variety of methods to correct this discomfort, such as sexual promiscuity, physical symptoms, clinging to the original family, and staying in a bad relationship with a married man or a dissolute boyfriend.

Most of the patients felt that valuable time was wasted encouraging withdrawn patients to participate. To reduce the tension of the group, the director made a deliberate effort to use the group as auxiliary egos when working with a withdrawn patient and to bring up a group problem—for example, emotional independence from mother. The therapeutic experience of becoming active agents in exerting an influence on a patient enhanced the members' sense of self-esteem, as well as giving them a chance to learn more of their own attitudes in relating to the problem.[3] Time, then, was well spent with the withdrawn patient.

The following is an example of a type of session, one that places a problem squarely on the patient and helps him with it. Direct and open management of the problem is demonstrated.

Case One: Feelings of Failure and Helplessness

Maria was a rather attractive twenty-six-year-old former nun. While she was a nun, Maria had lived in one community for seven years. Then she was transferred to a new community. This move precipitated a psychotic break. She was hospitalized because of her inability to adjust to life away from her old community. She complained of an inability to talk, of confusion, and of an internal churning excitement. After her release from the hospital, the psychiatrist referred her to our group as an outpatient. With the help of a friend she was able to work on a part-time basis. Her family, however, expected more than this and got her a full-time job as a filing clerk. She held this job, we think, through the support and encouragement of the group.

Maria posed practical problems, since most of her communications were blurred. She would blurt out, "I don't know how to tell you. I don't know what to say. Things are moving very fast inside me. I've been crying. I feel like a failure." The group members, on many occasions, were able to help her understand her feelings of bewilderment as being precipitated both by her high expectation of herself and by her high expectation of others. These general theories were put into actual situations. Many of the "ordinary experiences" of a filing clerk, such as misplacing a letter, became extraordinary events to her. Going to a baby shower given for her sister was an emotionally charged event in which she focused on being unable to talk to people, not on her feelings of isolation. Her most frequent despair was feeling inarticulate; she couldn't articulate what she wanted or what she didn't want from others.

Maria lived at home with her mother, father, and three sisters. All of them worked and were busy living their own lives—cooking, cleaning, shopping, dating, gossiping. Maria fit in with the cooking, cleaning, and shopping, but she felt unrelated to the gossiping and dating. Her most frequent complaint was, "They don't talk to me. They never ask my advice." One day she arrived in the group obviously excited. Invited to talk, she couldn't say more than, "It's my mother. If she wouldn't treat me like such a baby, I wouldn't be such a failure." She was incoherent and mixed up, first asking whether her mother had a right to pick her up by automobile when she visited her girl friends, then asking whether her mother wasn't wrong in not asking her about a present to be bought for her sister's baby shower. The director turned to the group and asked, "Is it clear to you what is bothering Maria?" The group began to respond with almost the same excitement as Maria. Each was thinking of mother, of some of the ways she hassled with her own mother. The director invited Maria to come to the stage area. Her speech was punctuated with frequent pauses, and her eyes were held in a stare.

MARIA	I want to move out. I want to get a different job.	
DIRECTOR	What would you like to do most— move out or get a new job?	*The director feels that it won't be possible for Maria to move until she gets a new job, and the job is certainly easier for her to deal with than her mother is.*

MARIA	I want to move out. I'm looking for an apartment.	
DIRECTOR	That would mean being independent of your mother. What is it that bothers you so much about her?	*The director accepts the conflict with mother and agrees to work it out.*
MARIA	She babies me.	
DIRECTOR	Janet, will you come and stand beside Maria and be her mother who babies her. (*Janet comes forward.*) What else does your mother do?	*The group members are clarifying Maria's blurred communications.*
MARIA	She criticizes me.	
DIRECTOR	Pat, you may be able to be the critical mother of Maria. Come and stand beside her. Maria, what else bothers you?	
MARIA	She doesn't think I can do anything. Like, when I wanted to do some volunteer work, she insisted that Dad pick me up, even though it was only ten o'clock at night.	*Maria means, "I'm afraid I can't do anything, and she thinks so, too."*
DIRECTOR	That belongs to the babying. Janet, there are some lines for you. What else does mother do, Maria?	
MARIA	She makes fun of Lynn (*a group member*), just because she's colored. She's very nice to her face, but as soon as she leaves, she warns me about feeling friendly with colored people.	*Maria says that people, especially her mother, are hypocrites.*

DIRECTOR

Who will be Maria's mother with prejudices? Will you, Rose? (*Rose comes forward.*) What else, Maria, does your mother do that bothers you?

MARIA

She is always picking on Dad —that's why he drinks too much.

DIRECTOR

Who will be the nagging mother?

The director is helping the patient channel her relationship to her mother. Each auxiliary ego symbolizes an attitude that distresses Maria. After all the areas have been assigned, including a mother who does not want her daughter to move, a double stands next to Maria to strengthen her position during the confrontation.

BABYING MOTHER

Maria, honey, what do you want for breakfast, eggs or cereal?

MARIA

(*With the help of the double.*) I wish you wouldn't make my breakfast; I'd feel more like an adult. I think when you make my breakfast it means that you think I don't know how to make breakfast.

BABYING MOTHER

Maria, I don't understand why you don't like for me to make your breakfast. No one else in the family objects. Why should you?

MARIA   That's one of the things that
                 bothers me. I'm not sure. If I
                 were sure of my
                 independence, it wouldn't
                 hurt. I mostly think that I
                 really can't cook, and I'll
                 never learn if you keep this
                 up.

CRITICAL MOTHER (*Jumps into the argument as
                 the babying mother stops
                 talking.*) You really never do
                 anything right. You're too
                 slow. The only thing you
                 really do right is shop and
                 spend money. What about
                 that bedroom set you bought?

MARIA   Why do you do this to me?
                 When I do something I like,
                 or when I say what I want,
                 you warn me, you confuse
                 me, you make me feel that
                 I'm doing the wrong thing.
                 Why couldn't you have
                 said it was a good idea for me
                 to buy the bedroom set?

CRITICAL MOTHER Maria, how else can you
                 learn to save money to
                 prepare for the future? I
                 love you, but anything I say
                 to you, you misunderstand.

On completion of the role playing, the auxiliary egos returned to the group. The relationship was pinpointed: Maria's mother had traditional values and wanted her daughter to be obedient; in return for this, the mother gave service and supervision. Maria was trying to change the relationship. A role transition is usually accompanied by stress, therefore, anger, but Maria ignored the central issue of the changing relationship.

In the interaction, the group observed that the double carried the conversation, while Maria was quiet without showing shyness, duplicating her pattern at home of disengagement in the midst of the family routine. She was asked when she first realized that her silence gave her a special place in the family. Her words and acts were more coherent, which showed that she was less resistant to revealing herself. The scene enacted, with the members of the group playing auxiliary roles, was of little Maria at bedtime in a room full of her sisters and cousins, playing, laughing, jumping from bed to bed. Her favorite aunt came into the room and said, "Quiet, children, it's sleep time." Maria was the first to be quiet, and her aunt recognized and praised her for this. This type of response—minding an admired authority—worked well until extra-familial encounters required a spontaneity Maria had not developed.

Any person who wants to move away from home into a new circumstance faces the task of confronting his parents with this decision. Maria was sure she would leave her mother's house. She had done it before. But her discomfort came from a too constricted view of how good other people should be. She resisted playing herself. Her preoccupation was with the misbehavior of her mother. This resistance was met by having her play a substitute role.[4] She was asked to be her mother telling *her* mother that she was leaving home. This opened the door for Maria; she stood up and talked clearly enough for all to make the connection that moving out is a stage of development that her mother faced with the help of a sister. While some wait for marriage to leave, others, in a burst of independence, move out on their own. In this instance, playing the role of mother had a normalizing effect, it reduced Maria's fears of being too weak and helpless to make it on her own. The beneficial effects were that she was able to enlist the support of one of the group members in getting a new job; her quietness was understood; and one member in the group became her particular friend.

It was after this session that Maria recalled a dream she had had when she first entered the group a year before: "I was at a party, and many people were sitting in a room at tables. I came in, and no one paid very much attention to me. I was ignored, and I felt it. I came with another person—a lady, I think. The hostess approached us and introduced herself, and, as the lady introduced me, she explained, 'This is Maria. She is engaged to Mrs. Starr's son.' The hostess's manner changed, and I became the center of everyone's attention."

When Maria was asked to change whatever displeased her in the dream, she refused. The dream was a successful experience. She said, "I felt lost, but then I found someone to help me." She had found a replacement for the group she had lost (the religious community).

Another indication of the value of a group approach with Maria was her ability to come to the group with this report of an experience on her new job: "I was tiptoeing down the hall at work, thinking that my heels were making too much noise, when the big boss came along and said, 'Maria, we don't have to tiptoe around this office.' I didn't know what to say to him, but I told him I didn't want to disturb anybody. For the next hour and a half, I wondered, 'Did I say the right thing or didn't I? Did I act crazy, or didn't I? Will they fire me because I didn't act right?' Then all of a sudden it stopped. I'm not sure I know why it stopped, but it did."

Maria moved away from her family. Her sisters, one by one, got married without threatening Maria's stability, and Maria, with the group's help, concluded: "I'm not ready for dating men. I may be sometime, but not now. I'm just learning how to make friends with women. There's no rush." She depended on the group to help her reorganize her life.

The use of multiple auxiliary egos helps define the problem and allows the dependency to be so vividly drawn that the patient is forced to see the development as a mutual transaction. There can be no bosses without willing servants. Sometimes the patient will need help in admitting this; then an excursion into the past directed toward the formation of a lifestyle arouses the patient to feel: "Help me be independent. I'm tired of being frightened." The director must be careful that the patient is portrayed in a good light, remembering, of course, that no light is really good enough. Still, the director must try to change a disturbing relationship into a healthy life experience.

Case Two: An Immediate Crisis

At times a patient would arrive at the clinic session with a freshly experienced crisis and ask for time to work it through with the group. The group was invaluable in sharing with the patient similar experiences that they had had and examining the problem with the group directors.

The future-projection technique is helpful with any crisis that has occurred, since it provides the patient with many different possible responses to a problem and offers a warm-up structure that helps the group membership explore with the patient the roles within the situation in relation to the difficult "other."

Meg was an easily excitable and dramatic young woman of twenty-five who felt stigmatized, when she joined the group eight months earlier, because she wasn't married. She finally became engaged to a "nice young man" who, she said, had yet to make his mark, but she was willing to help him. The group had shared the ups and downs of the dating period and were invited to the wedding. She rushed in with, "I just can't marry a man who cracks ice with his teeth and swishes it around in his mouth. It's too disgusting. The wedding is off. My father will have a fit. He'll be embarrassed to recall all the invitations—and furious about the money he put up for the hall." She was anxious about telling her father of the canceled wedding and was asked to soliloquize as she played the scene of breaking the news. (A double went along.)

It was clear from this trial run that her mind was racing with ways to justify her decision to her father. She didn't know where to begin. She was sure he would give her "holy hell." She faced her father, played by the co-director; he gave her hell, as she had anticipated. This was accomplished in a role reversal, as the patient played her father and the co-director became Meg. The father was furious at the wasted money and at the humiliating exposure before his friends of having a daughter who was so flighty as to break off a marriage at the last minute. This was the patient's view of her father's anticipated reaction.

While no one in the group had had a prior experience that exactly matched Meg's, they all understood the contempt someone is likely to feel from a family that is confronted with an example of bad judgment. The group began to offer other ways Meg could relate to her father and include her mother in order to lift the burden of Meg's position. One of the auxiliary egos represented a father who tried to persuade Meg to go through with the marriage. The enactment clarified the fact that Meg was firm in her decision not to marry. This gave the co-director an opportunity to close the session by playing the role of a father who was unhappy that the marriage had to be canceled, but glad that his daughter had discovered in time that it was a mistake. "After all, that's what the engagement period is all about, to test your capacities for getting along with each other. It's good to acknowledge that you made a mistake and to take steps to correct it."

The full effectiveness of the future-projection technique was revealed when Meg had a real meeting with her parents. Meg reported the following week that the news was met with anger, dismay, and finally a sensible approach to stopping the wedding plans, which included calling the young man, who seemed as relieved as Meg at the decision to have the marriage called off. This therapeutic effort was effective because it helped the patient examine, in a supportive emotional atmosphere, her fears about canceling the marriage, and helped her clarify her role in relation to her parents. This clarification led to a realization of feelings she had not completely formulated before the psychodramatic production; while her reasons for aborting the marriage were trivial, the role conflict was deep. Her panic reaction lessened as she realized that she was repulsed by immaturity, which she saw in her fiancé, and attracted to strong parental figures.

This was not enough, however. It wasn't long before Meg announced that she was leaving the group. Part of the agreement among members in the group was that one must discuss the reasons for one's decision to leave. Meg made a connection between group psychodrama and her recent episode of attempting to marry. She was going into individual therapy, away from all the emotional cripples in the group. This came as a bombshell that could have destroyed the spirit of the group; unless this negative expression could be counteracted with some positive understanding, others might have quit.

The director quickly considered the various approaches that might remedy this situation: (1) The director could ask for a double to warm up to Meg's onslaught and mirror her expression of "I see in you what I see and am repulsed by in myself." (2) The psychodramatist could ask for a role reversal; Meg could experience the hostility as another patient played Meg and tried to understand the source of the anger. She could be asked to reverse roles with each member of the group. (3) The director could ask Meg to move backward in time and show the events and influences that led to the decision. (4) Meg could be asked to place herself in the future and fantasize an "ideal" therapist and cure. (5) Meg could be seated in the antagonist's chair while the group, one by one, ventilated their disappointment and resentment of her derogatory evaluation of them.

But the real target of Meg's feelings, aroused by the group membership, had not been identified. Meg's accusation was general and diffuse. An empty chair was placed in the center of the room, and Meg was asked to imagine in the chair the person who bothered her the most and to express herself freely to the empty chair. She placed the codirector (a psychiatrist) in the chair. She saw him as withholding attention, knowledge, and directives from her since there were so many others able to capture his time and attention with their symptoms. This was an old story with Meg. She was an only child, and peer relations were difficult for her. The crisis was over, since the group understood this.

A format for separation from the group had been developed, providing constructive feedback of the separating patient's participation in the group. In a series of vignettes, in which one patient played Meg and another played himself, the members presented their first meeting with Meg, a clash involving Meg, and a friendly encounter with Meg. These formed a profile of growth. Meg could sit and watch as the scenes were played out or she could join in and add some useful or remembered information. The final scene invited Meg to tell the group how she saw herself in five years.

Case Three: A Vivid Recollection

Some sessions are vivid examples of an attempt to reach a patient. Such a session centered on Rys, an eighteen-year-old patient who had been referred by a psychiatrist. Rys was the youngest of three children; the two older ones were girls. His father was a maintenance engineer, and his mother was a soft-spoken housewife. At the age of sixteen, Rys threw his books around the schoolroom and rushed home to the attic, refusing to eat with the family. Rys was hospitalized for a time, given shock treatments, and released. He was still under treatment with a psychiatrist when psychodrama was recommended as an additional help.

The aim of therapy was to treat Rys's emotional withdrawal from his family group and his friends. His attitude toward them, regardless of how they treated him, was one of aloofness and suspicion. He had reorganized his social atom and related positively to painting, bicycling, and the great scientist, Albert Einstein. The director began therapy by entering into the situation as a person with whom Rys could experience a new relationship. The director was guided by Rys's spontaneous reactions. They indicated what would help Rys to form a less stereotyped attitude, first toward the director, then toward Rys's group.[5]

Rys came to the session carrying a bundle. He seemed so alone. The interview began.

DIRECTOR	Glad to see you, Rys. I see you brought some of your drawings along. Let's see them.	
RYS	(*Spreading them out.*) I think I have improved a lot over the summer. (*Pause.*) In fact, that one is my masterpiece, or rather one of	*He is saying, "I must be a successful person. My chance is in my talent." His self-esteem is related to the role of*

my masterpieces. I drew a series. The finest I sent to Professor Einstein, and he sent me a letter. I called the picture "Agony in the Garden." Here is the letter he sent me. "Dear Rys: Thank you for the drawings and the letter. Your pictures are interesting, artistically and psychologically. Albert Einstein."

artist. (The letter from Dr. Einstein was real.)

DIRECTOR

What an interesting summer you had! A wonderful letter from Professor Einstein, and to have been able to paint all these paintings! It really sounds like a good summer.

This stereotyped happy response dismays the patient.

RYS

Not at all, but I did get a new bicycle. You know I had my nose broken. Some men held me up and hit me three times on the head. I didn't even feel it.

"Things aren't that easy; in fact, they're awful."

DIRECTOR

That's too bad. Some bad things happened to you as well as good things. How are you getting on with your father?

RYS

If anything, worse. He tries to minimize everything. My letter . . .

"I'm having a rough time."

DIRECTOR

When did he minimize you, Rys? Who was in the room? You be your father and I'll be you.

RYS	My aunt and uncles, my sister, and mother. You know they show or are beginning to show real interest in my drawings. I walked into the room about there and laid my drawings and the letter near them on the radiator.	*His excitement grows as he anticipates reliving the disappointing attempts to deal with his family. The director takes the roles of Rys and the uncle, but the patient is so excited that he takes all the roles, including the father.*
RYS *(as uncle)*	Rys, what do you have there?	
RYS	(*Moving around the room as he plays the various roles.*) Some of my drawings and a letter from Professor Einstein.	
RYS *(as uncle)*	By gosh, let me read it. (*Reads it.*) By gosh, from Einstein—the authentic signature of the professor.	
RYS *(as aunt)*	Joe, who is Einstein?	
RYS *(as uncle)*	You haven't even heard of him? A great scientist.	
RYS	The greatest.	*Rys identifies with the greatest.*
RYS *(as dad)*	He must be a nice guy to send you a letter. Come on, Joe. I'll help you wash the car, if you want me to.	*The father is insensitive to his son but aware that a great man found the time to respond and encourage a troubled boy.*
RYS	(*To the director.*) He cut me off just like that. No, he said something about the army screening for communists.	*Rys worries about this meaning and loss of his father's respect.*
DIRECTOR	Shall I be your father, and you tell him he cut you off?	

RYS	(*Refuses by gazing off into space.*)	*He arranges not to improve the situation.*
DIRECTOR	I'll tell you what let's do. You be Einstein receiving the letter you sent him. I'll be one of his friends visiting.	*The director realizes that Rys wants to stay with the Einstein reverie. The focus now is on the patient's perception of Einstein's reaction to the letter.*
RYS	Oh, that's wonderful. (*Looks into space.*) I thought and thought about it. I even saw Einstein go to the mailbox and get the letter. (*He begins to become Einstein and reaches for the letter.*) Oh, here is a letter from Chicago. (*He opens the letter and reads.*) Do you believe in unified psychology? (*He reads silently, shaking his head all the while.*)	*My family is too much. He has found a replacement, someone he can relate to.*
DIRECTOR	Professor Einstein, do I disturb you? I would like to visit with you a bit.	
RYS	(*As Einstein.*) Come in and sit down. I just received a most interesting letter from a young man out in Chicago and some drawings. Very interesting. Listen to this. He says he is no communist. Neither am I. Do you suppose he means a synthesis when he says unified psychology? I would like to answer this letter in detail, a long, long letter. But I can't reveal myself. I am a mathematician and I must stay in my field. I'll read this letter over later. What can I do for you?	*Even here is disappointment.*

Rys then gathered his paintings, carefully put his letter that Einstein had sent him in his wallet, and left. In the psychodrama Rys realized his fantasy, which allowed him to express his feeling of self-satisfaction that his family did not provide. The schizophrenic often role plays great, noteworthy people (both in life and on the stage), but has few resources as an average man. Rys's productivity was all within the role of Einstein. It is easy for patients like Rys to have a dialogue with important figures on the thought level. The auxiliary ego interrupts and gives the patient warmth and interest, a transaction of acceptance with a real person. While Rys was no longer psychotic, he still felt more comfortable keeping distance between himself and the conventional. Rys got a letter and was pleased and excited with it; he was able to share this excitement by enacting Einstein receiving the letter. To bring about a favorable change in the patient, he was encouraged to practice and exercise social concern, and this was done in conjunction with others.

This roster of techniques and their application to specific cases has ended with a young man I have long remembered and his attraction to a great scientist. Even in that brief role-playing encounter, the quality of the encounter is sharp and enduring.

All the more so since I, too, in playing the role of Rys, experienced with Rys a great man's (Einstein's) social interest: the capacity to have sympathy, to encourage, and to be supportive to a troubled young man.

Menninger notes that "this is the deepest meaning of the therapeutic attitude" and puts this principle in a paragraph of directions for the workers in his psychiatric hospital: "If we can love: this is the touchstone. . . . To our patient who cannot love we must say by our actions that we do love him." Menninger adds that "hope is just as important as love in the therapeutic attitude."[6] Moreno emphasized that creativity and spontaneity affect the development of man's relationships, not only in the treatment of the ill, but also in dealing with the healthy.

It is natural to move from narration to acting, transforming an event of living into a performance that may be examined and changed if necessary. This book has illustrated appropriate uses of the various formats and techniques of psychodrama. While I have presented psychodrama from the viewpoint of a person who uses it as a principal method of therapy, I am aware that many will want to use it along with, and as a variation from, other forms of communication, to include it as a procedure in individual or group therapy. As in all matters psychological, the warehouse of information is open for all to take and use—judiciously, carefully, and slowly. This book encourages you to work in simple stages, to employ the methods with respect, and to recognize the complexity of the field.

To become a psychodramatist, one should train in directing and in becoming an auxiliary ego. Several institutes offer a course in psychodrama; usually, the students have a basic education in the mental health field. Generally, it is the person already in mental health as a nurse, psychologist, social worker, psychiatrist, or mental health worker that is attracted to psychodrama.

Another way to train is to work with patients on a unit with a good director and learn by sharing his or her expertise. This method can be supported and nourished by attending workshop seminars with peers. And there is no lack of these to attend. In-service training plus outside stimulation is the surest way to overcome the chief difficulty in the field of individuals doing psychodrama with little or no training.

In the first chapters, I expressed the hope of being able to write a manual on how to direct psychodrama in a wide variety of situations. If psychodrama is distinguished from other forms of therapy, it is because the participants act, not only for themselves, but for others. It is in the telling of real life situations and showing how to include imagery at the thought level that this book can be helpful to a student of psychodrama. Brander Matthews' advice to students of the drama, that they should train themselves to read plays by visualizing an actual performance, by translating the cold printed word into the warm action of a living performer, aptly applies to using this book. "He [the student] should call up a mental image of the scenes where the story is laid; and he should evoke moving pictures of the several characters, not merely with his eyes reading the dialogue, but with his ears hearing it as actors would speak it."[7] This is a warm-up that is difficult to improve on.

Notes

Introduction

1. Jules H. Masserman, *Modern Therapy of Personality Disorders* (Dubuque, Iowa: Wm. C. Brown, 1966), p. 83.

2. John Willett, *The Theatre of Bertolt Brecht* (London: Methuen & Co., 1959), p. 108.

3. Henry Thomas, *Stories of the Great Dramas* (New York: Garden City Pub. Co., 1939), pp. 371–76.

Chapter 1

1. Edgar F. Borgatta, "The Use of Psychodrama, Sociodrama, and Related Techniques in Social Psychological Research," *Sociometry* (Aug., 1950): 244–58.

2. Jacob L. Moreno, "The Triadic System, Psychodrama-Sociometry-Group Psychotherapy," *Group Psychotherapy and Psychodrama*, 23 (1970), no. 1 & 2.

3. Jacob L. Moreno, *Psychodrama,* vol. 1 (Beacon, N.Y.: Beacon House, 1946), pp. 356–61.

4. Ibid., p. 351.

5. Jules H. Masserman, "Humanitarian Psychiatry," *Bulletin of the New York Academy of Medicine,* 39(1963):533–44.

6. Borgatta, "Psychodrama, Sociodrama, and Related Techniques," p. 253.

7. Walter Bromberg, "Developments in Group and Action Methods," in *Progress in Psychotherapy*, vol. 5, ed. J. H. Masserman and J. L. Moreno (New York: Grune & Stratton, 1960), p. 60.

8. Alfred Adler, *What Life Should Mean to You* (New York: Little, Brown, 1931), pp. 40–42.

9. Bromberg, "Group and Action Methods," p. 61.

10. Jacob L. Moreno, *Sociometry Reader* (Glencoe, Ill.: Free Press, 1960), p. 59.

11. Bromberg, "Group and Action Methods," p. 65.

12. Rudolf Dreikurs, "Group Psychotherapy and the Third Revolution in Psychiatry," in *Group Psychotherapy and Group Approaches* (Chicago: Alfred Adler Institute, 1960), p. 44.

Chapter 2

1. Brander Matthews, *A Study of the Drama* (Cambridge: Houghton Mifflin, Riverside Press, 1910), p. 8.

2. Kenneth Burke, *Perspectives by Incongruity; Terms for Order,* ed. S. E. Hyman and B. Kormiller (Bloomington: Indiana University Press, 1964), p. 44.

3. Jacob L. Moreno, *Sociometry,* 17(1950):182.

4. Gregory Zilbourg, in collab. with G. W. Henry, *History of Medical Psychiatry* (New York: Norton, 1941), p. 287.

5. Henri Ellenberger, *Discovery of the Unconscious* (New York: Basic Books, 1970), pp. 367–71.

6. Kurt R. Eissler, *Goethe: Psychoanalytic Study,* vol. 1 (Detroit: Wayne State University Press, 1963), p. 230.

7. Gottfried Diener, "Relation of the Delusionary Process in Goethe's *Lila* to Analytic Psychology and to Psychodrama," *Group Psychotherapy and Psychodrama,* 24(1971).

8. Matthews, *Study of the Drama,* pp. 143–44.

9. Ibid., p. 146.

10. Ellenberger, *Discovery of the Unconscious,* p. 398.

11. B. J. Kenworthy, *George Kaiser* (Oxford: Basil Blackwell, 1957), p. 28.

12. Eissler, *Psychoanalytic Study of Goethe,* pp. 236–86.

13. Burke, *Perspectives by Incongruity,* p. 84.

14. Jules H. Masserman, "Humanitarian Psychiatry," *Bulletin of the New York Academy of Medicine,* 39(1963):533–44.

15. Kenworthy, *George Kaiser,* p. 44.

16. Sheldon Cheney, *A History of the Drama* (New York: Tudor Press, 1939), p. 95.

17. Burke, *Perspectives by Incongruity,* p. 143.

Chapter 3

1. Jurgen Ruesch and Gregory Bateson, *Communication of the Social Matrix of Psychiatry* (New York: W. W. Norton, 1951), p. 27.

2. Theodore R. Sarbin, "The Concept of Role-Taking," *Sociometry* 6(1943):273–84.

3. Henri Ellenberger, *Discovery of the Unconscious* (New York: Basic Books, 1970); p. 405.

4. George H. Mead, *Mind, Self, and Society* (Chicago: University of Chicago Press, 1934).

5. John C. McKinney, "A Comparison of the Social Psychology of G. H. Mead and J. L. Moreno," *Sociometry* 10(1947):338–49.

6. Jacob L. Moreno, *Psychodrama*, vol. 1 (Beacon, N.Y.: Beacon House, 1946), p. 157.

7. Ibid., p. 153.

8. Ibid., p. 77.

9. Ledford J. Bischof, *Interpreting Personality Theories* (New York: Harper & Row, 1964), p. 378.

10. Heinz L. Ansbacher and Rowena R. Ansbacher, *The Individual Psychology of Alfred Adler* (New York: Basic Books, 1956), p. 217.

11. Lewis Yablonsky, "An Operational Theory of Roles," *Sociometry* 16(1953):351.

12. Kenneth L. Artiss, ed., *The Symptom as Communication in Schizophrenia* (New York: Grune & Stratton, 1959), p. 19.

Chapter 4

1. Ira Greenberg, "Audience in Action," *Group Psychotherapy and Psychodrama*, 17(1964):119–21.

2. Jules H. Masserman, *The Practice of Dynamic Psychiatry* (Philadelphia: W. B. Saunders, 1955), p. 621.

3. Jacob L. Moreno, "Notes on Indicators and Contra-Indicators for Acting Out in Psychodrama," *Group Psychotherapy and Psychodrama*, 26 (1973), no. 1–2.

4. Zerka Toeman, "The Double Situation in Psychodrama," *Sociatry*, 1(1948):436–46.

5. Jacob L. Moreno, in collab. with Zerka Toeman Moreno and Jonathan Moreno, "The Discovery of the Spontaneous Man," in *Sociometry and the Science of Man* (Beacon, N.Y.: Beacon House, 1956), p. 162.

6. Lewis Yablonsky, "Humanizing Groups through Psychodrama," *Group Psychotherapy and Psychodrama*, 25(1972), no. 1–2.

7. Ledford J. Bischof, *Interpreting Personality Theories* (New York: Harper & Row, 1970), p. 377.

Chapter 5

1. Lloyd DeMause, "The History of Childhood: The Basis for Psychohistory," *History of Childhood Quarterly: The Journal of Psychohistory,* 1(1973):1.

2. Thomas Bulfinch, *Bulfinch's Mythology* (New York: Modern Library, 1934), p. 11.

3. Jacob L. Moreno, *Who Shall Survive?* (Beacon, N.Y.: Beacon House, 1953), p. 394.

4. Jerome Frank, *Persuasion and Healing* (New York: Schocken Books, 1963), p. 147.

5. Alfred Adler, *Understanding Human Nature* (New York: World Publishing Co., 1927), p. 42.

6. Gardner Murphy and Elizabeth Cattell, "Sullivan and Field Theory," in *The Contributions of Harry Stack Sullivan,* ed. Patrick Mullahy (New York: Science House, 1952), p. 6.

7. Ibid., p. 164.

8. Rowena R. Ansbacher, "Sullivan's Interpersonal Psychiatry and Adler's Individual Psychology," *Journal of Individual Psychology,* 27(1971): 86.

9. Murphy and Cattell, "Sullivan and Field Theory," p. 167.

10. Rudolf Dreikurs, "The Unique Social Climate Experienced in Group Psychotherapy," *Group Psychotherapy,* 3(1951):292.

11. Adler, *What Life Should Mean to You,* (New York: Little, Brown, 1931), p. 55.

12. Bulfinch, *Bulfinch's Mythology,* p. 11.

13. Frederick H. Allen, "Child Psychotherapy," in *Handbook of Psychiatric Therapies,* ed. Jules Masserman (New York: Grune & Stratton, 1966), p. 41.

14. Bina Rosenberg, "Family Counseling," in *Techniques for Behavior Change,* ed. Arthur G. Nekelly (Springfield, Ill.: Charles C. Thomas, 1971), pp. 117–23.

15. Rudolf Dreikurs and Loren Grey, "Understanding the Child's Personality," *Parents' Guide to Child Discipline* (New York: Hawthorn Books, 1970), p. 13.

16. Salvador Minuchin, *Families and Family Therapy* (Cambridge, Mass.: Harvard University Press, 1974), p. 58.

17. Rudolf Dreikurs, Bernice Bronia Grunwald, and Floyd C. Pepper, *Maintaining Sanity in the Classroom: Illustrated Teaching Techniques* (New York: Harper & Row, 1971), pp. 17–20.

18. Rudolf Dreikurs with Vicki Soltz, *Children: The Challenge* (New York: Duell, Sloan, and Pearce, 1964), pp. 190–91.

19. Carl A. Whitaker, "A Family Therapist Looks at Marital Therapy,"

in *Couples in Conflict, New Directions in Marital Therapy,* ed. Allan S. Gurman and David G. Rice (New York: Jason Aronson, 1975), p. 170.

20. Rosemary Lippitt, "Psychodrama in the Home," *Sociatry* 1(1947): 148.

21. Adaline Starr, "Sociometry of the Family," in *Alfred Adler: His Influence on Psychology Today,* ed. Harold H. Mosak (New York: Noyes Press, 1973). Reprinted in part with permission.

22. Ellen G. Ruderman and Sheldon Selesnick, "Multiple Avenues of Approach to a Child with a Chronic Stuttering," in *Science and Psychoanalysis,* vol. 14, *Childhood and Adolescence,* ed. Jules H. Masserman (New York: Grune & Stratton, 1969), p. 114.

23. Adaline Starr, "Psychodrama with a Child's Social Atom," *Group Psychotherapy,* 5(1953):222–25.

24. Adaline Starr, "Psychodrama with the Family," *Group Psychotherapy,* 12(1959):27–31.

Chapter 6

1. Jacob L. Moreno, "Sociometry and the Cultural Order," *Sociometry,* 6(1943):335.

2. Zerka Toeman, "Projects in Tests and Measurements," from the works of J. L. Moreno and the files of the Sociometric Institute, compiled by Zerka Toeman, *Sociatry,* 2(1948): no. 1 and 4.

3. Hannah B. Weiner and James M. Sacks, "Warm-Up and Sum-Up," *Group Psychotherapy,* 22(1969):91.

4. William C. Schutz, *Joy: Expanding Human Awareness* (New York: Grove Press, 1967), p. 131.

5. Jacob L. Moreno, *Who Shall Survive?* (Beacon, N.Y.: Beacon House, 1953), p. 703.

6. Lewis Yablonsky, "Sociopathology of the Violent Gang and Its Treatment," in *Progress in Psychotherapy,* vol. 5, ed. Jules H. Masserman and J. L. Moreno (New York: Grune & Stratton, 1960), p. 163.

7. David P. Ausubel, "Reciprocity and Assumed Reciprocity of Acceptance among Adolescents: A Sociometric Study," *Sociometry* 16(1953): 339–47.

8. Mary Northway, *A Primer of Sociometry* (Toronto: University of Toronto Press, 1952), p. 29.

9. Don Dinkmeyer and Rudolf Dreikurs, *Encouraging Children to Learn* (Englewood Cliffs, N.J.: Prentice-Hall, 1963).

10. Rudolf Dreikurs, Bernese B. Grunwald and F. Pepper, *Maintaining Sanity in the Classroom: Illustrated Teaching Techniques* (New York: Harper & Row, 1971), p. 98.

11. Moreno, *Who Shall Survive?*, p. 325.

12. Bernard H. Shulman, "The Family Constellation in Personality Diagnosis," *Journal of Individual Psychology*, 18(1962):35–47.

13. Mary Northway, *A Primer of Sociometry* (Toronto: University of Toronto Press, 1952), p. 34.

14. Ibid., p. 30.

Chapter 7

1. Adaline Starr, "Sociometry of the Family," in *Alfred Adler: His Influence on Psychology Today*, ed. Harold H. Mosak (Park Ridge, N.J.: Noyes Press, 1973), pp. 95–105.

2. Nathan W. Ackerman, "Family Diagnosis and Therapy," in *Handbook of Psychiatric Therapies*, ed. Jules H. Masserman (New York: Grune & Stratton, 1966), p. 349.

3. Zerka T. Moreno, "Basic Concepts of Sociometry and Group Dynamics," *International Handbook of Group Psychotherapy*, ed. J. L. Moreno (New York: Philosophical Library, 1966), p. 75.

4. Derek Miller, *Adolescence: Psychology, Psychopathology and Psychotherapy* (New York: Jason Aronson, 1974), p. 314.

5. Gustine Newman and Richard C. W. Hall, "Acting-Out: An Indication for Psychodrama," *Group Psychotherapy and Psychodrama*, 24 (1971):87–96.

6. Rudolf Dreikurs and Loren Grey, *A Parent's Guide to Child Discipline* (New York: Hawthorn Books, 1968), p. 13.

7. Ibid., p. 4.

8. Barbara Seabourne, "The Action Sociogram," *Group Psychotherapy*, 16(1963):145–55.

9. Ibid.

10. Loren D. Pankratz, "Extended Doubling and Mirroring 'In Situ' in the Mental Hospital," *Group Psychotherapy and Psychodrama* 24(1971): 150.

11. Jacob L. Moreno, *The Social Atom and Death* (Beacon, N.Y.: Beacon House, 1951), pp. 65–69.

12. Jules H. Masserman, *The Practice of Dynamic Psychiatry* (Philadelphia: W. B. Saunders, 1955), p. 210.

Chapter 8

1. Jerome Frank, *Persuasion and Healing* (Baltimore: Johns Hopkins Press, 1961), p. 173.

2. Jacob L. Moreno, "Theory of Spontaneity-Creativity," *Sociometry*

and the Science of Man, ed. J. L. Moreno (Beacon, N.Y.: Beacon House, 1956), p. 112.

3. Bernard H. Shulman, *Essays in Schizophrenia* (Baltimore: Williams and Wilkins, 1968), p. 184.

4. Moreno, "Theory of Spontaneity-Creativity," p. 112.

5. Ibid.

6. Ibid.

7. Ibid.

8. Ibid., p. 140.

Chapter 9

1. Jacob L. Moreno, *Who Shall Survive?* (Beacon, N.Y.: Beacon House, 1953), p. 702.

2. Marcia Robbins, "Psychodramatic Children's Warm-Ups for Adults," *Group Psychotherapy and Psychodrama* 26(1973), no. 1–2.

3. Walter Bromberg, "The Treatment of Sexual Deviates with Group Psychodrama," *Group Psychotherapy* 4(1952):274–89.

4. Rosemary Lippitt, "The Auxiliary Chair Technique," *Group Psychotherapy* 11(1958):8–26.

5. G. Douglas Warner, "The Didactic Auxiliary Chair," *Group Psychotherapy and Psychodrama,* 23(1970), no. 1–2.

6. Jonathan D. Moreno, "Philodrama and Psychophilosophy," *Group Psychotherapy and Psychodrama,* 24(1971), no. 1–2.

7. Rudolf Dreikurs, "Group Dynamics in the Classroom," in *Group Psychotherapy and Group Approaches* (Chicago: Alfred Adler Institute, 1960), p. 128.

8. Jules H. Masserman, *The Practice of Dynamic Psychiatry* (Philadelphia: W. B. Saunders, 1955), p. 167.

9. Rudolf Dreikurs, "Music Therapy with Psychotic Children," in *Child Guidance and Education* (Eugene, Ore.: Oregon Press, 1957), pp. 52–53.

10. Jacob L. Moreno, *Psychodrama,* vol. 1 (Beacon, N.Y.: Beacon House, 1946), pp. 277–84.

11. Doris Twitchell-Allen and Francis M. Stephen, "Some Theoretical and Practical Aspects of Group Psychotherapy," *Group Psychotherapy,* 4(1951):9–16.

12. Hannah B. Weiner and James M. Sacks, "Warm-Up and Sum-Up," *Group Psychotherapy,* 22(1969):88–99.

13. J. G. Rojas-Bermudey, "The Intermediary Object," *Group Psychotherapy,* 22(1969):149–54.

14. Weiner and Sacks, "Warm-Up and Sum-Up," p. 94.

15. Ibid.

Chapter 10

1. Helen H. Jennings, "Sociometric Choice Process in Personality and Group Formation," in *Sociometry Reader,* ed. J. L. Moreno (Glencoe, Ill.: Free Press, 1960), pp. 87–112.
2. Jacob L. Moreno, *Psychodrama* (Beacon, N.Y.: Beacon House, 1946), p. 210.
3. Raymond J. Corsini, with Samuel Cardone, *Roleplaying in Psychotherapy—A Manual* (Chicago: Aldine, 1966), p. 78.
4. Urie Bronfenbrenner and Theodore M. Newcomb, "Improvisations —An Application of Psychodrama in Personality Diagnosis," *Sociatry* 1 (1948):367–82.
5. Robert Bartlett Haas and Jacob L. Moreno, "Psychodrama as a Projective Technique," in *An Introduction to Projective Techniques,* ed. Harold H. Anderson and G. L. Anderson (Englewood Cliffs, N.J.: Prentice-Hall, 1961).
6. J. Del Torto and Paul Cornyetz, "Psychodrama as Expressive and Projective Technique," *Sociometry* 7(1944):356–75.

Chapter 11

1. Raymond J. Corsini, "The Behind Your Back Technique in Group Psychotherapy and Psychodrama," *Group Psychotherapy,* 6(1953):102–9.
2. Jacob L. Moreno and Zerka T. Moreno, "Dream Presentation," in *Psychodrama,* vol. 3 (Beacon, N.Y.: Beacon House, 1969), pp. 242–43.
3. Frederick S. Perls, "Dreamwork Seminar," in *Gestalt Therapy Verbatim,* ed. John O. Stevens (Lafayette, Calif.: Real People Press, 1969).
4. Jacob L. Moreno and Zerka T. Moreno, "Dream Retraining," *Psychodrama,* vol. 3 (Beacon, N.Y.: Beacon House, 1969), p. 243.
5. Robert W. Siroka and Gilbert Schloss, "The Death Scene in Psychodrama," *Group Psychotherapy,* 21(1968), no. 4.
6. James M. Sacks, "The Judgement Technique in Psychodrama," *Group Psychotherapy,* 18(1965):69–72.
7. Martin R. Haskell, "Psychodramatic Role Training in Preparation for Release on Parole," *Group Psychotherapy,* 10(1957):51–59.
8. Walter O'Connell, "Action-Oriented Methods," in *Techniques for Behavior Change,* ed. Arthur G. Nekelly (Springfield, Ill.: Charles C. Thomas, 1971), p. 89.
9. Jacob L. Moreno, "Psychodramatic Frustration Test," *Group Psychotherapy,* 6(1954):137–67.
10. Lucy K. Ackernecht, "Roleplaying of Embarrassing Situations," *Group Psychotherapy,* 20(1967):39–42.
11. Hannah B. Weiner and James M. Sacks, "Warm-Up and Sum-Up," *Group Psychotherapy,* 22(1969):97.

12. Tom Speros, "The Final Empty Chair," *Group Psychotherapy and Psychodrama*, 25(1972):32.

13. Delbert M. Kole, "The Spectrogram in Psychodrama," *Group Psychotherapy*, 20(1967):53.

14. Howard A. Blatmer, "The Technique of Sharing," in *Acting-In Practical Applications of Psychodramatic Methods* (New York: Springer Publishing Co., 1973), p. 82.

Chapter 12

1. Rudolf Dreikurs, *The Challenge of Marriage* (New York: Duell, Sloan and Pearce, 1946), pp. 32–41.

2. Ralph H. Turner, *Family Interaction* (New York: John Wiley, 1970), pp. 295–96.

3. Dreikurs, *Challenge of Marriage*, p. 42.

4. Bernard L. Greene, "Introduction: A Multi-Operational Approach to Marital Problems," in *The Psychotherapies of Marital Disharmony*, ed. Bernard L. Greene (New York: Free Press, 1965), pp. 1–9.

5. Salvador Munuchin, *Families and Family Therapy* (Cambridge, Mass.: Harvard University Press, 1974), p. 14.

6. Otto Pollak, "Sociological and Psychoanalytic Concepts," in *The Psychotherapies of Marital Disharmony*, ed. Bernard L. Greene (New York: Free Press, 1965), pp. 20–21.

7. Dreikurs, *Challenge of Marriage*, p. 121.

8. Jacob L. Moreno, "Psychodramatic Treatment of Marriage Problems," *Sociometry*, 3(1940):20.

9. Jules H. Masserman, *A Psychiatric Odyssey* (New York: Science House, 1971), pp. 274–76.

10. Rudolf Dreikurs, "Determinants of Changing Attitudes of Marital Partners toward Each Other," in *The Marriage Relationship*, ed. Salo Rosenbaum and Ian Alger (New York: Basic Books, 1968), p. 94.

11. Dreikurs, *Challenge of Marriage*, pp. 131–43.

12. Jacob L. Moreno, *Psychodrama* (Beacon, N.Y.: Beacon House, 1946), p. 206.

13. Lobitz and Lo Piccolo use role playing as "an adjunctive technique with the controlled and inhibited woman who has difficulty in accepting the uncontrollable movements and vocal release that often accompany their orgiastic responses. . . . In the presence of their husbands, they practice an exaggeration of their orgiastic response until they are completely comfortable with it." The mechanics of the sexual act are the center of this activity rather than the joyful process of erotic activity. Some changes in attitude can be achieved with sexual reconditioning and through improving the couple's ability to communicate affectionately in other areas. Thomas P. Laughren and David J. Kass, "Desensitization of Sexual Dysfunction: The

Present Status," in *Couples in Conflict, New Directions in Marital Therapy,* ed. Alan S. Gurman and David G. Rice (New York: Jason Aronson, 1975), p. 276.

14. Harold H. Mosak and Richard R. Kopp, "The Early Recollections of Adler, Freud, and Jung," *Journal of Individual Psychology,* 29(1973):157.

15. Gerald J. Mozdzier and Thomas J. Lattman, "Games Married People Play," *Journal of Individual Psychology,* 29(1973):182–94.

16. Rudolf Dreikurs, "The Private Logic," in *Alfred Adler: His Influence on Psychology Today,* ed. Harold H. Mosak (Park Ridge, N.J.: Noyes Press, 1973), p. 24.

17. Pitirim Sorokin, "Spontaneous Remarks on the Discovery of Spontaneous Man," *Group Psychotherapy,* 8(1955):327.

Chapter 13

1. Adaline Starr, "Psychodrama in the Child Guidance Centers," in *Adlerian Family Counseling,* ed. Rudolf Dreikurs, Raymond Corsini, Raymond Lowe, and Manford Sonstegard (Eugene, Ore.: University of Oregon Press, 1959), pp. 75–81.

2. Rudolf Dreikurs, Raymond Corsini, Raymond Lowe, and Manford Sonstegard, "Introduction," in *Adlerian Family Counseling* (Eugene, Ore.: University of Oregon Press, 1959), p. vii.

3. Rudolf Dreikurs, "Basic Principles in Dealing with Children," in *Adlerian Family Counseling* (Eugene, Ore.: University of Oregon Press, 1959), pp. 23–31.

4. Georgia Graven, "The Playroom and the Playroom Director," in *Adlerian Family Counseling* (Eugene, Ore.: University of Oregon Press, 1959), pp. 57–58.

5. Jacob L. Moreno and Florence B. Moreno, "Spontaneity Theory of Child Development," in *Sociometry and the Science of Man,* ed. J. L. Moreno (Beacon, N.Y.: Beacon House, 1956), p. 410.

6. Rosemary Lippitt and Catherine Clancy, "Psychodrama in the Kindergarten and Nursery School," *Group Psychotherapy* 6(1954):262–90.

7. Graven, "The Playroom and the Playroom Director," p. 58.

Chapter 14

1. Derek Miller, *Adolescence: Psychology, Psychopathology and Psychotherapy* (New York: Jason Aronson, 1974), p. 454.

2. Thomas Bulfinch, *Bulfinch's Mythology* (New York: Modern Library, 1934), pp. 131–34.

3. Karen Horney, *The Neurotic Personality of Our Times* (New York: W. W. Norton, 1937), p. 272.

4. W. Beran Wolfe, *How to Be Happy though Human* (New York: Farrar and Rinehart, 1931), p. 262.

5. Donald N. Lombardi, "The Psychology of Addiction," in *Alfred Adler: His Influence on Psychology Today,* ed. Harold H. Mosak (Park Ridge, N.J.: Noyes Press, 1973), pp. 71–75.

6. Aaron Stein and Eugene Friedman, "Group Therapy with Alcoholics," in *Comprehensive Group Psychotherapy,* ed. Harold I. Kaplan and Benjamin J. Sadok (Baltimore: Williams and Wilkins, 1971), pp. 652–60.

7. Joyce Lowinson and Israel Zwerling, "Group Therapy with Narcotics Addicts," in *Comprehensive Group Psychotherapy* (Baltimore: Williams and Wilkins, 1971), p. 602.

8. Hannah B. Weiner, "Treating the Alcoholic with Psychodrama," *Group Psychotherapy,* 18(1965):28–29.

9. Arnold Abrams, Dover Roth, and Benjamin Boshes, "Group Therapy with Narcotic Addicts, Method and Evaluation," *Group Psychotherapy,* 11 (1958), no. 3.

10. E. A. Eliasoph, "A Group Therapy and Psychodrama Approach with Adolescent Drug Addicts," *Group Psychotherapy,* 8(1955):161.

11. Howard T. Blane, *The Personality of the Alcoholic: Guises of Dependency* (New York: Harper & Row, 1968), p. 143.

12. Hendrik M. Ruitenbeck, *The New Group Therapies* (New York: Avon Books, 1970), p. 168.

13. Jules H. Masserman, *The Practice of Dynamic Psychiatry* (Philadelphia: W. B. Saunders, 1955), p. 480.

14. John A. Ewing and Ronald E. Fox, "Family Therapy of Alcoholism," in *Handbook of Psychiatric Therapies,* ed. Jules H. Masserman (New York: Grune & Stratton, 1966), pp. 275–80.

15. Douglas R. Bey, Jr., and Walter E. Smith, "Organizational Consultation in a Combat Unit," *American Journal of Psychiatry,* 128(1971): 405.

16. Blane, *Personality of the Alcoholic,* p. 18.

17. Sheila B. Blume, Joan Robins, and Arthur Branston, "Psychodrama Techniques in the Treatment of Alcoholism," *Group Psychotherapy,* 21 (1968):245.

18. Blane, *Personality of the Alcoholic,* p. 88.

19. Ibid., p. 74.

20. Peter Olson and Jerry Fankhauser, "The BUD and Its Resolution through Psychodrama," *Group Psychotherapy and Psychodrama,* 23(1970): 84.

21. Walter E. O'Connell, notes on action therapy and development group lecture, V.A. Hospital, Houston, Texas.

Chapter 15

1. Joyce Lowinson and Israel Zwerling, "Group Therapy with Narcotic Addicts," in *Comprehensive Group Psychotherapy,* ed. Harold I. Kaplan and Benjamin J. Sadock (Baltimore: Williams and Wilkins, 1971), pp. 603–7.

2. Rowena R. Ansbacher, "Interpersonal Psychiatry and Individual Psychology," *Journal of Individual Psychology,* 27(1971):94.

3. David Laskowitz, "The Adolescent Drug Addict, an Adlerian View," *Journal of Individual Psychology,* 17(1961):72.

4. Robert N. Rapoport, "The Community as Doctors, New Perspectives on a Therapeutic Community," in *Psychotherapy and Counseling: Studies in Technique,* ed. William S. Sahakian (Chicago: Rand McNally, 1969), p. 495.

5. Harrison J. Pope, *Voices from the Drug Culture* (Boston: Beacon Press, 1971).

6. Laskowitz, "The Adolescent Drug Addict, an Adlerian View," p. 69.

7. George Wiggins and Walter O'Connell, "Skin-Jumping Therapy: Creating Communal Cohesion," *St. Joseph Hospital Medical Surgical Journal,* 9(1974):38.

8. Herman P. Gladstone, "Youthful Offender in Psychotherapy," in *Handbook of Psychiatric Therapies,* ed. Jules H. Masserman (New York: Grune & Stratton, 1966), pp. 101–9.

9. Ledford J. Bischof, *Interpreting Personality Theories* (New York: Harper & Row, 1970), p. 400.

10. Alfred Adler, *What Life Should Mean to You* (New York: Grosset and Dunlap, 1931), p. 188.

11. Jules H. Masserman, *A Psychiatric Odyssey* (New York: Science House, 1971), p. 422.

12. Jordan Scher, *Drugs in Our Schools* (Chicago: National Council on Drug Abuse, 1972), p. 1204.

Chapter 16

1. Adaline Starr, "Psychodrama on a Hospital Ward: A Strategic Setting for Training," in *The International Handbook of Group Psychotherapy,* ed. J. L. Moreno, A. Friedemann, R. Battegay, and Zerka T. Moreno (New York: Philosophical Library, 1966), pp. 343–48.

2. Rudolf Dreikurs, "The Unique Social Climate Experienced in Group Psychotherapy," in *Group Psychotherapy and Group Approaches* (Chicago: Alfred Adler Institute, 1960), p. 46.

3. Jerome Frank, *Persuasion and Healing: A Comparative Study of Psychotherapy* (Baltimore: Johns Hopkins Press, 1961), p. 203.

4. Adaline Starr and Irving Chelnek, "Psychodrama at a Veterans Administration Hospital, Downey, Ill.," *Group Psychotherapy*, 8(1955): 20–24.

5. Bernard H. Shulman, *Essays in Schizophrenia* (Baltimore: Williams & Wilkins, 1968), p. 94.

6. Ibid., p. 160.

7. Ibid., p. 108.

8. Jurgen Ruesch and Gregory Bateson, *Communication: The Social Matrix of Psychiatry* (New York: W. W. Norton, 1951), p. 27.

9. Adaline Starr and Ernest Fogel, "Training State Hospital Personnel Through Psychodrama and Sociometry," *Group Psychotherapy*, 14(1961): 55–61.

Chapter 17

1. Jacob L. Moreno and Zerka T. Moreno, *Psychodrama*, vol. 3, (Beacon, N.Y.: Beacon House, 1969), p. 183.

2. Ibid., p. 196.

3. Alfred Adler, "Accusation," in *The Individual Psychology of Alfred Adler*, ed. Heinz L. Ansbacher and Rowena R. Ansbacher (New York: Basic Books, 1956), p. 271.

4. Bernard H. Shulman, *Essays in Schizophrenia* (Baltimore: Williams & Wilkins, 1968), p. 144; and Moreno and Moreno, *Psychodrama*, p. 184.

5. Moreno and Moreno, *Psychodrama*, p. 194.

6. Ibid., p. 190.

7. Ibid., p. 192. Also Joseph Mann, "The Incidental and the Planned Psychodramatic Shock and Its Therapeutic Value," in *The International Handbook of Group Psychotherapy*, ed. J. L. Moreno, A. Friedemann, R. Battegay, and Zerka T. Moreno (New York: Philosophical Library, 1966), p. 340.

8. Adler, "Feeblemindedness," in *The Individual Psychology of Alfred Adler*, p. 152.

9. Moreno and Moreno, *Psychodrama*, p. 188.

10. Harold M. Visotsky, "Modern Approaches to Community Mental Health," in *Handbook of Psychiatric Therapies*, ed. Jules H. Masserman (New York: Grune & Stratton, 1966), pp. 476–96. These conditions of a large patient population being cared for by an understaffed and overworked group prompted Harold Visotsky to undertake radical changes in the Illinois Department of Mental Health to bring about a more efficient and humane delivery of services to the mentally ill. This work is being further implemented by Leroy Leavitt.

11. Adaline Starr, "Psychodrama on a Hospital Ward: A Strategic Place for Training," in *The International Handbook of Group Psychotherapy*, pp. 342–48.

12. Jerome Frank, *Persuasion and Healing: A Comparative Study of Psychotherapy* (Baltimore: Johns Hopkins Press, 1961), p. 198.

13. Edgar F. Borgatta, "Analysis of Social Interactions and Sociometric Perception," *Sociometry,* 17(1954):7–32.

Chapter 18

1. Alfred Adler, "The Melancholic Fiction," in *The Individual Psychology of Alfred Adler,* ed. Heinz L. Ansbacher and Rowena R. Ansbacher (New York: Basic Books, 1956), p. 321.

2. Jacob L. Moreno, *Who Shall Survive?* (Beacon, N.Y.: Beacon House, 1953), p. 377.

3. Myrna M. Weissman and Eugene S. Paykel, *The Depressed Woman: A Study of Social Relationships* (Chicago: University of Chicago Press, 1974), p. 17.

4. Ibid., p. 148.

5. Edgar F. Borgatta, "A Diagnostic Note on the Construction of Sociograms and Action Diagrams," *Group Psychotherapy,* 3(1951):300.

6. Adler, "The Melancholic Fiction," p. 321.

7. Jacob L. Moreno and Zerka T. Moreno, *Psychodrama,* vol. 3 (Beacon, N.Y.: Beacon House, 1969), p. 235.

8. Ibid., p. 237.

9. William Offenkrantz in collaboration with Arnold Tobin, "Psychoanalytic Psychotherapy," *Archives of General Psychiatry,* 30(1974):600.

Chapter 19

1. Jerome Frank, "Group Psychotherapy with Psychiatric Outpatients," *Group Psychotherapy,* 16(1963):132.

2. Jay Haley, *Strategies of Psychotherapy* (New York: Grune & Stratton, 1963), p. 5.

3. Jerome Frank, *Persuasion and Healing* (Baltimore: Johns Hopkins Press, 1961), p. 190.

4. Marguerite Parrish, "Psychodrama: Description of Application and Review of Techniques," *Group Psychotherapy,* 6(1953):63–89.

5. Jacob L. Moreno, *Who Shall Survive?* (Beacon, N.Y.: Beacon House, 1953), p. 377.

6. Karl Menninger, *The Crime of Punishment* (New York: Viking Press, 1968), p. 260.

7. Brander Matthews, *A Study of the Drama* (Boston: Houghton Mifflin, 1910), p. 22.

Selected Bibliography

Books

Adler, A. *The education of children*. London: George Allen & Unwin, 1930. Reprinted 1947 and 1957.

Ansbacher, H. L. & Ansbacher, R. R. *The individual psychology of Alfred Adler*. New York: Basic Books, 1956.

Bach, G. R., & Deutsch, R. M. *Pairing*. New York: Avon Books, 1970.

Bach, G. R., & Wyden, P. *Intimate enemies*. New York: Avon Books, 1968.

Bischof, L. J. *Interpreting personality theories*. New York: Harper and Row, 1970.

Blatner, H. A. *Acting-in: practical applications of psychodramatic methods*. New York: Springer Publishing, 1973.

Burke, K. *Perspectives by incongruity*. Bloomington, Ind.: Indiana University Press, 1968.

Chapman, A. H. *The games children play*. New York: Berkley Medallion Books, 1971.

Chesler, M., & Fox, R. *Role-playing methods in the classroom*. Chicago: Science Research Associates, 1966.

Corsini, R. J. *Roleplaying in psychotherapy*. Chicago: Aldine, 1966.

Dreikurs, R. *Group psychotherapy and group approaches: collected papers*. Chicago: Alfred Adler Institute, 1960.

Dreikurs, R. Determinants of changing attitudes of marital partners toward each other. In S. Rosenbaum & I. Alger (Eds.), *The marriage relationship*. New York: Basic Books, 1968.

361

Dreikurs, R. *The challenge of marriage*. New York: Hawthorn Books, 1974.

Dreikurs, R., Grunwald, B. B., & Pepper, F. C. *Maintaining sanity in the classroom*. New York: Harper and Row, 1971.

Elam, H. P. Black pride and social interest. In H. H. Mosak (Ed.), *Alfred Adler: his influence on psychology today*. Park Ridge, N.J.: Noyes Press, 1973.

Fine, L. J. Action group processes and psychodrama in residency training. In G. M. Abroms & N. S. Greenfield (Eds.), *The new hospital psychiatry*. New York: Academic Press, 1971.

Frank, J. D. *Persuasion and healing*. New York: Schocken Books, 1963.

Halpern, M. Concordance requires discord: a theory of human relations. In J. H. Masserman & J. J. Schwab (Eds.), *Man for humanity*. Springfield, Ill.: Charles C. Thomas, 1972.

Jennings, H. H. *Leadership and isolation* (2nd ed.). New York: Longmans, Green and Co., 1950.

Laskowitz, D. Drug addiction. In A. G. Nikelly (Ed.), *Techniques for behavior change*. Springfield, Ill.: Charles C. Thomas, 1971.

Lobitz, C. W., & Lo Piccolo, J. New Methods in the behavioral treatment of sexual dysfunction. In A. S. Gurman & D. G. Rice (Eds.), *Couples in conflict*. New York: Jason Aronson, 1975.

Lombardi, D. *Search for significance*. Chicago: Nelson-Hall, 1975.

Lowen, A. *The language of the body*. New York: Collier, 1971 (1st ed. 1958).

Masserman, J. H. *The practice of dynamic psychiatry*. Philadelphia, London: W. B. Saunders, 1955.

Masserman, J. H. *A psychiatric odyssey*. New York: Science House, 1971.

Mathews, B. *A study of the drama*. Boston: Houghton Mifflin, 1910.

Mead, G. H. *Mind, self and society*. Chicago: University of Chicago Press, 1934.

Miller, D. *Adolescence: psychology, psychopathology, and psychotherapy*. New York: Jason Aronson, 1974.

Moreno, J. L. *Psychodrama* (Vol. 1). Beacon, N.Y.: Beacon House, 1946 (Rev. ed. 1964).

Moreno, J. L. *Who shall survive?* (Rev. ed.). Beacon, N.Y.: Beacon House, 1953.

Moreno, J. L. *Sociometry and the science of man*. Beacon, N.Y.: Beacon House, 1956.

Moreno, J. L. Fundamental rules and techniques of psychodrama. In J. H. Masserman & J. L. Moreno (Eds.), *Techniques of psychotherapy* (Vol. 3 of *Progress in psychotherapy*). New York: Grune and Stratton, 1958.

Moreno, J. L., in collaboration with Moreno, Z. T. *Psychodrama* (Vol. 3). Beacon, N.Y.: Beacon House, 1969.

Mosak, H. H. The controller—a social interpretation of the anal character. In H. H. Mosak (Ed.), *Alfred Adler: his influence on psychology today*. Park Ridge, N.J.: Noyes Press, 1973.

Munuchin, S. *Families and family therapy.* Cambridge, Mass.: Harvard University Press, 1974.

Northway, M. L. *A primer of sociometry.* Toronto: University of Toronto Press, 1952.

O'Connell, W. E. *Action therapy and Adlerian theory.* Chicago: Alfred Adler Institute, 1975.

Ossorio, A. G., & Fine, L. Psychodrama as a catalyst for social change in a mental hospital. In J. H. Masserman & J. L. Moreno (Eds.), *Review and integration* (Vol. 5 of *Progress in psychotherapy*). New York: Grune and Stratton, 1960.

Rapoport, R. N. The community as doctors, new perspectives on a therapeutic community. In W. S. Sahakian (Ed.), *Psychotherapy and counseling: studies in technique.* Chicago: Rand McNally, 1969.

Rose, W. *Men, myth and movements in German literature.* New York: Macmillan, 1931.

Schutz, W. C. *Here comes everybody.* New York: Harper and Row, 1971.

Shaftel, G., & Shaftel, F. *Roleplaying for social values.* Englewood Cliffs, N.J.: Prentice-Hall, 1967.

Shulman, B. H. *Essays on schizophrenia.* Baltimore: Williams and Wilkins, 1968.

Siroka, R. W., Siroka, E., & Schloss, G. (Eds.). *Sensitivity training and group encounter—an introduction.* New York: Grossett and Dunlap, 1971.

Stanislavski, C. *An actor prepares.* New York: Theatre Arts Books, 1948.

Willett, J. *The theatre of Bertolt Brecht* (3rd ed. rev.). New York: New Directions, 1968.

Yablonsky, L. *Psychodrama.* New York: Basic Books, 1976.

Yalom, I. D. *The theory and practice of group psychotherapy.* New York: Basic Books, 1970.

Periodicals

Kefir, N., & Corsini, R. J. Dispositional sets: A contribution to typology. *Journal of Individual Psychology,* 1974, *30* (2), 163–78.

Korn, R. R. The self as agent and the self as object. *Group Psychotherapy and Psychodrama,* 1975, *28,* 184–210.

Mosak, H. H. Strategies for behavior change in schools: Consultation strategies. *The Counseling Psychologist,* 1971, *3,* (1), 58–62.

Papanek, H. Group psychotherapy interminable. *International Journal of Group Psychotherapy,* 1970, *20,* 213–23.

Shulman, B. H. The use of dramatic confrontation in group psychotherapy. *Psychiatric Quarterly Supplement,* 1962 (Part 1), *36,* 93–99.

Weiner, H. B. & Sacks, J. M. Warm-up and sum-up. *Group Psychotherapy,* 1969, *12* (1 and 2), 85–102.

Author Index

Subject Index

About the Author

Adaline Starr is a psychodrama consultant to Veterans Administrations hospitals in Illinois and to many Chicago area hospitals. She has worked on the staffs of the Northwestern University Medical School's department of psychiatry and the Alfred Adler Institute. A pioneer in the field of psychodrama, Starr has authored a number of articles in major psychological and psychiatric journals. She is an active member of the Illinois Group Psychotherapy Society, the International Association for Social Psychiatry, the American Society of Adlerian Psychology, and the International Committee of Adlerian Summer Schools and Institute, and a fellow of the American Society of Group Psychotherapy and Psychodrama.